'This is a new book by prolific author I
attainment gaps at school for minority e
dents. The focus is on England, but ther
tries and education systems. Using a com
professional experience, the book looks in detail at how ethnic attainment gaps can be, and in some cases have been, successfully addressed. It moves from description to analysis and practical recommendations. Its main audience will be policymakers, school leaders, and other practitioners. But it will be of great interest to anyone concerned with improving outcomes for any disadvantaged groups, including parents, activists, and the public more generally.'

Stephen Gorard, *Professor of Education and Public Policy, Director of the Durham University Evidence for Education, UK*

'This is a timely, contemporary, and relevant examination of Black and Ethnic Minority Achievement. What makes Feyisa Demie important is his career and research in local authorities, which has given him over 30 years of access to culturally diverse schools and classrooms. This is a key text in education and the wider social sciences, not only for undergraduate and postgraduate students but significantly for teachers and everybody who works and cares for children and young adults.'

Dr. Richard Race, *Senior Lecturer in Education, Teesside University, UK*

'This is an excellent book that is firmly located in the "what works" approach to education. It should be a must read for staff in schools who are teaching diverse pupil communities. It offers a wide range of effective strategies and good practices to address disadvantage and tackle educational inequality. It should prove invaluable to classroom teachers, school leaders, and school improvement professionals alike.'

Sean Hayes *was a local authority educational researcher for over 30 years and is an Honorary Fellow at the Education Department of Durham University.*

BLACK AND ETHNIC MINORITY ACHIEVEMENT IN SCHOOLS

This eminently timely volume explores the successful practice and effective intervention strategies in schools to drive school improvement and close the achievement gap for Black and minority ethnic students.

Representing a seminal publication in the literature, this book collates 20 years of original research into race, achievement, and educational equality in schools in England to find out what's really working in education and identify the key areas for improvement. Looking at leading issues such as the curriculum, school exclusions, and language barriers, chapters focus on the lived experiences of headteachers, teachers, parents, pupils, and other school staff obtained through focus groups and interviews. Presenting longitudinal evidence from school surveys and the National Pupil Database, the book considers:

- The scale of the achievement gap and educational inequality
- The barriers to learning for Black and ethnic minorities
- The experience of raising achievement in successful multicultural schools
- Strategies and success factors to drive improvement in schools
- Targeted intervention to tackle inequality
- The international experience to close the achievement gap
- Lessons learned from successful schools to inform policy and practice

Ultimately tackling educational inequality head-on, the book demonstrates concrete strategies for how to close the achievement gap for Black and ethnic minority students and will therefore be essential reading for academics, policymakers, and school staff involved with multicultural education, education policy and politics, and school improvement and effectiveness, as well as race and ethnicity studies more broadly.

Feyisa Demie is Honorary Professor at Durham University, UK, and a Fellow of the Academy of Social Science (FAcSS).

BLACK AND ETHNIC MINORITY ACHIEVEMENT IN SCHOOLS

Strategies and Successful Practice to Tackle Inequality

Feyisa Demie

Routledge
Taylor & Francis Group
LONDON AND NEW YORK

Designed cover image: © Getty Images

First published 2025
by Routledge
4 Park Square, Milton Park, Abingdon, Oxon OX14 4RN

and by Routledge
605 Third Avenue, New York, NY 10158

Routledge is an imprint of the Taylor & Francis Group, an informa business

© 2025 Feyisa Demie

The right of Feyisa Demie to be identified as author of this work has been asserted in accordance with sections 77 and 78 of the Copyright, Designs and Patents Act 1988.

All rights reserved. No part of this book may be reprinted or reproduced or utilised in any form or by any electronic, mechanical, or other means, now known or hereafter invented, including photocopying and recording, or in any information storage or retrieval system, without permission in writing from the publishers.

Trademark notice: Product or corporate names may be trademarks or registered trademarks, and are used only for identification and explanation without intent to infringe.

British Library Cataloguing-in-Publication Data
A catalogue record for this book is available from the British Library

ISBN: 978-1-032-81395-0 (hbk)
ISBN: 978-1-032-80204-6 (pbk)
ISBN: 978-1-003-49963-3 (ebk)

DOI: 10.4324/9781003499633

Typeset in Sabon
by SPi Technologies India Pvt Ltd (Straive)

For Margaret, Ibsa, and Kulani with much love

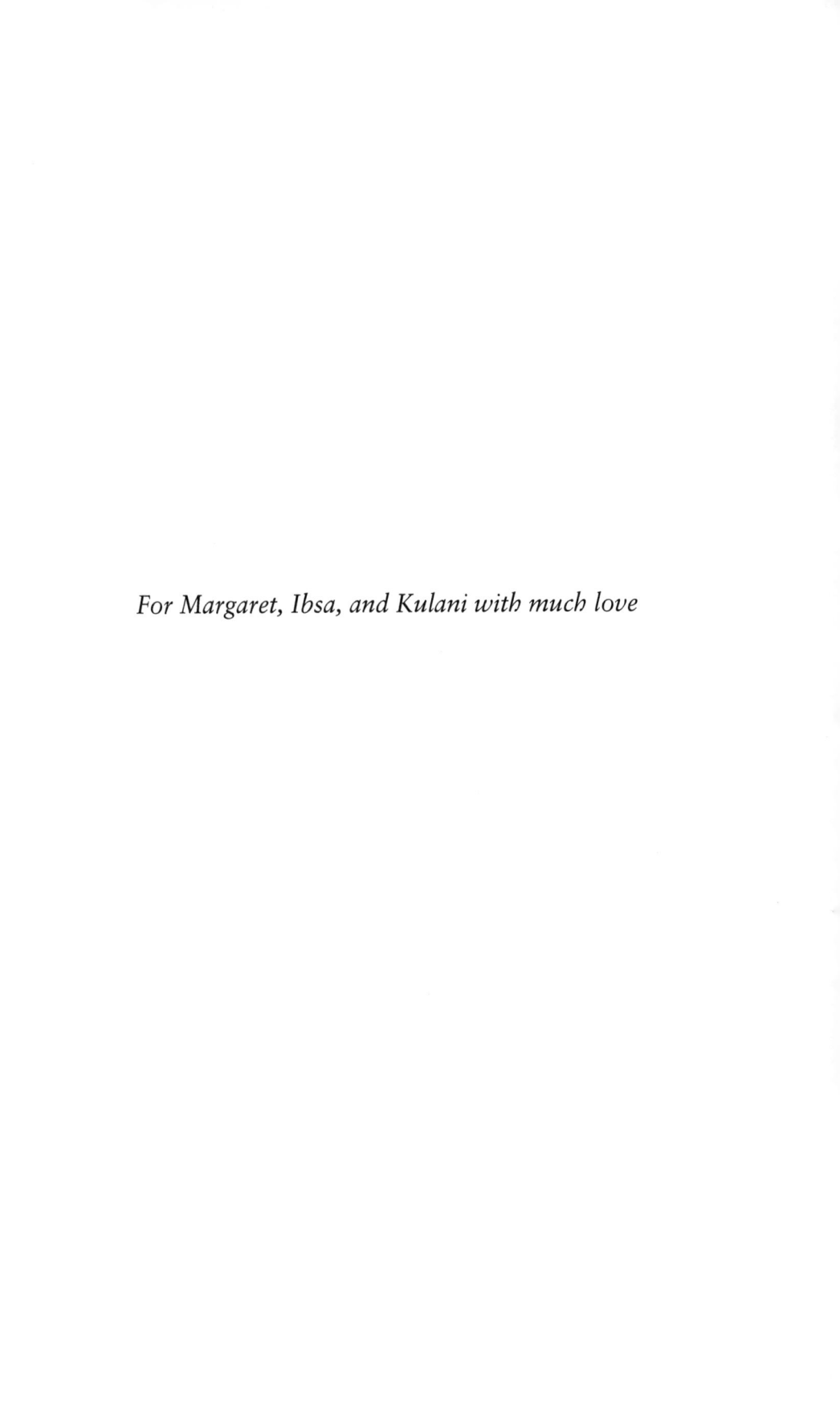

CONTENTS

List of figures   *xv*
List of tables   *xvi*
List of abbreviations   *xvii*
About the author   *xix*
A note on terminology and code used in the book   *xx*
Acknowledgement   *xxi*

PART I
Introduction: Black and Ethnic Minority Educational Achievement Issues, Debates, and Policy Concerns   1

1 Introduction: Policy Concerns and Challenges   3
   Why is there an interest in Black and ethnic minority achievement? 3
   What does research tell us about strategies to raise achievement and tackle inequality? 8
   The aims of the book 10
   Research methods 11
   The structure of the book 13
   Notes 16
   References 17

2 The Achievement Gap: The Empirical Evidence   23
   Introduction 23
   Why does the achievement gap matter? 23
   *The attainment performance measures and national
      curriculum 27*
   *The ethnic achievement gap and inequality
      in education 28*
      *The gender achievement gap by ethnic background
         and inequality 31*
   *The socioeconomic achievement gap and inequality in
      education 32*
      *The attainment of disadvantaged pupils: the KS2 and
         GCSE evidence 32*
      *The attainment of disadvantaged pupils by ethnic
         background 32*
      *The gender achievement gap and inequality
         in education 35*
   Conclusions 36
   References 38

3 Barriers to Learning   40
   Introduction 40
   Factors associated with barriers to learning 41
      A lack of funding for education 42
      Poverty factor 44
      Low literacy level and language barriers 45
      Lack of parental engagement 47
      The lack of parental aspiration 48
      Lack of diversity 49
      Curriculum barriers and relevance 50
      School exclusions 52
      Racism 53
      Teachers low expectations 54
      Other factors 55
   Conclusions 56
   References 57

PART II
The Experience of Raising the Achievement of Black and Ethnic Minority Students in Schools   **61**

4 Success Factors in Improving Leadership and Teaching to Raise Achievement   63
Introduction 63
Success factors and intervention strategies used in schools 63
  Providing strong school leadership 66
  High-quality teaching and learning 72
  Effective use of data 74
Conclusions 78
References 80

5 Targeted Intervention Strategy to Raise Achievement   83
Introduction 83
The school survey evidence on effective intervention strategies in schools 84
The London challenge evidence on effective intervention strategies in schools 90
The EEF evidence on effective intervention strategies in school 94
Conclusions 96
Notes 97
References 98

6 Strategies and Success Factors to Raise Pupils with English as an Additional Language Achievement   101
Introduction 101
The achievement of pupils with EAL in schools by language diversity 103
The achievement of pupils with EAL in schools by stages of English proficiency 105
Success factors and school strategies in raising the achievement of EAL pupils 109
  Strong leadership in school that supports pupils with EAL 110

Effective EAL teaching and learning in the classroom 111
Targeted support for EAL pupils 115
Targeted support from EAL coordinators and EAL teachers 116
Targeted support from EAL support staff 118
Effective use of assessment data for monitoring EAL pupils 119
Conclusions 121
References 122

PART III
Good Practice in Parental Engagement, Use of Inclusive Curriculum, and School Exclusions — 125

7 The Experience of Parental Engagement: Teachers, Headteachers, Parents, and Pupils View — 127
Introduction 127
Teachers and headteachers' views about partnerships with parents 128
Parents view on the partnership with schools 135
The pupil's views on parental engagement 141
Celebration of cultural diversity 142
Conclusions 143
References 144

8 Inclusive Curriculum to Raise Achievement: Teachers and Headteachers' Perspectives — 146
Introduction 146
Why does curriculum diversity matter? 146
Effective use of inclusive multicultural curriculum: evidence from the case study schools 149
Approaches used in diversifying the curriculum in schools: evidence from a school survey 156
Conclusions 159
References 161

9 Tackling School Exclusions of Ethnic Minority Pupils 163
   Introduction 163
   Tackling school exclusions 165
      Effective use of inclusive and nurturing 169
      Restorative approach 170
      Effective use of LAs and multiagency team 171
      Trauma-informed practice 172
      Effective behaviour management 172
   Conclusions 174
   References 175

PART IV
The International Experience in Raising the Achievement of Black and Ethnic Minority Students 179

10 The International Experience in Raising the
   Achievement of Black and Ethnic Minority Students 181
   Introduction 181
   The racial achievement gap in the USA 181
   Factors associated with the achievement gap in the USA 184
   Effective strategies to tackle educational inequalities
      and the racial achievement gap 193
      Closing the school readiness gap in the early years 194
      Closing the achievement gap in school 195
      Providing effective leadership 196
      High quality in teaching and learning 196
      Using a rigorous, inclusive curriculum 197
      Small class size 198
      Effective use of assessment data and test results
         to improve 198
      Teacher's continuous professional development
         (CPD) programme 199
      Other intervention strategies 199
   The achievement gap in other English-speaking
      countries 199
   Summary and conclusions 201
   References 203

PART V
What Are the Lessons for Those Concerned with Black and Ethnic Minority Achievement?   213

11 Summary, Conclusions, and Lessons to Raise Achievement and Tackle Inequality   215
Introduction 215
Summary and conclusions 216
  The barriers to learning: challenges 216
  Success factors in closing the achievement gap: good practice 216
  Targeted intervention strategies in addressing inequality 218
Lessons to raise achievement and tackle inequality in schools 218
  The experience in English schools 218
  The international experience 220
  The lessons to be drawn from successful schools 222
References 223

12 Implications for Policy and Practice   227
Introduction 227
Implications for schools 227
Implications for headteachers and teachers 229
Implications for central government 229
Implications for local education authorities and multi-academy trusts 230
Implications for diversifying the curriculum 231
Implications for the research community 232
References 234

Index   237

FIGURES

1.1	GCSE achievement gap by ethnic background	5
1.2	Ethnic minority population in schools	6
2.1	The achievement gap between pupils eligible for free school meals (FSM) and non-FSM pupils in England (% 5+ A* to C including English and Maths 2005–2023)	30
3.1	Main barriers to learning	42
4.1	A survey of the factors that contributed to improving ethnic minority and disadvantaged pupils' achievement	65
4.2	Ofsted judgements about teaching and leadership quality in the schools	68
4.3	Five Stages of the school improvement cycle	69
5.1	A survey of the targeted intervention strategies used by schools to raise attainment	85
5.2	Mapping the London Challenge	91
5.3	The impact of the London Challenge in closing the ethnic minority gap	92
5.4	GCSE Black Caribbean and White British achievement gap in England (5+A*-C incl. English and Maths)	93
5.5	Interventions strategies to close the achievement gap of disadvantaged pupils	95
9.1	Trend in permanent exclusions in England by main ethnic groups	165
10.1	Trends in out-of-school suspension rates in K-12 schools by race and ethnicity, 1973–2018	192

TABLES

2.1	KS2 and GCSE performance by ethnic origin in English schools (%)	29
2.2	KS2 (expected level) and GCSE 5+ A*–C performance in England by gender and ethnic background (%)	31
2.3	Disadvantaged pupils KS2 and GCSE performance in England, 2011–2023	33
2.4	KS2 and GCSE performance in England by ethnic background (%), 2023	33
2.5	GCSE achievement gap of disadvantaged pupils by ethnic background and FSM (%)	34
2.6	Percentage of pupils eligible for FSM reaching the expected standard in RWM at KS2	34
2.7	KS2 and GCSE achievement of pupils in England by gender (%)	36
6.1	Attainment by main languages spoken in the LA at end of KS2 and GCSE, 2023	104
6.2	English proficiency stage and EAL attainment at KS2 (% reaching expected standard)	107
6.3	English Proficiency and EAL Attainment at GCSE	108
9.1	Exclusions by pupil characteristics in schools in England, percentage of population 2021/2022	166
10.1	The National Assessment of Educational Progress (NAEP) trend in reading and mathematics average scores for Black, Hispanic, and White students in the USA	183

ABBREVIATIONS

In English education, there is a tendency in schools and in central and local government to use acronyms in written and spoken communication. The following list explains what some of the common acronyms used in this study mean for international readers:

CAT	Cognitive ability test
CPD	Continuing professional development
DCSF	Department for Children, Schools and Families
DfE	Department for Education
EAL	English as an additional language
EEF	Education Endowment Foundation
EMAG	Ethnic Minority Achievement Grant
ESOL	English for speakers of other languages
EYFS	Early years foundation stage
FSM	Free school meals
FSP	Foundation stage profile
GCSE	General Certificate of Secondary Education
HMI	Her Majesty's Inspector
HLTA	Higher-level teaching assistant
ICT	Information and communications technology
KS1	Key stage 1
KS2	Key stage 2
KS3	Key stage 3
KS4	Key stage 4
LA	Local authority
LSA	Learning support assistant

NQT	Newly qualified teacher
NLE	National leader of education
NPD	National pupil database
NQT	Newly qualified teacher
NVQ	National Vocational Qualification
Ofsted	Office for Standards in Education, Children's Services and Skills
PP	Pupil premium
PPF	Pupil premium funding
PPG	Pupil premium grant
PPR	Pupil performance review
PSHE	Personal, social, health, and economic education
RWM	Reading, writing, and mathematics
SAT	Standard attainment test
SEN	Special educational needs
SENCO	Special educational needs coordinator
SFR	Statistical first release
SLE	Specialist leader of education
SLT	Senior leadership team
SMT	Senior management team
TA	teaching assistant

ABOUT THE AUTHOR

Feyisa Demie is Honorary Professor at Durham University, UK, and a Fellow of the Academy of Social Science (FAcSS). He has worked extensively for over 30 years with local authorities, government departments, and schools on using research and data to drive school improvement. He also runs annual school improvement conferences and school-focussed training programmes on using achievement data and 'what work' research evidence for headteachers, teachers, governors, and policymakers to support school self-evaluation.

A NOTE ON TERMINOLOGY AND CODE USED IN THE BOOK

1. **Ethnic minorities:** The term 'ethnic minorities' is used in the book refers to all ethnic groups in the UK 2021 census except the white British group.
2. **White British** refers to English, Welsh, Scottish, Northern Irish, or British.
3. **BAME** is used to emphasize all Black, Asian, and all other Minority ethnic groups.
4. **Black and ethnic minority** has been used as an inclusive term for Black Africans, Black Caribbean, Any other Black background, and other ethnic minorities in the census such as mixed ethnic groups, Asian, Other White, and other minority ethnic groups.
5. **Disadvantaged pupils** refer to pupils from low-income backgrounds who are eligible for a free school meal. This differentiates between pupils eligible for FSM and those who are not.
6. **Pupil Premium refers to** additional funding given to publicly funded schools in England to raise the attainment of disadvantaged pupils to close the achievement gap between those on free school meals and their peers.
7. **School case studies** in the book are coded alphabetically.
8. **Survey respondents** in the book are coded numerically and only the respondent's code of those who made additional comments in the survey is used.

ACKNOWLEDGEMENTS

This book is based on original research conducted by the author over the last two decades into what works in the achievement of Black and ethnic minority students in multicultural schools. The empirical evidence of the book is based on case studies of schools and school surveys.

The authors would like to thank the headteachers, teachers, parents, pupils, and school governors who participated in various research activities, including case studies, school surveys, and focus groups. We are grateful for welcoming us into their schools and classrooms, year after year, generously giving their time for interviews and offering thoughtful comments about strategies and successful practice to raise achievement. Unfortunately promises about confidentiality prohibit us from naming them here. The school and staff interviewed are coded and given pseudonyms.

Our investigation of learning barriers and strategies that have improved the academic performance of Black and Ethnic Minority students over the past two decades gave rise to the book. Some of the extracts and quotations are also drawn from the author's previous corpus of reports, research publications, and articles including:

Demie, F. (2023) 'Tackling educational inequality: Lessons from London schools.' *Equity in education & society* 2(3): 243–266.

Demie, F. (2023) *Raising the Achievement of Black Caribbean pupils: Barriers and Good Practice in Schools*, School Research and Statistics Service.

Demie, F. (2022) *Understanding the Causes and Consequences of School Exclusions: Teachers, Parents and Schools' Perspectives*. London: Routledge.

Demie, F. (2019) *Educational Inequality: Closing the gap*. London: UCL IOE Press.

Demie, F. (2018) 'English as an Additional Language and Attainment in Primary Schools in England' *Journal of Multilingual and Multicultural Development*, 39(7):641–653.

Demie, F and Lewis, K. (2018) 'Raising the achievement of English as additional language pupils in schools: implications for policy and practice', *Educational Review*, 70(4):427–446.

We have also used a systematic review of the literature listed in the references. All extracts and quotations from the review are referenced and acknowledged as appropriate.

I want to thank the editors of all journals and publications cited in the reference. Thanks to Taylor and Francis, for publishing my articles and this book. Many thanks also to those who edited this book.

PART I

Introduction

Black and Ethnic Minority Educational Achievement Issues, Debates, and Policy Concerns

1
INTRODUCTION
Policy Concerns and Challenges

Why is there an interest in Black and ethnic minority achievement?

Black and ethnic minority communities have been settled in the UK for centuries. Still, the presence has been long characterised in negative terms, with concerns about achievement and their potential negative impacts on White pupils as the result of their identities and backgrounds. Much of the research has documented how discrimination against minority ethnic groups was implemented within British education for decades (Swann, 1985; Rampton, 1981; Archer and Francis, 2007; Demie and Mclean, 2017). Evidence from the research shows that race and ethnicity were ignored within education policy but were acknowledged in the context of underachievement (Archer and Francis, 2007; Demie, 2019a, b; Gillborn, 2002; MacPherson, 1999). Undoubtedly, some Black and ethnic minority pupils' underachievement in the last decade of the twentieth century saw much debate among schools, academic researchers, and policymakers about the achievement of Black and ethnic minority pupils in British schools.

The relative underachievement of ethnic minority pupils has also been a major issue in national education policy formulation. The government set up an inquiry committee and reported on the issue of underachievement twice during the 1980s. The first recognition of the problem was the Rampton Report (1981), which looked into the education of children of ethnic minority groups. This report dealt in detail with the underachievement of pupils with Black backgrounds and concluded, 'West Indian children are underachieving in our education system' (Rampton, 1981, p. 80). The Swann Report (Swann, 1985) also gives a good deal of attention to the underachievement of pupils of

Caribbean backgrounds and confirms the findings of the Rampton report. Thus, the Swann Report concludes, 'There is no doubt that the West Indian children, as a group and on average, are underachieving, both by comparison with their school fellows in the White majority as well as in terms of their potential, notwithstanding that some are doing well' (Swann, 1985, p. 81).

There is now much research to show that Black students are underachieving within the education system and that they are less likely to achieve their full potential at school (Demie 2003, 2001; Gillborn and Mirza, 2000; OFSTED, 2002b; Coard, 1971; Cook, 2013; Crozier, 2005; Demie, 2020; Demie & Lewis, 2013;Gillborn & Youdell; 2000; Greaves et al. 2014; Hutchings & Mansaray 2013);Hutchings et al. 2012; Maylor et al. 2009;Milliard et al. 2018; Richardson, 2005; Tomlinson, 1983). Other research in the 1990s also reflected earlier findings, with Black Caribbean and African students continuing to make less progress on average than other students (Gillborn and Gipps, 1996; Gillborn and Mirza, 2000; Demie, 2005, 2003, 2001). These studies show considerable underachievement by Black Caribbean and Black African students in comparison with the achievement of White British, Indian, and Chinese students. Similarly, recent EPI (2019) research also confirms that there are huge disparities between pupil groups by ethnic background. By the end of secondary school, Chinese and Indian pupils perform significantly better than their White British peers; Black pupils; Pakistani, mixed-race, and gypsy/Roma pupils; and other White, Black, and mixed-race pupils have continued underachieving. Figure 1.1 and research into other ethnic minority achievement and educational attainment have also highlighted the importance of addressing underachievement in schools to close the gap (see Demie 2019a; Strand, 2015, 2012; Ofsted, 2010, 2009, 2002b; EPI 2023; Choudry 2021).

It is interesting to note here that most of the research on race and ethnicity in England is concerned with the largest ethnic minority communities: people of Indian, Black Caribbean, African, Pakistani, and Bangladeshi ethnicities, Chinese, and other White ethnic groups. They all argued that the performance in GCSE examinations at 16 can be vital to young people's future educational and employment chances. Results of all previous studies show that except for Indians and Chinese, most ethnic minority groups are underachieving compared to White British (Demie, 2019a,b; Strand, 2012; Gillborn and Gipps, 1996; Gillborn and Mirza, 2000; Demie, 2005, 2003, 2001). Particularly, Black Caribbean pupils have not shared equally in the increasing rates of educational achievement, and they are significantly lower than other groups. The achievements of Black Caribbean, White other, and mixed-race children are particularly cause for concern. There is a growing gap between the achievements of Black, Pakistani, and mixed-race students and their peers (Demie and Mclean 2017; Demie 2003). Overall, previous research and available data show the gap in achievement between the highest- and lowest-achieving ethnic groups is growing (see Choudry, 2021;

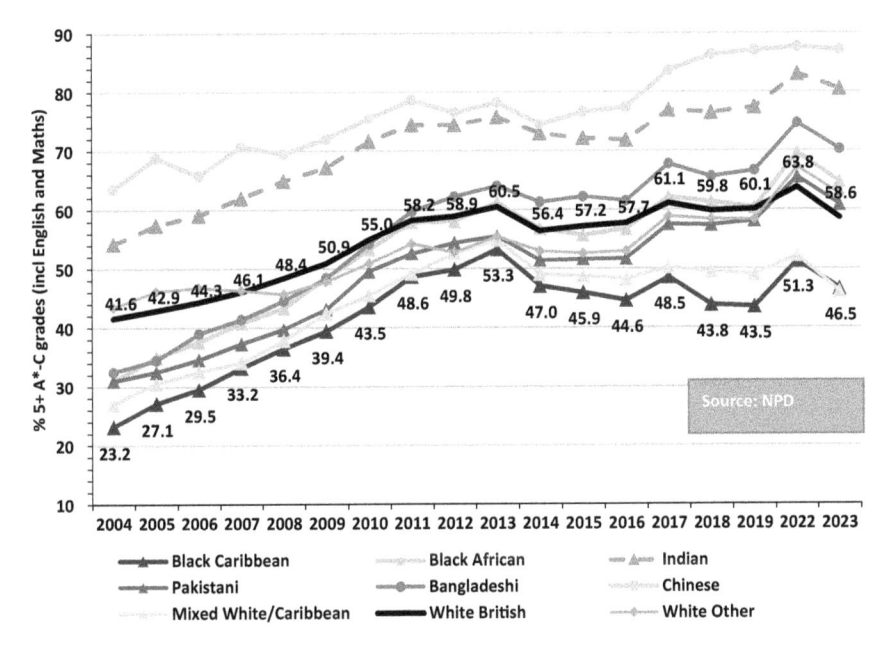

FIGURE 1.1 GCSE achievement gap by ethnic background.
Source: DfE 2017 and Demie, 2023:4.

Demie, 2019a; Demie and Mclean, 2017; Archer and Francis, 2007; EPI, 2023). This is also supported by an IFS comprehensive study showing entrenched inequalities in educational attainment and that education in the UK is not tackling inequality (IFS, 2022). The explanations for the underachievement of some ethnic minorities tended to centre on cultural and family differences, language barriers, curriculum issues, schools and teachers' low expectations, institutional racism, a lack of diversity in the school workforce, the effects of poverty, and a lack of targeted support as possible contributing causes to low achievement (Tomlinson, 2008; Swann, 1985; Rampton, 1981; Modood, 2011; Igbal, 2019; Demie, 2022a,b, 2019a, 2023; Demie and Mclean, 2017; Race, 2024).

As the ethnic minority population has grown in England, policymakers are also concerned about how to tackle diversity issues. The government data shows the ethnic minority population is growing, and currently 37% of the school population is considered an ethnic minority (see Figure 1.2.). Recent Census data shows the total school population of England was over 8 million. Of this, about 64% are White British pupils and Asian ethnic groups (12.3%), Black ethnic groups (5.8%), mixed other groups (5.6%), and other ethnic groups (2.2%).

6 Black and Ethnic Minority Achievement in Schools

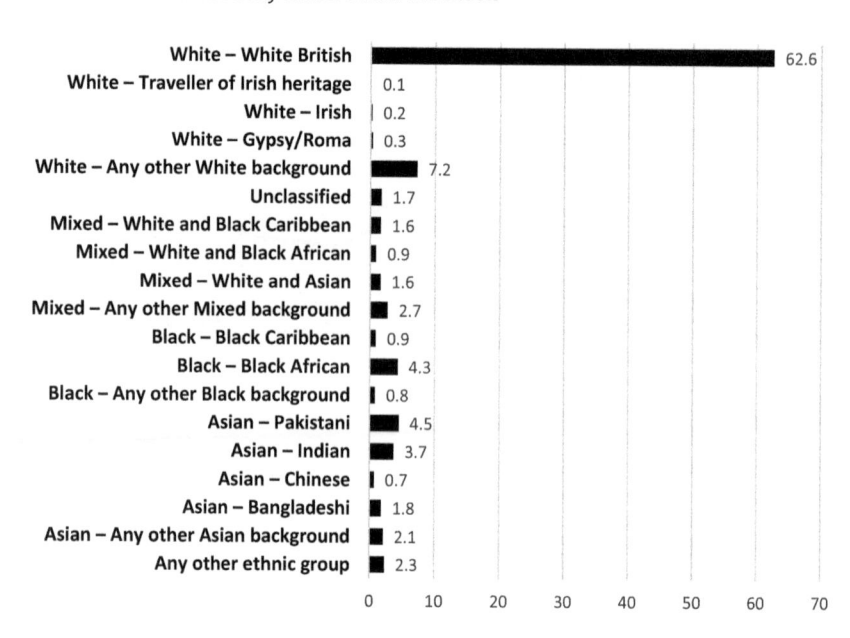

Ethnic group	%
White – White British	62.6
White – Traveller of Irish heritage	0.1
White – Irish	0.2
White – Gypsy/Roma	0.3
White – Any other White background	7.2
Unclassified	1.7
Mixed – White and Black Caribbean	1.6
Mixed – White and Black African	0.9
Mixed – White and Asian	1.6
Mixed – Any other Mixed background	2.7
Black – Black Caribbean	0.9
Black – Black African	4.3
Black – Any other Black background	0.8
Asian – Pakistani	4.5
Asian – Indian	3.7
Asian – Chinese	0.7
Asian – Bangladeshi	1.8
Asian – Any other Asian background	2.1
Any other ethnic group	2.3

FIGURE 1.2 Ethnic minority population in schools.
Source: DfE (2003) January 2023 census.

To tackle the growth of the ethnic minority problem, policymakers in England looked at the various education policies and approaches to settling new communities in England, ranging from assimilation policy (1950–1960), integration (1966–1970), multiculturalism (1970–1980), Every Child Matters, and community cohesions between 1980 and 2010 (see Modood, 2011; Race 2024). Tomlinson's (1982:1; 2008) research shows the worrying picture that in 'Britain, the education system is only just beginning to come to terms with the changes necessary for the successful incorporation of ethnic minority children and the creation of a multiracial and multicultural society that offers equal opportunities to all.' There has been a battle in implementing multicultural education and replacing the current monocultural and Euro-centric curriculum that does not recognise diversity in Britain (Swann, 1985; Tomlinson, 2008) and multicultural education to educate all children within a culturally diverse framework. The inequalities faced by Black and minority ethnic communities have been deepened by the lack of an inclusive curriculum in the English education system and the failure of the national curriculum to adequately reflect the needs of a diverse, multi-ethnic society (Demie 2022a,b, 2019a,b; Gillborn and Mirza 2000; Macpherson 1999; Demie and Mclean 2017; Demie 2005; Mortimore 1999; Swann 1985; Rampton 1981). Recently, despite stark race inequalities, the national policy has been largely one in which there is a refusal to acknowledge the impact of race and identity on the lives of ethnic minority families and within education. These government policies and approaches resulted in many debates and issues that need to be addressed in the education of ethnic minority pupils in England, including Black and ethnic minority underachievement issues, racism, curriculum barriers and relevance, teachers' lower teacher expectations, diversity issues, multicultural education, and how to promote equality of opportunities (Swann 1985; Rampton 1981; Demie 2003, 2019a,b, 2023; Demie and Mclean 2017; Race 2024; Archer and Francis, 2007; Macpherson, 1999; and Gillborn and Mirza, 2000).

Despite reports related to these issues and government enquiries, the issue of the underachievement of many Black and ethnic minority pupils continued. The lack of recognition of the diversity of the backgrounds of ethnic minority pupils in the national curriculum and the under-representation of ethnic minority teachers remained. There is still a growing debate on the role of schools in tackling educational underachievement. What is worrying is that little progress has been made in addressing race and ethnic-based inequalities in schools to tackle the underachievement of some ethnic minority groups. A well-established body of research evidence shows that inequality in educational outcomes has grown for some groups over the last decade, and a large number of ethnic minority children are underachieving, yet policy does little to tackle it because of a lack of good practices to drive improvement. Of particular concern is the growing inequality in educational outcomes for some disadvantaged groups, such as Black Caribbean, Pakistani, mixed-race, and other White pupils (Demie 2022a,b,2019a,b,2005, 2003, 2001; Demie and Mclean 2017).

Researchers now agree that the biggest obstacles to raising Black and ethnic minority achievement are the 'colour blind' approach, which has put the group at a disadvantage, and the failure of the national curriculum to adequately reflect the needs of a diverse, multi-ethnic society (Gillborn, 2002; MacPherson, 1999). All government education reform acts and White papers failed to explore the specific needs of Black and ethnic minority pupils. Recently, the government has adopted standard rhetoric for all and the market alternative in policy-making, which has resulted in the fragmentation of the education systems (Ball, 1993). As a result, the government was unable to act decisively against the significant and growing inequalities that now characterise the system. Ball (1993) highlighted this problem with standard rhetoric and market approach policy and argued that school competition and reducing State intervention in education planning in England has failed to address inequality in education. Although previous governments have added inequality of education attainment between social groups into their policy statements on social justice and inclusion, there has been no strong lead given to address the issues of the underachievement of Black and ethnic minority pupils by the central government since 2010. Governments have failed to recognise that children of minority ethnic origin, such as Black Caribbean and Pakistani, have particular needs that are not being met by the school system. Evidence from the national data suggests that the performance gap is widening and that some ethnic minority children in England's schools are not sharing the higher educational standards achieved over the last decade in England. Such evidence reinforces the findings of previous research, which identified serious concerns about the extent to which the education system and schools were meeting the needs of Black and ethnic minority children (Gillborn and Mirza 2000; Rampton 1981; Swann 1985; Gillborn and Gipps 1996; Demie 2003 and 2005). These concerns persist. Research also shows both failure and success in education, but a wide-ranging attempt to address ethnic diversity and underachievement is long overdue in schools (Demie, 2003 and 2005). However, in contrast, research has begun to examine the benefits of addressing diversity and tackling educational inequality. To address the issue, researchers started to look at the school's good practices that provide an environment in which ethnic minority pupils flourish against the odds (Mongon and Chapman, 2008; Ofsted, 2009; Demie and Lewis, 2010a,b; Demie and Mclean, 2015a, b, 2017, 2019; Baars et al., 2014). The next section will review previous research about the school's strategies and good practices to raise school achievement.

What does research tell us about strategies to raise achievement and tackle inequality?

There is now a growing acceptance that research into what works in driving school improvement and tackling educational inequality among ethnic minority pupils provides valuable background and useful insights for those concerned with improvement in schools (see Edmonds 1982; Hopkins et al. 1994; Sammons et al. 1995; Reynolds and Sammons 1996; Mortimore, 1999; Mortimore et al. 1988; Rutter et al. 1979; Sammons 1999; Stoll and Fink, 1994; Muijis et al. 2004; Blair and Bourne 1998; Demie and Lewis 2010a,b; Demie and Mclean 2015a, 2016, 2017).

However, Thrupp (1999; Mortimore and Whitty 1997; Demie 2019a; Gorard 2000, 2010) has argued that research in the school effectiveness and improvement field has taken insufficient account of socioeconomic and ethnic background context. They also suggested that schools can make a difference, albeit with certain limits, and that school effectiveness and school improvement research is downplaying the significance of social factors, race, and ethnic background (Edmonds, 1982; Hopkins et al., 1994; Sammons et al., 1995; Reynolds and Sammons, 1996; Mortimore, 1999; Mortimore et al., 1988; Rutter et al., 1979; Thrupp, 1999; Demie, 2019a; Gorard, 2000, 2010). Mortimore's research (1999:300) endorses all previous research on school effectiveness and school improvement studies that show that schools can make a difference, but 'the effect of poverty cannot be dismissed as irrelevant; just some schools in disadvantaged areas can promote exceptional progress.' Researchers have now accepted that much of the differences in pupil outcomes are due to school intake characteristics, and the family social and ethnic background, neighbourhood where pupils live, and types of school attended can have a detrimental impact on their educational achievement and progress (Reynolds and Sammons 1996; Sammons 1999; Mortimore and Whitty 1997; Rasbash et al. 2010; Clifton and Cook 2012; Ofsted 2014; Gorard 2000, 2010; Strand 2015; Demie 2019a).

In particular, in the UK and the USA, the link between ethnic background and poor educational attainment is greater than in almost any other developed country (Demie 2019a; Hutchinson et al. 2019; EPI 2019; Leach and Williams, 2007). Educational inequality starts early, continues, and widens throughout school and impacts a child's life when measured by social, economic, and ethnic background. Research also shows inequality in education outcomes has grown for Black and ethnic minority groups in the last three decades (Demie 2019a; Hutchinson et al. 2019; Demie and Mclean 2017). Yet despite this, policymakers do little to tackle the growing ethnic inequality in education, particularly with Black Caribbean, Pakistani, and other underachieving groups.

Drawing on past research that suggests schools can make a difference in driving school improvement and closing the achievement gap, this book is about the achievement of Black and ethnic minority students in schools. There is well-established research to show that African and Caribbean pupils are underachieving within the education system and that they are not achieving their full potential at school (Demie and Mclean 2017). The government-funded inquiry committee on this issue looked twice during the 1980s and gave a good deal of attention to the underachievement of pupils of Black Caribbean backgrounds. The committee of inquiry report shows that Black Caribbean and Black African children are underachieving within the British education system (Rampton, 1981; Swann, 1985). The concerns persist. Other research in the 1990s and 2000s also confirmed earlier findings, with Black students continuing to make less progress on average than other ethnic groups (Demie, 2023; Gorard et al., 2023; Strand, 2012; Gillborn and Mirza, 2000; Demie, 2005, 2003, 2001). All the previous studies showed considerable underachievement of Black Caribbean, Black African, and mixed-race pupils when compared to the achievement of White British, Indian, and Chinese pupils.

However, the situation is not all doom and gloom. There is no inherent reason Black African and Black Caribbean children should not achieve as well as the majority of other children. Research shows that schools can make a difference in raising achievement (Mortimore, Sammons et al., 1988; Sammons, 2007; Tikly et al., 2006; Strand, 2012, 2014; Demie and Mclean, 2007;

Ofsted, 2002a,b 2009; Ofsted, 2013; Demie, 2005, 2022b; Baars et al., 2014), and Black children buck the national trend. Furthermore, in recent years, the need for a detailed case study of successful schools in raising the achievement of African and Black Caribbean pupils has become apparent as a means of increasing our understanding of how schools can enhance pupils' academic achievement. Several previous research studies looked at examples of schools that provide an environment in which Black Caribbean, Black African, and Bangladeshi pupils flourish and identified key characteristics of successful schools in raising achievement, including strong leadership, high expectations, effective teaching and learning, effective use of inclusive curriculum, diversity in the school workforce, effective use of data to track students achievement by ethnic background, the ethos of respect with a clear approach to racism and bad behaviour, and parental involvement (see for details) (Demie 2005, DfES 2003, McKenley et al. 2003, Blair and Bourne 1998; Demie and Mclean 2007, 2015a, 2017, 2016; DfE 2010; Baars et al. 2014; Ofsted 2002a,b 2009, 2013; EEF 2019; Boyle & Humphreys, 2012; Burgess, 2015; Rhamie & Hallam, 2010). There is a growing synthesis of evidence of what works to raise the achievement of Black and ethnic minority students. The key challenge is finding out what strategies schools can use to make a difference for Black students nationally and internationally. A growing body of research now argues the need to explore further the barriers to learning and school strategies to close the achievement gap (Demie 2005, 2015, 2019a, 2022b; DfE 2010; Demie Mclean 2017; Miller 2019).

This book gives an account of what works in tackling Black and ethnic minority students' educational inequality with insights and understanding about educational success for Black and ethnic minority students. It also aims to illustrate good practice models from England that make a difference in the UK and beyond. Above all, it is an important contribution to theoretical knowledge, policy, and practice and challenges policymakers and school leaders on their current practice with recommendations on what needs to be done to improve education policy and drive school improvement.

The aims of the book

The research in this book is rooted in the theory of the fields of school effectiveness and school improvement, which is concerned with making schools 'better places for pupils, teachers, and the wider community and providing evidence of good practice in schools that are closing the achievement gap' (Hopkins et al. 1994:3). The book arose from our research into the barriers to learning and what works to raise the achievement of Black and ethnic minority students in the last 20 years. This book argues that Black and minority ethnic students' educational inequality matters. It aims to provide empirical evidence and good practices in successful schools for closing the achievement gap for Black and ethnic minority students. The book looks to answer, in detail, a number of questions, including:

- What does education policy tell us about race and inequality?
- What is the empirical evidence for educational inequality?
- What are the barriers to learning?
- What are strategies and good practices for addressing inequality and closing the gap?
- What is the international experience of tackling educational inequalities?
- What are the implications for policy and practice?

The book addresses these questions and engages with any contentious debates in this area in several chapters at national and international levels. Drawing on original evidence of KS2 and GCSE attainment data from the National Pupil Database (NPD), case studies, focus groups, and interviews with headteachers, teachers, school staff, policymakers, parents, pupils, and governors, the author tries to chart the road to improvement and tackle inequality in education. It also draws on international comparative literature on Black and minority ethnic groups' achievement in the various studies he has been involved with and his 20 years of experience working within local authorities (LAs), the London Challenge, government departments, national strategies, schools, and governors as a researcher, school adviser, and CPD trainer.

This book is also unique as it takes a reflective, longer-term overview of the educational experiences in schools of addressing educational inequality and closing the achievement gap of Black and ethnic minority students. It also offers readers and schools the chance to engage with the experiences of successful schools and consider what lessons can be drawn for future policy and practice to drive school improvement.

Research methods

The methodological approach used to gather evidence for the book is mixed-methods research that combines qualitative and quantitative research elements to understand the educational achievement and inequality issues of Black and ethnic minority students. These include a review of the literature that reflects each chapter, case studies of selected schools, focus group interviews, school survey evidence, and achievement gap data analysis. Each of the four complementary methodological approaches used in the book contributes a particular set of data to the study, and the details are given below.

First, a review of the literature was undertaken to examine racial and socioeconomic gaps at the national and international levels, including the barriers and what works in closing the achievement gap and tackling educational inequality.

Second, detailed case study research was conducted to study the strategies to close the achievement gap. A structured questionnaire was used to interview headteachers, teachers, parents, school governors, and pupils. A focus group of parents, pupils, and governors was also conducted to ascertain their views on barriers and strategies that worked to raise achievement. Topics explored as part of the case study schools include the quality of school leadership and management, the school curriculum, the quality of teaching and learning, pupil performance, targeted intervention strategy and support, English as an Additional Language (EAL) pupils assessment and support, school exclusions, pupils' views about the school, race and ethnicity in the curriculum, and school parental engagement and diversity in the school workforce.

Thirteen schools (eight primary and five secondary schools) were selected for case studies. Purposive sampling is used to select schools and respondents for the case study. This sampling approach is widely used in qualitative research to identify and select information-rich case studies for the most effective use of limited resources. The key criteria for the selection of schools were those with a very high proportion of pupils with ethnic minority heritage, an above-average proportion of students who are eligible for free school meals and EAL, good KS2 and GCSE results, and outstanding Ofsted inspection reports. The case study schools are the most ethnically, linguistically, and culturally diverse schools, with African pupils comprising 24% of the ethnic group., followed by Black Caribbean with 17%, White British 15%, mixed-race 13%, White other 8%, Portuguese 6%, and other Black 6%. There are also a small number of Indian, Bangladeshi, Pakistani, Irish, and Turkish pupils in schools. Almost half of the students (47%) are EAL and speak a language other than English at home, and about 34% of pupils are taking up free school.

As part of the research, a variety of members of school staff and parents were interviewed to get a range of perspectives on the main practices in the case study schools. These included headteachers and deputy headteachers; class teachers; EAL teachers and special educational needs coordinators; teaching assistants and learning support teachers; family support workers, governors, and pupils. Each case study school was visited at least once every year as part of the research between 2010 and 2022 to monitor what worked and what did not work in driving school improvement and tackling inequality. The author also worked as a school self-evaluation advisor for the schools. There have been good opportunities to know and record information about the school's achievements and challenges over the years. The case study schools in the book are coded alphabetically from school A to school Y to ensure unanimity. Case study schools: 'A, B, C, D, G, J, W, and Y are primary schools, and E, H, F, O, and R' are secondary schools.

Third, a questionnaire survey was undertaken to collate the views of headteachers and teachers on barriers and good practice. The survey asked the respondents how much they felt each of the factors contributed to barriers to learning, good practices to raise achievement, and strategies for targeted interventions to close the achievement gap (see for details, Figures 3.1, 4.1, and 5.1). Using a 7-point scale, it was then grouped into strongly disagree, disagree, agree, and strongly agree. We also asked additional open-ended questions to describe the key factors that they felt contributed to barriers to learning, good practices, and strategies for targeted intervention. Survey responses were received from 183 headteachers, the senior management team, and school staff from various schools and phases. The survey respondents (SPs) are coded with numerical numbers from SP1 to SP183 to ensure confidentiality. About 61% of the respondents were headteachers, and 17% were deputy headteachers and assistant headteachers. The reminders were EAL coordinators, SENCO, and the teacher with lead responsibilities. Of the respondents to the survey, 74% represented the primary phase and 21% the secondary phase, followed by 3.6% all through primary and secondary and 1.2% nursery and special. Almost all the respondents worked over 3 years, with 10% between 3 and 10 years, 24% between 12–20 years, 43% between 20–30 years, 19% between 30–40 years, and over 4% for over 40 years (see Demie, 2024).

The findings that emerged from the study based on the above research approach are given in the following chapters.

The structure of the book

The book seeks to provide answers to these and other questions. It draws on two decades of the author's research in London. The book is relevant to education, sociology, economics, and human geography courses. It is also relevant to a range of researchers and academics, students, teachers, school leaders, practitioners, education professionals, and policymakers. We concentrate in this book on the school sector in England but also draw experience from the UK and other countries when it is relevant.

The book has three parts and twelve chapters, depending on the readers' roles, interests, and needs. Each part or chapter can be read from start to finish and may be read in any order. The following outline of the report structure is intended to help readers navigate their way through the text.

Black and ethnic minority achievement in British schools cannot be understood in isolation from the numerous education policy directives that have been pursued by successive governments over decades about ethnic minorities' education and underachievement. The first part of Chapters 1–3 therefore explores Black and ethnic minority educational achievement issues, debates, and policy concerns. The rest of the book is concerned with factors associated with barriers to learning and success factors in schools in tackling educational inequality and targeted intervention strategies to drive improvement in successful schools.

Chapter 1 provides the introduction. It sets the scene for the book and discusses the policy context of Black and ethnic minorities' achievement issues in schools in England. Key literature was reviewed on policy concerns and challenges to the achievement of Black and ethnic minority students. The chapter also maps out key debates within the field, including why there is interest in diversity and Black and ethnic minority achievement, what research tells us about strategies to tackle educational inequality, the book's aims, research methods, and structure.

Chapter 2 explores educational inequality and the achievement gap. This chapter asks the key question critical for chapters to follow: What is the empirical evidence for educational inequality and the achievement gap? Drawing on longitudinal KS2 and GCSE NPD data, it examines in detail the attainment patterns by gender, ethnic background, and socioeconomic status to measure the impact of government policy over the past decades on educational inequality and closing the achievement gap.

Chapter 3 investigates the factors associated with barriers to learning and the reasons for Black students' underachievement. Drawing on case studies, focus groups, and school surveys, this chapter presents key evidence and explanations of factors associated with barriers to learning and underachievement, including teachers' low expectations, poor leadership, institutional racism, curriculum barriers, language barriers, poverty, a lack of targeted support, diversity, funding, and parental engagement. These reasons for barriers to learning are supported by evidence collected during the research from school leaders, teachers, parents, governors, and pupils.

The next 4–6 chapters in Part 2 look at the experience of raising the achievement of Black and ethnic minority students in schools by looking into what works in driving school improvement and closing the achievement gap. Using the review of the literature of the published research I have been involved in the last 20 years, this part discusses in detail 'what works' in schools in tackling educational inequalities and closing the achievement gap for Black and ethnic minority students. It draws on various good practice studies and school surveys collected during the research from school leaders, teachers, parents, governors, and pupils.

Chapter 4 explores good practices for raising the achievement of Black and ethnic minority students and the lessons from schools. The main aim is to explore how students from Black and ethnic minority backgrounds are helped to achieve high standards in school and to identify the factors that contribute to the success of raising achievement. This chapter also asks, 'What strategies does your school use to raise achievement and close the gap for black students?' Drawing on evidence collected through case study interviews, surveys of headteachers, teachers, and school staff, and a review of literature, the specific success factors and strategies explored in this chapter include providing strong school leadership, effective teaching and learning, effective use of inclusive curriculum, diversity in the teaching workforce, and the use of data for monitoring and tracking pupil progress.

Chapter 5 explores the school's targeted intervention strategy to raise achievement and close the gaps. Drawing on evidence collected through case study interviews, focus groups, and surveys of headteachers, teachers, and school staff, and a review of literature, the following sections provide the views and experiences of relevant stakeholders in schools, including the school survey evidence on effective targeted intervention strategies, the London Challenge evidence on effective intervention strategies, and the EEF evidence on effective intervention strategies.

Chapter 6 discusses school strategies for raising the achievement of pupils for whom English is an Additional Language (EAL). Drawing on the author's research evidence conducted in the last decades, it will look into attainment and success factors for raising students' achievement with EAL.

Chapters 7–9 examine the experiences of headteachers, teachers, parents, pupils, and school staff with Black and ethnic minority achievement, parental engagement, school curriculum, and school exclusions, using evidence collected through case study interviews, focus groups, and school surveys.

Chapter 7 explores the experience of parental engagement. Drawing on evidence collected through interviews and focus groups, it will cover teachers' and headteachers' views on partnerships with parents and parents' and pupils' views on partnerships with schools.

Chapter 8 examines the experience with the British curriculum. Using evidence collected through case study interviews, focus groups, and surveys, it will provide the views and experiences of headteachers, teachers, parents, governors, and students on an effective inclusive curriculum to support Black and ethnic minority pupils.

Chapter 9 looks into the experiences of Black and ethnic minority students with school exclusions. There is now a growing body of research that argues the need to explore the reasons for Black pupils' over-representation and what needs to be done to tackle disproportionality in school exclusions, as they affect the academic achievements of students of colour. Drawing on nationally available trending statistical data and case studies, it will provide the scale of the exclusions problem and some approaches and good practices to tackle school exclusions.

Chapter 10 in Part 3 explores the international experience in raising the achievement of Black and ethnic minority students.

Chapter 10 explores the international experience of raising achievement and closing the achievement gap. It looks for evidence using a systematic review of the literature. Based on the findings from the review of literature on the Black and ethnic minority experience in the USA and other English-speaking countries, it will cover the racial and ethnic achievement gap, factors associated with the gap, and effective strategies to tackle educational inequalities.

Chapter 11 gives a summary, conclusions, and what we have learned from the research over the previous 20 years about raising achievement and addressing educational inequality. It provides a summary and conclusion related to barriers to learning, success factors to close the achievement gap, targeted intervention strategies, and lessons from English and international experience.

The last chapter, Chapter 12, draws implications of the findings for schools, governments, school improvement practitioners, headteachers and teachers, LAs, and multi-academy trusts, diversifying the curriculum, parental engagement, and the research community.

Notes

* In addition to the original case studies, school survey, and achievement data that are used as evidence to write the book, I also carried out systematic literature reviews for reports related to the racial and ethnic achievement gap in education and strategies to tackle educational inequalities to identify other relevant studies. This literature review produced pre-existing literature amounting to a total of around 20,000 distinct reports. The reports were in several electronic databases and search engines, including Google and Google Scholar. The bulk of the relevant references came from the main educational, sociological, and psychological databases.

As the purpose of this literature review was to understand the scale of the achievement gap in education and to identify schools' strategies to tackle the racial and socioeconomic gap, the following keywords were used as inclusion criteria to search:

- The achievement gap in education
- Studies on the socioeconomic achievement gap
- Studies of the racial/ethnic achievement gap
- Closing the achievement gap
- School strategies to raise achievement and tackle inequality
- Targeted intervention strategies to close the achievement gaps
- School good practices to drive school improvement
- Parental engagement
- School curriculum
- School exclusions and suspensions
- Relevant to research questions

As exclusion criteria, studies were excluded if they were:

- Studies on non-educational inequalities
- Studies that do not include Black and ethnic minority groups
- Studies on interventions that are not in school or higher education
- Studies on gender differences
- Studies on special education
- Studies on health equality
- Studies that do not describe strategies or interventions in school education
- Not published or reported in English

The literature review involved mainly reports of research available in English over the past 20 years. In the first stage, studies were screened for duplication and relevance based on the title and abstract to delete further reports found not to meet the search criteria in practice or the focus of the book. This led to thousands of reports for each review. The next stage is to apply inclusion and exclusion criteria based on the keywords used before screening. Only studies that were related to the research questions in each chapter were retained. The remaining piece was used for a literature review with a focus on England and international experience.

As a result of the systematic review of literature and reading abstracts, we finally identified 500 publications that are relevant to this study. This includes government publications and data, research published in refereed journals, research reports, and theses in England, the USA, Australia, Canada, and New Zealand, and at the international level. These are used as references in writing the book.

References

Archer, L. & Francis, B. (2007) *Understanding Minority Ethnic Achievement: Race, Gender, Class and Success*. London: Routledge.

Baars, S., Bernardes, E., Elwick, A., Malortie, A., McAleavy, T., McInerney, L., Menzies, L. & Riggall, A. (2014) *Lessons from London Schools*. London: CfBT and Centre for London.

Ball, S. (1993) Education markets, choice and social class: The market as a class strategy in the UK and the USA. *British Journal of Education* 14(1): 13–19.

Blair, M. & Bourne, J. (1998) *Making the Difference: Teaching and Learning Strategies in Successful Multi-Ethnic Schools*. London: Department for Education and Employment Publication Research Report RR59.

Boyle, A. & Humphreys, S. (2012) *Transforming Education in Hackney*. London: Hackney Learning Trust. https://www.learningtrust.co.uk/Documents/10%20Years%20in%20Hackney.pdf

Burgess, S. (2015) *Understanding the Success of London; schools*. Bristol: University of Bristol. https://www.bristol.ac.uk/media-library/sites/cmpo/migrated/documents/wp333.pdf

Choudry, S. (2021) *Equitable Education: What Everyone Working in Education Should Know About Closing The Attainment Gap*. Critical Publishing.

Clifton, J. & Cook, W. (2012) *A Long Division: Closing the Attainment Gap in England's Secondary Schools*. London: Institute for Public Policy Research (IPPR).

Coard, B. (1971) *How the West Indian Child is Made Educationally Subnormal in the British School System*. London: New Beacon Books.

Cook, C. (2013) *London School Children Perform the Best*. London: Financial Times, 13 January 2013. https://www.ft.com/content/8f65f1ce-5be7-11e2-bef7-00144feab49a

Crozier, G. (2005) There is a war against our children: Black educational underachievement revisited. *British Journal of Sociology of Education* 26(5): 585–598.

Demie, F. (2001) Ethnic and gender difference in educational achievement and implications for school improvement strategies. Educational Research 43(1): 91–106.

Demie, F. (2003) Raising the achievement of Black Caribbean pupils in British schools: unacknowledged problems and challenges for policy makers. London Review of Education 1(3): 229–248.

Demie, F. (2005) Achievement of Black Caribbean pupils: Good practice in Lambeth schools. *British Educational Research Journal* 31(4): 481–508.

Demie, F. (2015) Language diversity and attainment in schools: implication for policy and practice. Race Ethnicity and Education 18 (5): 723–737. Doi: 10.1080/13613324.2014.946493

Demie, F. (2019a) *Educational Inequality: Closing the Gap*. London: UCL IOE Press, July. https://www.ucl-ioe-press.com/books/social-justice-equality-and-human-rights/educational-inequality/

Demie, F. (2019b) Raising the achievement of Black Caribbean pupils: Good practice for developing leadership capacity and workforce diversity in schools. *Journal School Leadership & Management* 39(1): 5–25.

Demie, F. (2020) *What Works in Driving School Improvement-_Lessons From London Schools*. London: Lambeth School Research and Statistics Unit.

Demie, F. (2022a) *Understanding the Causes and Consequences of School Exclusions: Teachers, Parents and Schools' Perspectives*. London: Routledge.

Demie, F. (2022b) 'Tackling teachers' low expectations of Black Caribbean students in English schools. *Equity in Education & Society* 1(1): 32–49 https://doi.org/10.1177/27526461211068511

Demie, F. (2023) *Raising Achievement of Black Caribbean Pupils: Barriers and Good Practice in Schools*. London: Lambeth school Research and Statistics Unit. https://www.ucl-ioe-press.com/books/social-justice-equality-and-human-rights/educational-inequality/

Demie, F. (2024) *A Survey of Barriers to Learning, Success Factors, and Intervention Strategy in London Schools to Raise Achievement and Tackle Educational Inequality*. London: Lambeth Schools Research and Statistics Unit, April draft.

Demie, F. & Lewis, K. (2010a) *Outstanding Secondary Schools: Good Practice*. London: School Research and Statistics Unit.

Demie, F. & Lewis, K. (2010b) Raising the achievement of Portuguese pupils in British schools: A case study of good practice. *Educational Studies* 36(1): 95–109.

Demie, F. & Lewis, K. (2013) *Outstanding Secondary Schools: A Study of Successful Practice*. London: Lambeth School Research and Statistics Unit.

Demie, F. & Mclean, C. (2007) Raising the achievement of African heritage pupils: A case study of good practice in British schools. *Educational Studies* 33(4): 415–434.

Demie, F. & Mclean, C. (2015a) Tackling disadvantage: What works in narrowing the achievement gap in schools. *Review of Education* 3(2): 138–174. https://doi.org/10.1002/rev3.30

Demie, F. & Mclean, C. (2015b) *Narrowing the Achievement Gap: Good Practice in Schools*. London: Lambeth Research and Statistics Unit.

Demie, F. & Mclean, C (2016) Tackling disadvantage: what works in narrowing the achievement gap in schools. Review of Education 3 (2): 138–174. https://doi.org/10.1002/rev3.30

Demie, F. & Mclean, C. (2017) *Black Caribbean Underachievement in Schools in England*. London, London: Schools Research and Statistics Unit.

Demie, F. & Mclean, C. (2019) *Tackling Educational Disadvantage: What Works in Schools*. London: Lambeth Schools Research and Statistics Unit.

DfE. (2010) *Making an Impact on Black children's Achievement: Examples of Good Practice from the Black Children's Achievement Programme*. London: Department for Education.

DfE (2017) *National and LA KS2 and GCSE performance table 2005-2017, SFR*. London: Department for Education.

DfES (2003) *Aiming High: Raising the Achievement of Minority Ethnic Pupils*. London: DfES Consultation.

Edmonds, R. (1982) Programs of school improvement: An overview. *Educational Leadership* 40(3): 8–11.

EEF. (2019) *Teaching and Learning Tool Kit*. London: Education Endowment Fund. https://educationendowmentfoundation.org.uk/evidencesummaries/teaching-learning-toolkit/

EPI. (2019) *Education in England: Annual Report 2019*. London: Education Policy Institute. https://epi.org.uk/publications-and-research/annual-report-2019/

EPI (2023) *Education in England: Annual Report 2023*. London: Education Policy Institute, 26th August. https://epi.org.uk/publications-and-research/education-in-england-annual-report-2023/

Gillborn, D. (2002) *Education and Institutional Racism, Inaugural Professorial Lecture*. London: Institute of Education, University of London.

Gillborn, D. & Gipps, C. (1996) *Recent Research on the Achievement of Ethnic Minority Pupils*. London: OFSTED Reviews of Research, HMSO.

Gillborn, D. & Mirza, H.S. (2000) *Educational Inequality: Mapping Race and Class*. London: Office for Standards in Education.

Gillborn, D. & Youdell, D. (2000) *Rationing Education: Policy, Practice, Reform and Equity*. Buckingham: Open University Press.

Gorard, S. (2000) *Education and Social Justice*. Cardiff: University of Wales Press.

Gorard, S. (2010) *Education can Compensate for Society - A Bit*. London: British Journal of Educational Research, Taylor and Francis.

Gorard, S., Siddiqui, N., See, B.H., Tereschenko, A. & Demie, F. (2023) *Ethnic Proportionality of Teachers and Students, and the Link to School-Level Outcomes*. Durham University Evidence Centre for Education, Education Sciences. https://www.mdpi.com/2227-7102/13/8/838

Greaves, E., Macmillan, L. & Sibieta, L. (2014) *Lessons from London Schools for Attainment Gaps and Social Mobility*. London: Social Mobility and Child Poverty Commission.

Hopkins, D., Ainscow, M. & West, M. (1994) *School Improvement in an Era of Change*. London: Cassell.

Hutchings, M., Greenwood, C., Hollingworth, S., Mansaray, A., Rose, A. & Glass, K. (2012) *Evaluation of the City Challenge Programme*, London Metropolitan University & Coffey International Development.

Hutchings, M. & Mansaray, A. (2013) *A Review of the Impact of the London Challenge (2003–2008) and the City Challenge (2008–2011)* Ofsted.

Hutchinson, J., Bonetti, S., Crenna-Jennings, W. & Akhal, A. (2019) *Education in England: Annual Report 2019*. London: Education Policy Institute.

IFS (2022) *Education Inequalities*. IFS Deaton Review of Inequalities. https://ifs.org.uk/inequality/chapter/education-inequalities/

Igbal, K. (2019) *British Pakistan Boys, Education and the Role of Religion*. London: Routledge.

Leach, M.T., & Williams, S.A. (2007) The impact of the academic achievement gap on the African American Family: a social inequality perspective. Journal of Human Behaviour in the Social Environment 15(2–3): 39–59. https://doi.org/10.1300/J137v15n02_04

Macpherson, W. (1999) *The Stephen Lawrence Inquiry*. London: The Stationery Office.

Modood, T. (2011) *Multiculturalism and Integration: Struggling with Confusion*. https://assets.qmul.ac.uk/migration/pdf/QMUL%20Talk%201%20November%202011.pdf

Maylor, U., Smart, S., Kuyok, K.A., et al. (2009) *Black Children's Achievement Programme Evaluation*. London: Department for Children and Schools.

McKenley, J., Power, C., Ishani, L. & Demie, F. (2003) *Raising the Achievement of Black Caribbean Pupils in British Schools: Good Practice in Lambeth Schools*. London: Lambeth Research and Statistics Unit.

Miller, P. (2019) *'Tackling' Race Inequality in School Leadership: Positive Actions in BAME Teacher Progression – Evidence from Three English Schools*. London. https://doi.org/10.1177/1741143219873098

Milliard, W., Brown-Viner, K., Baars, S., et al. (2018) *Boys on Track Improving Support for Black Caribbean and Free School Meal Eligible White Boys in London A Research Report*. London: Greater London Authority (GLA).

Mongon, D. & Chapman, C. (2008) *Successful leadership for promoting the achievement of White Working Class pupils*. National College for School Leadership (NCSL).

Mortimore, P. (1999) *The Road to Improvement: Reflections on School Effectiveness*. London: Taylor & Francis.

Mortimore, P., Sammons, P., Stoll, L., Lewis, D. & Ecob, R. (1988) *School Matters: The Junior Years*. Wells: Open Books.

Mortimore, P. & Whitty, G. (1997) *Can School Improvement Overcome the Effects of Disadvantage?* London: Institute of Education, University of London.

Muijis, D., Harris, A., Chapman, C., Stoll, L. & Russ, J. (2004) Improving schools in socioeconomically disadvantage areas - A review of research evidence. *School Effectiveness and School Improvement* 15(2): 149–175.

Ofsted. (2002a) *Achievement of Black Caribbean Pupils: Three Successful Primary Schools*. Ofsted Publications HMI 447, April.

Ofsted. (2002b) *Achievement of Black Caribbean Pupils: Good Practice in Secondary Schools*. London: Office for Standards in Education, HMI 448, April.

Ofsted. (2009) *Twelve Outstanding Secondary Schools: Excelling Against the Odds.* London: Office for Standards in Education, HMI: 080240. https://dera.ioe.ac.uk/id/eprint/11232/2/Twelve.pdf

Ofsted. (2010) *London Challenge.* https://webarchive.nationalarchives.gov.uk/ukgwa/20141107033128/http://www.ofsted.gov.uk/resources/london-challenge

Ofsted. (2013) *A Review of the Impact of the London Challenge (2003–2008) and the City Challenge (2008–2011).* https://kclpure.kcl.ac.uk/portal/en/publications/a-review-of-the-impact-of-the-london-challenge-20038-and-the-city-challenge-200811(075d012d-8209-4aa9-ab46-a60f5800a1fc).html

Ofsted (2014) Written evidence to House of Commons Education Select Committee. In *Education Committee (2014). Underachievement in Education by White Working Class Children*, London: House of Commons 142, The Stationery Office Limited.

Race, R. (2024) *Multiculturalism and Education.* London: Open University.

Rampton, A. (1981) *West Indian Children in our Schools.* Cmnd 8273. London: HMSO.

Rasbash, J., Leckie, G., Pillinger, R. & Jenkins, J. (2010) Children's educational progress: partitioning family, school and area effects. *Journal of the Royal Statistical Society* 173 (3): 657 –682.

Reynolds, D. & Sammons, P. (1996) School effectiveness and school improvement in the UK. *School Effectiveness and School Improvement* 7(2): 133–158.

Rhamie, J. & Hallam, S. (2010) An investigation into African-Caribbean academic success in the UK. *Race Ethnicity and Education* 5(2): 151–170.

Richardson, B. (2005) *Tell it like it Is: How Our Schools Fail Black Children.* Bath: Bath Press.

Rutter, M., Maughan, B., Mortimore, P. & Ouston, J. (1979) *Fifteen Thousand Hours: Secondary Schools and Their Effect on Children.* London: Open Books.

Sammons, P. (1999) *School Effectiveness: Coming of Age in the Twenty-first Century.* Lisse: Swets and Zeitlinger.

Sammons, P. (2007) *School effectiveness and equity: making connections - a review school effectiveness and improvement research-its implications for practitioners and policymakers.* Reding: CFBT Education Trust.

Sammons, P., Hillman, J. & Mortimore, P. (1995) *Key characteristics of effective schools: Review school effectiveness research.* London: Ofsted.

Stoll, L. & Fink, D. (1994) Views from the field: Linking school effectiveness and school improvement. *School Effectiveness and School Improvement* 5(2): 149–177.

Strand, S. (2012) The White British-Black Caribbean achievement gap: Tests, tiers, and teacher expectations. *British Educational Research Journal* 38(1): 75–101.

Strand, S. (2014) School effects and ethnic, gender and socio-economic groups in educational achievement at age 11. *Oxford Review of Education* 40(2): 223–245.

Strand, S. (2015) *Ethnicity, Deprivation, and Educational Achievement at Age 16 in England: Trends Over Time.* Oxford: University of Oxford.

Swann, L. (1985) *Education for All: Final Report of the Committee of Inquiry into the Education of Children from Ethnic Minority Groups.* Cmnd 9453. London: HMSO.

Thrupp, M. (1999) *School Makes a Difference: Let Us Be Realistic!* Open University Press.

Tikly, L., Haynes, J., Caballero, C., Hill, J. & Gillborn, J. (2006) *Evaluation of Aiming High: African Caribbean Achievement Project.* London: DfES Research Report 801.

Tomlinson, S. (1982) A note on the education of ethnic minority children in Britain. *The International Migration Review* 16(3): 646–660. Sage Publications, Inc.

Tomlinson, S. (1983) *Ethnic Minorities in British Schools: A Review of Literature 1960–82*. Policy Studies.

Tomlinson, S. (2008) *Race and Education: Policy and Politics*. Open University.

2
THE ACHIEVEMENT GAP
The Empirical Evidence

Introduction

This chapter asks the key question, which is critical for chapters to follow: does the achievement gap matter? What is the empirical evidence for educational inequality and the achievement gap? Drawing on longitudinal KS2 and GCSE NPD data, it examines in detail the attainment pattern by ethnic background and socioeconomic status to measure the impact of government policy in England over the past decades on educational inequality and closing the achievement gap.

Two methodological approaches are used. First, we examine the gap in educational achievement between ethnic minorities and the majority group in England. Second, we look at the achievement gap between disadvantaged pupils and their peers to gain further insight into the effects of social background and educational inequality.

Why does the achievement gap matter?

The achievement gap refers to any significant and persistent disparity in academic performance or educational attainment between different groups of students with various ethnic and socioeconomic backgrounds. A growing body of educational research confirmed the existence of widespread school achievement gaps between groups (EPI, 2017, 2020; Demie, 2019; Cassen and Kingdon, 2007). One of the most enduring debates in education in this area has been on how to close the achievement gap between White students on the one hand and Black and Hispanic students in the USA and the UK (Demie 2019; EPI 2020; Gorard et al. 2023). Researchers argued that the

DOI: 10.4324/9781003499633-3

academic gap exists in virtually every measure of educational progress, including grade point average (GPA) and standardised tests (EPI 2020; IFS 2022), between students of certain races of colour and White students in the USA. In addition, other researchers assert that low-socioeconomic status (SES) youth and children of colour are the most crucial for the USA and the UK educational system (Demie 2019). Previous research highlights the concern of the socioeconomic and racial achievement gap.

There are several explanations for the existence of the gap. A long-standing gap is the racial gap – Black/White academic performance gap. EPI (2020) research in the UK confirms that

- Gypsy/Roma pupils are almost three years (34 months) behind White British pupils at GCSE level. In contrast, Chinese pupils are two whole years (23.9 months) ahead of White British pupils in learning at this stage of their education.
- Some ethnic groups have experienced growing inequalities over recent years. Black Caribbean pupils were 6.5 months behind White British pupils in 2011, but this gap has now regressed to 10.9 months, meaning that the gap has widened for Black Caribbean pupils by well over four months in the last eight years.
- Gaps have also widened for pupils from other black backgrounds, and for pupils with English as an additional language who arrived late to the school system.

(EPI 2020: 3)

The USA studies also show a similar large gap. In the USA context, this gap is manifested in measures such as test scores, grades, college completion and dropout rates, and selection of courses and has often been used to draw attention to the concerning differences in performance between African Americans and Latinos and their non-Hispanic White counterparts. The evidence from the USA suggests that Hispanic and African American students have persistently lagged behind Whites in academic matters, triggering heated policy discussions. Some studies in the USA also support the notion that these gaps have been declining in the last three decades (Kao and Thompson, 2003).

In the UK, there has been a wide variability in progress by ethnic minorities between 1992 and 2004. All ethnic groups experienced an increase in the proportion of pupils obtaining at least five General Certificate of Secondary Education (GCSE) grades of A* to C grades at the end of compulsory schooling. The Indian and Chinese pupils now outperform the dominant White group, while Black Caribbean, Bangladeshi, Pakistani, and Black pupils still present lower outcomes than the dominant White group.

Another factor identified in the research is the socioeconomic achievement gap. The EPI (2017) research that looked at the achievement gap between disadvantaged pupils (those eligible for the pupil premium) and their peers suggests how that gap varies over time. Indeed, despite significant investment and targeted intervention programmes,

> The gap between disadvantaged 16-year-old pupils and their peers has only narrowed by three months of learning between 2007 and 2016 in the UK. In 2016, the gap nationally, at the end of secondary school, was still 19.3 months. Disadvantaged pupils fall behind their more affluent peers by around 2 months each year throughout secondary school. Over the same period (2007–2016), the gap by the end of primary school narrowed by 2.8 months and the gap by age 5 narrowed by 1.2 months. At current trends, we estimate that it would take around 50 years for the disadvantage gap to close completely by the time pupils take their GCSEs. For pupils who are persistently disadvantaged (i.e. those who have been eligible for free school meals for 80 percent or longer of their school lives), the gap at the end of secondary school has widened slightly since 2007, by 0.3 months. In 2016, it stood at 24.3 months, equivalent to over two years of learning.
>
> *(EPI 2017:6)*

Research by IFS (2022) on the attainment gap between poorer pupils and their better-off classmates shows it is still as large as it was 20 years ago. The study also found that disadvantaged pupils start school behind their better-off peers, and those inequalities persist through their school years and beyond. The Institute for Fiscal Studies (IFS) argues that there is overwhelming evidence that the education system in England leaves too many young disadvantaged people behind despite decades of policy focus.

> Despite decades of policy attention, there has been virtually no change in the 'disadvantage gap' in GCSE attainment over the past 20 years. While GCSE attainment has been increasing over time, 16-year-olds who are eligible for free school meals are still around 27 percentage points less likely to earn good GCSEs than less disadvantaged peers.
>
> *(IFS, 2022:2)*

Demie and Mclean's (2016a,b) research shows the inequality of outcomes for pupils on free school meals; Black Caribbean and Pakistani pupils have grown between 2006 and 2016. They concluded that children in poorer homes do worse educationally than their peers, with 38% of pupils eligible for free school meals achieving 5+A*-c, including English and maths, compared to 65% of better-off pupils. The evidence from this research suggests that there is a significant gap between free school meals (FSM) and non-FSM pupils. This has not changed. Other research also suggests that the eligibility for FSM is strongly associated with low achievement and also notes similar evidence suggesting that 'fsm pupils are in fact half as likely as no-fsm pupils to score 5+A*-c results in GCSE' (Cassen et al., 2015:3–4)

Recent studies by Gorard et al. (2023) also suggest that:

> There has been a marked drop in the attainment gap at KS1 in England since pupil premium funding was introduced, there was the beginning of a reduction in the attainment gap at KS2, and the picture at KS4 is more mixed. The achievement gap dropped and began to grow from 2014 onwards.
>
> *(Gorard et al., 2023:201)*

In the USA, also groups in disadvantaged socioeconomic terms tend to display, on average, a lower academic achievement than their non-disadvantaged groups.

> In both the United States and England, for example, it is estimated that the attainment of high-school students from low-income households lags behind that of their counterparts from higher-income households by the equivalent of more than two and a half years of schooling.
>
> *(Easterbrook and Hadden, 2021: 181)*

Several studies have attempted to explain the many factors associated with the achievement gap for disadvantaged and ethnic minority pupils. UK and international evidence suggest that disadvantaged pupils at school face several problems, including poverty across generations, lack of parental engagement, and negative attitudes towards education (Mongon and Chapman, 2008; Demie and McLean, 2015). There is a consensus that poverty and home and community factors impact the academic achievement of students and contribute to the achievement gap. Despite average overall improvements in test scores, large differences in educational achievement according to socioeconomic status persist (Mongon and Chapman, 2008; Strand, 2014). The attainment gap widens at each key stage as children pass through the education system, with pupils eligible for FSM falling behind their peers.

The effect of poverty on learning dominates the outcomes (Andrews et al., 2017; Demie and McLean, 2015, 2017; Hutchinson et al., 2016; Cassen and Kingdon, 2007; Cassen et al., 2015; Strand, 2014) and is the greatest cause for concern. Other factors than poverty do affect outcomes, such as lack of parental engagement and negative attitudes towards education. Hutchinson et al. list them as:

> Limited language, restricted vocabulary; poor attendance; mobility – many moves between schools; poor nutrition; low aspirations; low expectations;

narrow range of opportunities outside school; lack of role models, especially male role models; lack of self-confidence and self-esteem; poor social skills; and inadequate support from teachers and teaching assistants.

(Hutchinson et al., 2016:29–30)

There is now a growing body of research that argues the need to explore the achievement gap by race/ethnic groups in the USA and the UK (Darling-Hammond, 1998; Ladson-Billings, 2006; Gorard et al. 2023). We would argue that disparities in opportunity and outcomes along race, socioeconomic background, and social class begin early and often persist throughout students' primary and secondary education years and beyond since the racial and SES achievement gap is vital in unequal educational outcomes. Researchers have provided numerous explanations for the existence of the achievement gap, related to SES (Hung et al., 2020; White et al., 1993; Ofsted, 2013; Mortimore and Whitty, 1997; Ofsted, 2013; Education Committee, 2014), and yet the gap for these disparities is less documented or under-researched using available national data in England.

This chapter examines what the data tells us about the standard of achievement of all pupils in English schools at the end of KS2 and GCSE, including

- The achievement gap in education: The KS2 and GCSE trend data evidence.
- The Black and ethnic minority students' achievement gap by ethnic background and inequality.
- The Black and ethnic minority students' socioeconomic achievement gap and inequality.
- The Black and ethnic minority students' gender gap and inequality.
- Conclusions and implications of the data evidence.

The attainment performance measures and national curriculum

The strength of the research is its data source, the National Pupil Database (NPD). The NPD is a pupil-level database that matches data on pupil and school characteristics to pupil-level attainment. The number of pupils who completed GCSE in summer 2023 was 643,095, and of those who completed KS2 in 2023, about 673,120. The data on state schools is accurate and has several key features. First, this census dataset of information about the population of all pupils in state schools is more helpful, for a variety of analyses, than a dataset based on just a sample of schools, as it provides a much richer set of data on school and pupil characteristics. The dataset includes information on the language spoken at home, ethnicity, FSM, gender, and results at key stages 2 and 4. Second, data has been drawn from DfE statistical first releases (SFRs), although some statistics have been calculated directly from the NPD files. The lists that the SFRs draw on to collate data on achievement are given in the references.

It is important to note that in the English education system, pupils aged 5 to 16 years old are taught the national curriculum. It covers national curriculum subjects such as English, mathematics, and science. There are four key stages: KS1 (primary Years 1 and 2); KS2 (Primary Years 3 to 6); KS3 (Secondary Years 7 to 9); and KS4 (Secondary Years 10 and 11), where assessments are undertaken. Until 2015, pupils in key stages 1 to 3 were given levels ranging from 1 to 8. In key stages 1 and 2, results are reported for reading, writing, and math. Thus, a typical seven-year-old is expected to reach level 2B at KS1, an 11-year-old (end of KS2) level 4, and a 14-year-old level 5 at KS3. At the end of KS4, pupils take the GCSE exams. These are the main qualifications attempted by pupils at the end of compulsory schooling at the age of 16 and consist of examinations in the curriculum subjects the pupils have been studying. The measure of performance used in this book is the percentage of pupils gaining Level 4 or above at KS2 in reading, writing, and maths, and for GCSE it was the national measure of the percentage of pupils gaining five or more good GCSEs, including English and maths (5+ A*–C). However, in 2016, the measures used to discuss attainment changed, and a new version of the national curriculum assessment was introduced that removed the attainment levels. Instead, tests and teacher assessments are available for reading, writing, and mathematics, as follows:

- Working above the expected standard
- Working at the expected standard
- Working towards the expected standard
- Below the expected standard

The ethnic achievement gap and inequality in education

The 1990s and 2000s saw a dramatic improvement in the proportion of pupils completing their compulsory schooling with five or more GCSE higher-grade passes, including English and maths. In England, more pupils have been achieving 5+ A*–C grades year on year, from 20 percent in 2000 to 60 percent in 2023. This is an improvement of 40 percent over the period, suggesting a remarkable transformation. The key question is, Which students made such an improvement?

A striking finding from the trend data is that members of every main ethnic group are more likely to attain five higher grades than ever before (see Figure 1.1). This evidence shows that levels of attainment can be improved for every ethnic group and there are considerable differences in attainment between different ethnic groups. It also reveals pupils of different ethnic origins do not experience equal educational opportunities. Additionally, compared to their

White, Chinese, and Indian counterparts, Black African, Pakistani, and Bangladeshi students have a significantly lower chance of earning five higher-grade GCSEs.

The above pattern of improvement is related to education reform and significant government policy measures during the period to raise achievement in schools (Demie and McLean, 2015). However, there is a significant difference between different ethnic groups, and not all ethnic groups share equally in the overall improvement in attainment. As we argue next, government policy measures have also had a negative impact: they have increased inequalities between different ethnic groups. Table 2.1 shows the KS2 and GCSE results for each group at the national level. The KS2 data also shows that 75% of Black Caribbean pupils achieved the expected standard compared with 80% for England as a whole. Similarly, at GCSE, 46% of Black Caribbean pupils achieved 5+ A*–C, including English and maths, compared with the national average of 54%. However, nationally there are marked differences in performance between different ethnic groups. Broadly speaking, Chinese-, Indian-, and White-heritage pupils are the highest-achieving groups at GCSE, followed by Black African and Bangladeshi. Black Caribbean and Pakistani are the lowest-achieving groups. The national data in England also suggests that Black Caribbean underachievement in education is real and persistent, and Black Caribbeans remain the consistently lowest-performing group in the country. The real concern is that the difference between their educational performance and that of other groups is larger than for any other ethnic group.

TABLE 2.1 KS2 and GCSE performance by ethnic origin in English schools (%)

Ethnicity	Key Stage 2 results (reading, writing, and maths)				GCSE 4–9 English and maths			
	2018	2019	2022	2023	2018	2019	2022	2023
Bangladeshi	69%	70%	67%	68%	69%	70%	78%	74%
Black African	66%	67%	62%	63%	65%	64%	73%	69%
Black Caribbean	55%	56%	49%	50%	49%	48%	56%	52%
Chinese	81%	80%	70%	69%	87%	89%	89%	88%
Indian	76%	76%	74%	73%	79%	80%	85%	83%
Pakistani	61%	62%	59%	60%	61%	62%	69%	66%
Mixed White/Black Caribbean	57%	59%	49%	51%	54%	54%	56%	51%
White British	64%	65%	58%	59%	64%	65%	67%	63%
White Other	61%	63%	61%	60%	62%	62%	70%	66%
All pupils	64%	65%	59%	60%	64%	65%	64%	61%

Source: DfE (2018–2023).

30 Black and Ethnic Minority Achievement in Schools

As at GCSE, Black Caribbean pupils are the lowest-achieving group at KS2 (see Table 2.1). Previous studies also came to similar conclusions (Demie, 2001; Gillborn and Mirza, 2000) suggesting Black Caribbean underachievement. Perhaps the most important new finding from the national data is that there is now some evidence that Chinese-, Bangladeshi-, and Indian-heritage pupils are improving more rapidly and narrowing the gap with White pupils. However, Black Caribbean pupils have not improved enough to narrow the gap (see Figure 2.1). The empirical evidence highlights a particular concern and disadvantage experienced in the English education system by Black Caribbean pupils (Demie, 2001; Gillborn and Mirza, 2000). To date, it has been difficult to draw generalised conclusions from research on Black Caribbean educational achievement, but the new national data is at least helpful and confirms that Black Caribbean children have not shared equally in the increasing rates of achievement at KS2 and GCSE (see Table 2.1 and Figure 1.1). These findings have important implications for strategies for raising achievement. The findings make it at least easier for researchers to examine the differences in performance between pupils from different ethnic

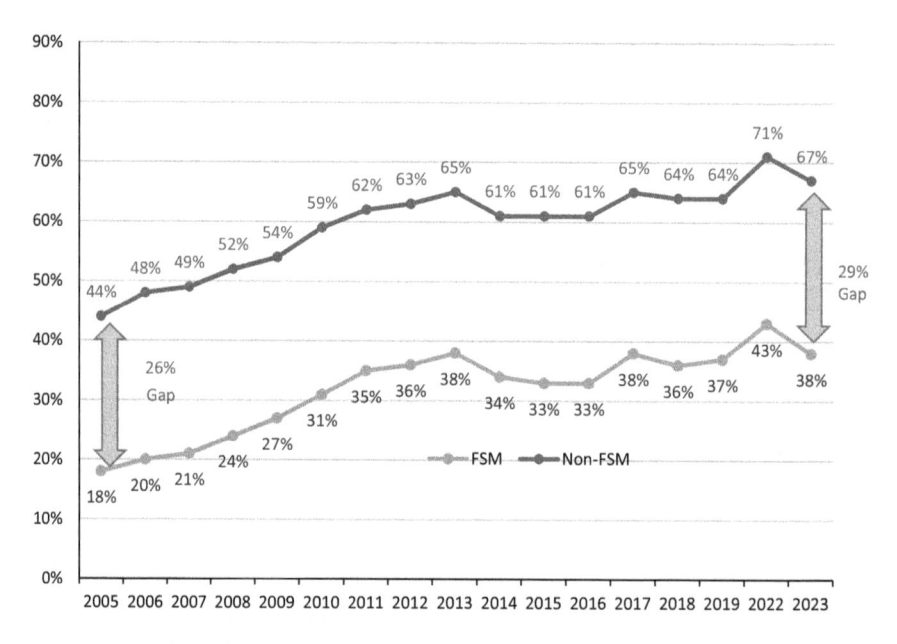

FIGURE 2.1 The achievement gap between pupils eligible for free school meals (FSM) and non-FSM pupils in England (% 5+ A* to C including English and Maths 2005–2023).

Source: DfE, 2017, 'National and LA KS2 and GCSE performance table 2005–2017,' SFR. DfE (2015). SFR06/2015; DfE (NPD 2016).

groups and for practitioners to identify appropriate strategies to tackle perceived problems.

Overall, the national data supports some of the research findings in the field that the gap between the highest- and lowest-achieving ethnic groups is growing. It also shows Black Caribbean-heritage pupils are achieving on average significantly below the level of other main ethnic groups at KS2 and GCSE (Table 2.1).

The gender achievement gap by ethnic background and inequality

The debate around underachievement by gender, particularly boys, is well established in the UK, the USA, and Australia (see Francis and Skelton, 2005; Gorard et al. (2023); Arnot et al., 1998; Demie 2019, 2001). In the UK, the gender data is presented in the national league table data, but there is no league table data that examines gender and ethnicity. Previous research in the UK has shown ethnicity and social class continue to be stronger predictors of educational achievement than gender (see Strand, 2014). I would argue, therefore, knowing gender achievement by ethnic background provides useful information to understand the achievement patterns in the UK.

Table 2.2 repeats the pattern established earlier, in which girls tend to outperform boys at each key stage (see Demie, 2001 and Gillborn and Gipps, 1996). Overall, girls achieve higher averages than boys by a noticeable margin. This is true for African, Caribbean, and White British pupils at all key stages. It also confirms that for Black Caribbean pupils, the gap in performance

TABLE 2.2 KS2 (expected level) and GCSE 5+ A*–C performance in England by gender and ethnic background (%)

Ethnic group	KS2 reading, writing, and maths			GCSE 4–9 English and maths		
	Boys	Girls	Gap	Boys	Girls	Gap
Bangladeshi	65%	72%	7%	73%	76%	3%
Black African	59%	72%	13%	65%	73%	8%
Black Caribbean	45%	72%	27%	46%	57%	11%
Chinese	64%	72%	8%	85%	92%	7%
Indian	69%	72%	3%	82%	85%	3%
Pakistani	56%	72%	16%	64%	68%	4%
Mixed White and Black Caribbean	47%	72%	25%	48%	54%	6%
White British	56%	72%	16%	61%	67%	6%
White Other	56%	72%	16%	64%	69%	5%
All	56%	63%	7%	62%	67%	5%

Source: DfE (2018–2028).

between boys and girls is higher than for Black African and White British pupils, suggesting the lower achievement of boys. Overall, these findings question some of the previous studies which argued that only Black boys, and not girls, faced inequalities. The data in Table 2.2 confirms that both girls and boys of Black Caribbean heritage were lagging behind White British boys, and all three groups were some distance behind White girls. There are few exceptions where the data also shows a small gap for Chinese and Indian between boys and girls at both KS2 and GCSE.

The socioeconomic achievement gap and inequality in education

The attainment of disadvantaged pupils: the KS2 and GCSE evidence

Poverty is certainly a major factor influencing the performance of disadvantaged pupils (see Cassen and Kingdon, 2007). The FSM variable is often used as a proxy measure of the extent of social deprivation in the pupils' backgrounds and has been linked to underachievement (see Gillborn and Youdell, 2000; Demie, 2001). Figure 2.1 shows a significant gap, with only 38% of pupils on FSM gaining 5+ A*–C, compared to 65% of those who were not. Overall, the findings from the national data confirm that pupils eligible for FSM did considerably less well than their more affluent peers in England (see Figure 2.1).

The attainment gap between children eligible and not eligible for FSM is also apparent in the age 11 KS2 national tests in the average marks for reading, writing, and maths. At the end of primary education in 2023, 43% of eligible pupils achieved the expected standard, whereas 66% of pupils who were not eligible achieved this level (Table 2.3). The GCSE evidence also shows that at the end of secondary education, 43% of school meals achieved 4–9 grades compared to 72% of non-FSM. It is not just achievement that is affected: pupils eligible for FSM generally have lower rates of progress (see DfE, 2023).

The attainment of disadvantaged pupils by ethnic background

Tables 2.3–2.6 indicate that there is a marked difference in KS2 and GCSE performance between pupils eligible for FSM and the more economically advantaged groups in schools. There is a significant difference in attainment between pupils eligible for FSM and those who are not at the end of primary education. About 43% of Black Caribbean eligible pupils achieve the expected standard in KS2, whereas 57% of pupils who are not eligible achieve this level. The GCSE data also shows a significant gap, with only 41% of pupils on FSM gaining 5+ A*–C, compared to 59% of those who are not.

TABLE 2.3 Disadvantaged pupils'* KS2 and GCSE performance in England, 2011–2023

	KS2 performance (RWM)				GCSE performance in England 4–9 English and maths			
	All pupils	FSM	Non-FSM	Gap	All pupils	FSM	Non-FSM	Gap
2011	67%	49%	71%	22%	59%	35%	63%	27%
2012	74%	59%	78%	19%	59%	37%	63%	26%
2013	75%	60%	79%	19%	61%	39%	66%	27%
2014	78%	64%	82%	18%	59%	37%	63%	26%
2015	80%	66%	83%	17%	59%	36%	63%	27%
2016	53%	35%	57%	22%	63%	39%	67%	28%
2017	61%	43%	64%	21%	64%	40%	68%	27%
2018	64%	46%	68%	22%	64%	40%	68%	28%
2019	65%	47%	68%	21%	65%	42%	69%	27%
2022	59%	42%	64%	22%	64%	47%	75%	28%
2023	60%	43%	66%	23%	61%	43%	72%	29%

Note:

* Disadvantaged pupils are those in receipt of free school meals.

Source: DfE (2011–2023).

TABLE 2.4 KS2 and GCSE performance in England by ethnic background (%), 2023

	KS2 (RWM)			GCSE 4–9 grade English and maths		
	FSM	Non-FSM	Gap	FSM	Non-FSM	Gap
Bangladeshi	63%	71%	8%	67%	78%	11%
Black African	58%	65%	7%	61%	73%	12%
Black Caribbean	43%	57%	14%	41%	59%	18%
Chinese	71%	69%	–2%	84%	89%	5%
Indian	60%	74%	14%	69%	85%	16%
Pakistani	53%	62%	9%	57%	69%	12%
Mixed White/Black Caribbean	41%	60%	19%	51%	72%	21%
Mixed White/Black African	51%	67%	16%	37%	61%	24%
White British	40%	66%	26%	36%	71%	35%
White Other	42%	65%	23%	49%	70%	21%
National	43%	66%	23%	44%	73%	29%

Source: DfE 'National and LA KS2 and GCSE performance, SFR.; DfE, NPD 2023.

TABLE 2.5 GCSE achievement gap of disadvantaged pupils by ethnic background and FSM (%)

	2011	2012	2013	2014	2015	2016	2017	2018	2019	2022	2023
White British	29%	31%	33%	31%	31%	34%	35%	34%	36%	40%	36%
Mixed White/Black Caribbean	34%	37%	39%	35%	33%	37%	35%	37%	37%	42%	37%
Mixed White/Black African	44%	46%	50%	44%	46%	48%	50%	49%	50%	56%	51%
Indian	58%	58%	62%	57%	58%	62%	63%	64%	67%	72%	69%
Pakistani	44%	47%	48%	44%	44%	47%	50%	52%	52%	60%	57%
Bangladeshi	57%	59%	60%	58%	58%	61%	64%	60%	63%	71%	67%
Black Caribbean	38%	41%	43%	39%	35%	39%	41%	34%	38%	66%	41%
Black African	48%	49%	52%	49%	48%	53%	55%	55%	55%	45%	64%
Chinese	74%	68%	77%	70%	75%	79%	79%	79%	83%	82%	84%
FSM – all	35%	37%	39%	37%	36%	39%	40%	40%	42%	47%	43%
Non-FSM – all	63%	63%	66%	63%	63%	67%	68%	68%	69%	75%	72%
All pupils	59%	59%	61%	59%	59%	63%	64%	64%	65%	64%	61%

Source: DfE. 2011–2023.

TABLE 2.6 Percentage of pupils eligible for FSM reaching the expected standard in RWM at KS2

	2011	2012	2013	2014	2015	2016	2017	2018	2019	2022	2023
Bangladeshi	63%	74%	72%	76%	80%	52%	59%	63%	66%	63%	63%
Black African	56%	66%	68%	72%	75%	46%	54%	57%	60%	56%	58%
Black Caribbean	52%	61%	62%	66%	67%	35%	46%	47%	48%	41%	43%
Chinese	77%	83%	87%	84%	85%	67%	66%	77%	75%	75%	71%
Indian	64%	73%	71%	78%	75%	47%	58%	61%	62%	59%	60%
Pakistani	52%	63%	65%	68%	72%	39%	49%	53%	55%	51%	53%
Mixed White/Black Caribbean	51%	62%	63%	64%	67%	34%	44%	44%	47%	39%	41%
Mixed White/Black African	57%	64%	66%	70%	71%	42%	50%	51%	53%	50%	51%
White British	46%	56%	58%	61%	63%	32%	39%	43%	44%	38%	40%
White Other	52%	61%	57%	60%	64%	38%	45%	48%	49%	44%	42%
FSM – all	49%	59%	60%	64%	66%	35%	43%	46%	47%	42%	43%
Non-FSM – all	71%	78%	79%	82%	83%	57%	64%	68%	68%	64%	66%
National – all	67%	74%	75%	78%	80%	53%	61%	64%	65%	59%	60%

Source: DfE, 2011–2023.

This national data confirms that Black Caribbean pupils eligible for school meals did considerably less well than their more affluent peers: the gap at GCSE is 18%.

There are also significant differences when the data is analysed by ethnic background and eligibility for FSM at GCSE. Table 2.5 shows that 36% of White British pupils eligible for FSM achieved 5+ A*–C. This is a huge underachievement when compared to 71% of White British, not FSM pupils. The White-British difference is higher, with a gap of 26 percentage points at KS2 and 35 at GCSE. However, the gaps for Chinese, Bangladeshi, Pakistani, and Black African pupils at KS2 are narrower. This is despite more of these pupils than White British being on FSM. This finding underlines the importance of treating with scepticism any measure of school performance which does not allow for the influence of background factors such as social class and deprivation. Social class data is particularly significant for the analysis of the performance of White British and Black Caribbean pupils in addition to other factors of disadvantage. As we have argued, our analysis is not complete for White British because of the lack of data on social class. It is therefore difficult to generalise from this study to a wider context without social class data. Further research in school populations outside London is required. The main finding from analysing the national FSM data confirms that:

- Black Caribbean and White British children eligible for FSM are consistently the lowest-performing ethnic groups of children from low-income households.
- More than any other ethnic group, the achievement difference between children eligible for FSM and the rest is greater for Black Caribbean, White British, and mixed White and Black Caribbean youngsters.
- The gap widens even more at the end of secondary education for White British and mixed White and Black Caribbean pupils.
- Chinese and Indian disadvantaged pupils tend to significantly outperform the White British majority.

It is a matter of concern that the gap widens rather than narrows during schooling for Black Caribbean, White British, and Mixed White and Black Caribbean children more than for any other ethnic group. This indicates the failure of the English education system to address those pupils' needs and to establish fairness for all.

The gender achievement gap and inequality in education

Table 2.7 repeats the pattern established earlier, whereby girls tend to outperform boys at every key stage (see Demie, 2019, 2001; Arnot et al., 1998). Overall, the results at different key stages indicate that girls achieve higher

TABLE 2.7 KS2 and GCSE achievement of pupils in England by gender (%)

	KS2 performance 2017 (RWM)				GCSE performance in England 4–9 English and maths			
	All pupils	Girls	Boys	Gap	All pupils	Girls	Boys	Gap
2011	49%	54%	44%	10%	35%	38%	32%	6%
2012	59%	64%	54%	10%	37%	41%	33%	8%
2013	60%	65%	56%	9%	39%	43%	34%	9%
2014	64%	68%	59%	9%	36%	40%	32%	8%
2015	66%	70%	62%	8%	36%	39%	32%	7%
2016	35%	39%	32%	7%	39%	43%	35%	8%
2017	43%	47%	39%	8%	40%	44%	36%	8%
2018	46%	51%	41%	10%	40%	44%	36%	8%
2019	47%	53%	42%	11%	41%	46%	37%	9%
2022	42%	46%	38%	8%	47%	50%	44%	6%
2023	43%	47%	40%	7%	43%	46%	40%	6%

Source: DfE, 2018–2023.

averages than boys by a noticeable margin. This is true at all key stages. It also confirms that the gap in performance between boys and girls is wide, suggesting that boys underachieve. Generally, these findings question some of the previous studies which argued that boys, but not girls, face inequalities. The data in Table 2.4 confirms that disadvantaged girls and boys were lagging behind the national average.

Conclusions

Educational researchers and practitioners have long been concerned with identifying policy instruments to reduce the racial achievement gap in the UK. A review of previous research shows the link between poverty and achievement by ethnic background (see 2005; Cassen and Kingdon, 2007; Mortimore and Whitty, 1997; Ofsted, 2013). There is no clear evidence that suggests socioeconomic inequities are the most significant contributor to the achievement gap. This chapter asks the key question, 'What is the empirical evidence for educational inequality in England?' Drawing on longitudinal KS2 and GCSE data, we have examined in detail the achievement pattern and evidence by ethnic background, gender, and disadvantage, to show the impact of government policy over the past decades on educational inequality. We used trend data to analyse the achievement gaps between White British and minority students over time in recognition of this. The national data suggests that the pattern of comparative underachievement in some ethnic groups through English schooling is strong and persistent. Their trend analysis shows the change in the achievement gap over time between White and different ethnic minority groups. The data confirm that Chinese, Indian, Bangladeshi, and African pupils tend to significantly outperform the White British majority while Black Caribbean, Pakistani, Traveller, and Gypsy children tend to underperform. Moreover, worryingly, the gap in Black Caribbean achievement increases rather than narrows as a child progresses through compulsory education.

The empirical evidence also confirms that disadvantaged pupils' underachievement in education is real and persistent and that they are consistently the lowest-performing group in the country. It shows that:

- Chinese and Indian disadvantaged pupils tend to significantly outperform the White British majority.
- Black Caribbean, Traveller, and White British children eligible for FSM are consistently the lowest-performing ethnic groups of children from low-income households.
- The attainment gap between children eligible for free school meals and the remainder is wider for Black Caribbean, Traveller, White British, and Mixed White and Black Caribbean than for any other ethnic group.
- The gap widens, particularly at the end of secondary education, for White British and Mixed White and Black Caribbean pupils.

At the current rate of progress, it would take a full 50 years to reach an equitable education system where disadvantaged pupils did not fall behind their peers during formal education to age 16.
(EPI, 2017; see also Hutchinson et al., 2016)

Indeed, despite these differential patterns in school achievement in England, there is a tendency to downplay the issue of inequalities with British education research and policy. As noted by some researchers (Demie 2019, 2023; Majors 2001) the British government policy tended to maintain the 'colour-blind' approach. At present there is not any evidence that the government is willing to set targets for improvement and closing the gap between ethnic groups. Despite the current situation, it is important to recognise there has been a great deal of analysis of the education policy concerning 'race' issues. In 1979, the Rampton inquiry was set up to investigate the causes of minority ethnic underachievement with a focus on the Black Caribbean and this was followed by the Swann report. These reports at least bring the issue of 'race' and racism into the mainstream education policy and the differential achievement.

The next chapters look in detail at the barriers to learning and the strategies and good practices in driving improvement in schools.

References

Andrews, J., Robinson, D. & Hutchinson, J. (2017) *Closing the Gap? Trends in Educational Attainment and Disadvantaged.* London: Education Policy Institute, https://epi.org.uk/publications-and-research/closing-gap-trends-educational-attainment-disadvantage/

Arnot, M., Gray, J., James, M. & Rudduck, J. (1998) *Recent Research on Gender and Educational Performance, Ofsted.* London: The Stationery Office.

Cassen, R. & Kingdon, G. (2007) *Tackling Low Educational Achievement.* Joseph Rowntree Foundation.

Cassen, R., McNally, S., & Vignoles, A. (2015) *Making a difference in Education: What the evidence says.* London: Routlege.

Darling-Hammond, L. (1998) *Unequal Opportunity: Race and Education.* Brookings. https://www.brookings.edu/articles/unequal-opportunity-race-and-education/

Demie, F. (2001) Ethnic and gender difference in educational achievement and implications for school improvement strategies. *Educational Research* 43(1): 91–106.

Demie, F. (2019) *Educational Inequality: Closing the Gap.* London: UCL IOE Press, July.

Demie, F. (2023) Tackling educational inequality: Lessons from London schools. *Equity in Education & Society*, https://doi.org/10.1177/27526461231161775

Demie, F. & Mclean, C. (2015) *Narrowing the Achievement Gap: Good Practice in Schools.* London: Lambeth Research and Statistics Unit.

Demie, F. & Mclean, C. (2016a) Tackling disadvantage: what works in narrowing the achievement gap in schools. *Review of Education* 3(2):138–174. https://doi.org/10.1002/rev3.30

Demie, F. & Mclean, C. (2016b) *What Works in School Improvement: Examples of Good Practice.* Lambeth LA: Lambeth Research and Statistics Unit.

Demie, F. & Mclean, C. (2017) *Black Caribbean Underachievement in Schools in England.* Lambeth LA: Lambeth Research and Statistics Unit.

DfE (2015) *Supporting the attainment of disadvantaged pupils: articulating success and good practice Research report.* London: Department for educations, November

DfE (2017) *National and LA KS2 and GCSE performance table 2005-2017, SFR.* London: Department for Education.

DfE (2023) *Schools, pupils and their characteristics*: January 2023. London: Department for educations, June.

Easterbrook, M. J., and Hadden, I. R. (2021) Tackling educational inequalities with social psychology: identities, contexts, and interventions. *Social Issues and Policy Review* 15, 180–236. https://doi.org/10.1111/sipr.12070.3

Education Committee. (2014) *Underachievement in Education by White Working Class Children, HC 142.* London: The Stationery Office Limited.

EPI. (2017) *Closing the Gap? Trends in Educational Attainment and Disadvantage.* https://epi.org.uk/wp-content/uploads/2017/08/Closing-the-Gap_EPI-.pdf

EPI. (2020) *Education in England: Annual Report 2020.* https://epi.org.uk/publications-and-research/education-in-england-annual-report-2020/

Francis, B. and Skelton, C. (2005) *Reassessing Gender and Achievement: Questioning Contemporary Key Debates.* London: Routledge, https://doi.org/10.4324/9780203412923

Gillborn, D. & Gipps, C. (1996) *Recent Research on the Achievement of Ethnic Minority Pupils.* London: OFSTED Reviews of Research, HMSO.

Gillborn, D. & Mirza, H.S. (2000) *Educational Inequality: Mapping Race and Class*. London: OFSTED.

Gillborn, D. & Youdell, D. (2000) *Rationing Education: Policy, Practice, Reform and Equity*. Buckingham: Open University Press.

Gorard, S., See, B.H. & Siddiqui, N. (2023) *Making Schools Better for Disadvantaged Students: The International Implications of Evidence on Effective School Funding*. London: Routledge.

Hung, M., Smith, W.A., Voss, M.W., Franklin, J.D., Gu, Y. & Bounsanga, J. (2020) Exploring Student Achievement Gaps in School Districts Across the United States. *Education and Urban Society* 52(2): 175–193.

Hutchinson, J., Dunford, J. & Treadway, M. (2016) *Divergent Pathways: The Disadvantage Gap, Accountability and the Pupil Premium*. London: Education Policy Institute. https://epi.org.uk/wp-content/uploads/2018/01/disadvantage-report.pdf

IFS. (2022) '*Education Inequalities*', IFS Deaton Review of Inequalities. https://ifs.org.uk/inequality/chapter/education-inequalities/

Kao, G. & Thompson, J. (2003) Racial and ethnic stratification in educational achievement and attainment. *Annual Review of Sociology* 29: 417–442. https://doi.org/10.1146/annurev.soc.29.010202.100019

Ladson-Billings, G. (2006) From the Achievement Gap to the Education Debt: Understanding Achievement in US Schools. *Educational Researcher* 37(7): 3–12.

Majors, R. (2001) ed. *Educating our black children*. London: Routledge Falmer.

Mongon, D. & Chapman, C. (2008) *Successful Leadership for Promoting the Achievement of White Working Class Pupils*. Nottingham: National College for School Leadership (NCSL).

Mortimore, P. & Whitty, G. (1997) *Can School Improvement Overcome the Effects of Disadvantage?* London: Institute of Education, University of London.

NPD. (2016) National pupil Database, Department for Education.

NPD. (2023) National pupil Database, Department for Education.

Ofsted. (2013) *Unseen Children: Access and Achievement 20 Years on*. Ofsted. http://www.ofsted.gov.uk/resources/unseen-children-access-and-achievement-20-years

Strand, S. (2014) School effects and ethnic, gender and socio-economic gaps in educational achievement at age 11. *Oxford Review of Education* 40(2): 223–245. Oxford. https://doi.org/10.1080/03054985.2014.891980

White, S.B., Reynolds, P.D., Thomas, M.M. & Gitlaff, N.J. (1993) Socioeconomic status and achievement revisited. *Urban Education* 28(3): 328–343.

3
BARRIERS TO LEARNING

Introduction

This chapter investigates the factors associated with barriers to learning and the reasons for Black and ethnic minority students' underachievement. Drawing on previous research and school surveys, this chapter presents key evidence and explanations of factors associated with barriers to learning and underachievement.

A growing body of research suggests many factors contribute to the underachievement of Black and ethnic minority pupils in schools. Within education literature recently, barriers to learning and underachievement have been influenced by factors such as teachers' low expectations, institutional racism, lack of diversity in the school workforce, lack of parental engagement, lack of parental aspiration, single-parent households, low literacy levels, poverty, lack of positive role models, a social class issue, curriculum barriers, lower tier entry in school ability groups, and school exclusions (see Gillborn and Youdell, 2000; Maylor et al., 2009; DCSF, 2008; Gillborn, 1995; DfE 2000; EHRC, 2016; MacPherson, 1999; DfES, 2006a; Demie 2005, 2003; 2022a,b,c; Race, 2024). Other researchers also noted the lack of adequate support for schools from parents, economic deprivation, poor housing, and home circumstances (Rampton, 1981a,b; Swann, 1985) and the failure of the national curriculum to adequately reflect the need for a diverse and multi-ethnic society (Macpherson, 1999; Gillborn, 2002; and Demie and Mclean, 2017). These research findings are supported by other surveys (see Demie, 2023,b) of headteachers and teachers in Inner London schools that asked, 'What are the main barriers to learning for disadvantaged and ethnic minority pupils in schools?' The survey identified, in addition to the factors listed

DOI: 10.4324/9781003499633-4

above, poverty, a lack of parental involvement, parental numeracy issues, curriculum barriers, racism, and a lack of funding.

Several studies have attempted to explain the many factors associated with barriers to learning and low achievement. UK and international evidence suggests disadvantaged and ethnic minority pupils face many problems, including poverty across generations, a lack of parental engagement, negative attitudes towards education, home, and community factors (Mongon and Chapman, 2008; Demie and Mclean, 2017). This finding of the literature review related to barriers to learning has led us to develop several explanatory factors that we believe have contributed to barriers to learning and the underachievement of disadvantaged and ethnic minority pupils in schools. This has also helped us identify several factors that need to be included in any further survey questionnaire. To investigate barriers to learning, we asked headteachers and senior management teams in schools to complete a survey (Demie 2024). We wanted to establish whether issues covered in our literature reviews were also raised as key factors by the school staff. The survey asked the respondents how much they felt each of the factors contributed to barriers to learning and underachievement, using a 7-point scale that was then grouped into 'strongly disagree, disagree, agree, strongly agree.' The findings that emerged from the study based on the above survey approach, which are outlined in Chapter 1, are discussed below.

Factors associated with barriers to learning

The main findings of the survey results on barriers to learning are given in Figure 3.1, showing the factors that contributed to barriers to learning and the underachievement of pupils. This is a response to the question, 'What are the main barriers to learning for BAME and disadvantaged pupils in your school?'

Further analysis of the evidence in Figure 3.1 by those who responded as agree and strongly agree in the survey also confirms that the factors that respondents rated as having the most contribution to underachievement and barriers to learning were:

- lack of funding (92%),
- socioeconomic poverty (87%),
- lack of parental engagement in schooling (69%),
- low literacy level (68%),
- lack of family support (66%),
- attracting and retaining good teaching staff (64%),
- lack of parental aspirations (63%),
- pupil aspiration (61%),
- social class issues (60%),

42 Black and Ethnic Minority Achievement in Schools

Barrier	Disagree	Strongly disagree	Agree	Strongly agree
Teacher training and professional development opportunities	40%	38%	20%	2%
Attracting and retaining good teaching staff	22%	13%	41%	23%
Attracting and retaining good support staff	16%	27%	27%	30%
Lack of diversity in the school workforce	35%	44%	20%	
Lack of positive role models	27%	43%	25%	5%
Lack of funding		8%	19%	73%
Lack of sufficient tracking and monitoring systems	56%	26%	18%	
Curriculum barriers	23%	46%	27%	5%
Socioeconomic poverty	5%	9%	37%	50%
Pupil aspiration	21%	19%	42%	19%
Social class issues	16%	24%	35%	25%
Low literacy level	14%	19%	39%	29%
Setting in lower stream ability groups	55%	18%	23%	4%
School exclusions	51%	28%	18%	3%
Racism	53%	29%	17%	1%
Lack of parental engagement in schooling	9%	23%	43%	26%
Lack of parental aspirations	13%	24%	37%	26%
Parental negative attitudes to education	16%	25%	38%	21%
Lack of family support	12%	22%	40%	26%

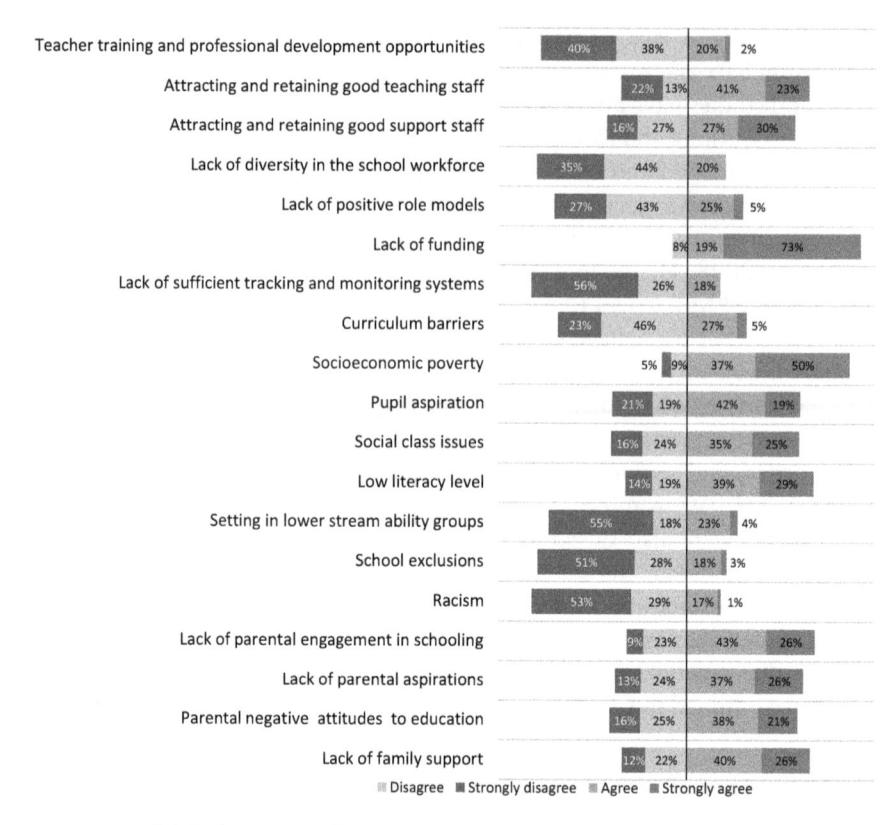

FIGURE 3.1 Main barriers to learning.

- parental negative attitudes towards education (59%),
- and attracting and retaining good support staff (57%).

(see also Demie 2024)

It was agreed that these were the main barriers to learning reported by the respondents, with factors such as curriculum barriers (32%), lack of positive role models (30%), setting in lower stream ability groups (27%), teacher training and professional development opportunities (22%), school exclusions (21%), lack of diversity in the school workforce (20%), racism (18%), and lack of sufficient tracking and monitoring systems (18%) contributing less than 50% (see also Demie 2024).

There were several barriers to learning that the survey respondents added and commented on in the questionnaire including the following.

A lack of funding for education

The main factor identified as a barrier to learning from the survey is a lack of funding, which is having serious consequences for schools' ability to support children's education and learning. All headteachers who commented raised funding as a major factor and barrier to learning. Some of the respondents who highlighted funding as a barrier stated that:

> Schools need the funding to employ and keep good teachers! Current academic-based qualifications at GCSE do not meet the needs of all, especially disadvantaged students.
>
> *(Headteache.r, SP45)*

> Money is the biggest factor; we know what we want to do, we know what we should do, but we can't afford to do it.
>
> *(SENCO, SP74)*

> Chronic underfunding of education impacts not only all pupils but also disadvantaged pupils. We are no longer able to afford any extra teaching or support staff beyond class teachers and 1:1 support LSAs. We have a specialist resource provision and are seeing children with increasingly severe mental health issues both within our provision and in the mainstream. We are no longer able to afford our school counsellor, which we know will impact support for some of our most vulnerable pupils. As school leaders, we are having to spend an increasing amount of time covering classes as there is no money to supply teachers. The system is at a breaking point, and it is the next generation who will suffer.
>
> *(Deputy Headteacher, SP28)*

> There is a lack of funding to support SEND pupils in schools. The increase in ASC and sensory needs is causing issues for all mainstream schools. The lack of funding for support for these children, combined with the lack of places for children who need a different environment, is having an impact on the availability of quality teaching and support for other children with a lower threshold of need but who are still underachieving.
>
> *(SENCO, SP36)*

> Some schools are reluctant to take SEND children on a roll because of a lack funding and staff cuts.
>
> *(SENCO, SP84)*

> There is no one there to support EAL and SEND children because of a lack of funding.
>
> *(Headteacher, SP35)*

> Schools do not have enough money to pay specialist teachers to work with pupils with challenging behaviours and SEN pupils.
>
> *(SENCO, SP84)*

School leaders are extremely concerned about the lack of funding and cuts in schools. There is no one there to support schools and families because of budget cuts. The lack of funding is clearly at the top of the survey lists.

Poverty factor

The second most important factor associated with barriers to learning in the survey is poverty. Persistent socioeconomic disadvantage has a negative impact on the life outcomes of many Black and ethnic minority children. In Britain, poverty rates were higher for children living in households headed by someone from an ethnic minority (41.9%), Pakistani or Bangladeshi (43.8%), Black Caribbean (39.4%), mixed-race (26.5%), or Indian (24.9%) compared with someone from a White group (24.5%) (see EHRC 2015). Poverty is seen to play a major role in underachievement for Black and ethnic minorities (Demie and Mclean, 2017). Black people lack sufficient income to be able to participate fully in society, and they are 'socially excluded'. The head teachers and teachers who responded to our survey also commented on how poverty affects learning. They argued that:

> Poverty is an issue in London, and schools are underachieving because of poverty.
>
> *(Headteacher, SP9)*

> Black and ethnic minority families live mainly in deprived areas, and pupils also go to school in deprived areas. I think geographical areas affect them.
>
> *(Headteacher, SP95)*

> Just because a family is poor does not mean they do not have aspirations for their children. The problem is that in primary school, particularly, the curriculum is too crowded with too many objectives for reading, writing, and math. It would be better to teach less but teach deeper. Children need to learn how to be learners and also be given opportunities to develop in the arts and creative subjects. Poverty can look very different depending on where you are located. For example, you can be poor in London but come out of the door and within a few minutes see thriving businesses, whereas in more northern areas this is not always the case.
>
> *(Headteacher, SP37)*

> Our barriers to learning are constant mobility, children newly arriving in the country, which then takes away precious resources for non-mobile children, budget constraints, etc.
>
> *(Headteacher, SP21)*

Disadvantage and poverty are complex issues involving many factors. Disadvantaged children and their families, as an ethnic group, are disproportionately impacted by low income, mental health, poor housing, and mobility. The children at our school who do not attain as well as their peers are.

(Headteacher, SP23)

We have a black family on the local estate. The children are excluded from school. All linked to poverty and social factors.

(Headteacher, SP12)

The above views on the effect of poverty on BAME are also supported by previous research. For example, EHRC (2015) and Demie and Mclean (2017), all argue that economic deprivation appears widely prevalent among Black groups. Many Black and ethnic minority children are further disadvantaged by the fact that they attend under-resourced and less successful schools in inner cities.

Low literacy level and language barriers

Low literacy affects learning. Research has now generally agreed that literacy is critical for learning and can significantly impair children's overall learning as well as English classes.

These are only a few instances of literacy learning obstacles. Students who require additional learning help, for instance, could find it difficult to learn at the same rate or use the same instructional strategies as their classmates. Students who have educational obstacles like dyslexia or visual impairments need to be given equal support to learn. Disadvantaged pupils may also experience learning barriers to literacy through a lack of access to the correct equipment or materials for learning, such as books and computers. During the interviews and survey, we learned that many children in schools are recent arrivals who lack familiarity with standard English.

A number of headteachers and teachers also commented in another study (Demie and Mclean, 2017:72–73) and summed it up succinctly:

Poorly spoken English may be a source of disadvantage to ethnic minority children.

We have a problem where pupils are struggling with literacy; it is because their parents are

Illiterate.

Parents who have very poor literacy skills themselves cannot fill out forms or read newsletters.

Some parents require basic knowledge of math, reading, and writing. Some parents say the way we teach is so different from the way they were taught at school, and they cannot understand it. We struggle to get parents on board sometimes. I think this links to parents' literacy skills.

There is evidence from the survey and comments made by headteachers and teachers that literacy is a barrier to learning and there is a lack of academic language to access the national curriculum.

In addition to low literacy levels, this research also identifies language learning barriers that have a negative impact on children's education. Two major language barriers to learning can be observed in the context of the English education system. This is particularly key for English as an Additional Language (EAL) pupils and parents who do not have a strong command of the language of instruction; language barriers can impede understanding and communication, making it difficult to engage with the curriculum. The British research suggests that students who are exposed to English as an additional language can encounter challenges according to their proficiency in communicating and understanding. Similarly, parents who are not fluent in the language spoken at school might not be fully involved in the student's performance due to a lack of communication with the teacher.

The headteachers and teacher respondents to the survey argued that:

For EAL learners, particularly new arrivals, parents are unable to access information from the school or the homework that the children are set. This is a large barrier to their learning. Parents and carers are often unaware of the resources and support available, so it is important that we help them feel empowered to reach out, even with a translated email. Targeted help could help to challenge the barriers related to accessing the curriculum for EAL proficiency for parents and pupils.

(EAL coordinator and teacher, SP75)

Moreover, learners using EAL will need differentiated work and home learning. Unfortunately, not all teachers feel confident differentiating work for EAL learners; the language barrier scares them. This means that staff need to be trained adequately and have routine reminders. In South London schools, we receive many new starters who cannot speak English, and it is vital that children feel safe and settled before they start. Investing in well-trained support staff, translators, and intervention programmes has made it easier and more efficient to support these new English learners. Targeted support for EAL to improve English proficiency is critical for them to access the national curriculum.

(EAL coordinator and teacher, SP75)

Lack of parental engagement

Extensive research literature published over the years indicates that parental involvement is an important element of effective education for children of all ages (Lambert et al., 2022; Hornby and Ian Blackwell, 2018). This includes home-based parent engagement, such as listening to children read, and school-based parent involvement, such as attending parent-teacher meetings.

The effectiveness of parental engagement in facilitating academic achievement has been reported by many reviews and meta-analyses of the literature (Jeynes, 2012; Cooper et al., 2010; Hill and Tyson, 2009; Barton et al., 2004). There is evidence from the research that shows successful schools reported engaging parent involvement using:

- 'Regular newsletters, leaflets, information sheets, and letters home
- Websites used to give information to parents
- teacher-parent meetings
- having an active parent association
- open days/evenings
- new parents' evenings
- school performances, celebration events, and assemblies
- Pupils exhibitions
- school fairs
- sports days
- language day
- parent education classes, such as focussing on math, Information Communication Technology (ICT), literacy, and EAL teaching.
- Texting and emails between teachers and parents
- being open longer hours for breakfast clubs and extending the day to when parents collect their children to allow for conversations between teaching staff and parents.'

(see Hornby and Ian Blackwell, 2018:11)

Successful schools encourage parents to take part in assemblies, special events, parent education classes, and school trips. However, despite this, our survey suggests there is a lack of parental engagement, which is a barrier to learning for children. Research suggests that parental involvement has been further complicated by factors such as family socioeconomic status, cultural differences, social class, and racial-ethnic backgrounds (McDermott and Rothenberg, 2000). School leaders reported parents' own negative experiences of school as barriers to parental engagement, as indicated below.

Parents who had negative school experience assume their children's experience will be the same.

(Headteacher, SP2)

There's an element of parents who had a bad experience of school' and are scared of school settings.

(Headteacher, SP60)

Some parents have low literacy levels as a result reluctant to engage with the school.

(Headteacher, SP50)

Some parents have had a difficult life. This sometimes has a negative impact on the child.

(Headteacher, SP120)

Parents who do not engage in our school tend to be people with a lot of social care issues.

(SP70)

Some parents have EAL issues which can be a barrier to learning.

(Headteacher, SP75)

Some White working-class families and parents do not engage and they do not send their children to booster classes as they do not see the point. They say lack of education has not done them any harm.

(Headteacher, SP23)

We have parents here who have very low aspirations.

(Headteacher, SP26)

We have parents on free school meals, benefits and most of them are single parents. There is a strong sense of isolation in the community and poor engagement with schools.

(Headteacher, SP23)

The lack of parental aspiration

The lack of aspiration among White working-class families is also raised as a concern to those involved in raising the achievement of disadvantaged pupils. Headteachers expressed their concern at the gap between the high aspirations for children's learning held by the school and the low aspirations of parents.

Headteachers highlighted the lack of education of White working-class parents as a causative factor for low aspirations.

> White working-class students are the hardest students to reach. Easy access to low-skilled work but a relatively high salary means that they are not motivated to do well in school. Our non-white working class, especially students whose families originate from Asia or Africa, is much more motivated to do well and is engaged. Often, research puts the two groups together, yet there is a huge difference between the strategies each group requires.
> *(Headteacher, SP23)*

> Many white working-class parents and the disadvantaged are on benefits. There is a vicious cycle of poverty that keeps them on benefits.
> *(Headteacher, SP23)*

> Education does not have a priority for whites working at home, and this has an impact on how the children feel about their work in school.
> *(Headteacher, SP23)*

One headteacher argued that there are limited or no 'enrichment opportunities that raise aspiration.'

> Schools do offer a range of enrichment opportunities, trips, and visits that raise the aspiration of black pupils. It is important to tackle barriers to learning at school and also provide cultural, artistic, and sporting experiences that pupils are unlikely to encounter at home or in the community, widening horizons and heightening their aspirations and expectations, and giving them access to opportunities that they may take up later in life. This provides opportunities to develop greater self-confidence for black pupils.
> *(Headteacher, SP72)*

Lack of diversity

The survey shows there is a lack of diversity in the school workforce. In England, schools have not yet recruited teaching and non-teaching staff that reflect the language, culture, and ethnic background of the pupils in the schools. The evidence from school workforce data shows that in England, '86% of teachers, 91% of the leadership, 87% of teaching assistants, and all other school staff are white British. Only 0.8% of school leaders and 1% of teachers are Black Caribbean.' It also clearly shows that there is a growing mismatch between the ethnic diversity of the pupil population and that of the teachers in their schools.

Headteachers in another research study and survey (see Demie 2023:16a) also commented:

> Diversity is a key problem not only in London but also nationally.
> Lack of diversity and cultural understanding within SLT.
> School diversity does not reflect the language, culture, and ethnic background of the pupils in the schools. There is a huge disproportionality between the school workforce and the student population. Diversity issues must be addressed to tackle the barriers to learning and underachievement for ethnic minority pupils.

A teacher of one school pointed out further concern about the diversity of ethnic minority leadership in their school and argued.

> Not enough black and ethnic minority in senior leadership.
> *(teacher, Demie, 2023:16a)*

The study's evidence and previous research suggest that diversity matters and is at the heart of the work of schools. In general, increasing the diversity of the teaching force can help to tackle educational inequality, raise aspiration, reduce school exclusions, and promote learning for students and high achievement. It also helps in promoting cultural diversity and tackling the shortage of teachers in disadvantaged areas (see Demie, 2019; Demie, 2023, b).

Curriculum barriers and relevance

The survey also identified curriculum barriers and relevance as barriers to learning. The headteachers and teachers who responded to another survey commented on the curriculum barriers to learning and on the importance of diversifying the curriculum to address diversity in multicultural Britain as follows:

> The relevance of the curriculum to ethnic minorities and addressing diversity is the subject of much concern. There is a need to decolonise the English curriculum'. The black and ethnic minorities' experience needs to be used to enrich the curriculum in art, dance, music, geography, and history.
> *(Headteacher)*

> In the classroom, I always wanted to know about my culture and background'. It was ridiculous what I was taught in the history class. We wanted to do African or Blak history but were not taught.

Frustrations were expressed by teachers at the constant changes to the curriculum in the UK. There is not a consistent approach to initiatives and education. Something starts and it gets taken away.

(Teacher)

The government does not make it easier by constantly changing the curriculum, assessment, etc. It makes it difficult to recruit staff and retain them.'
' The government changes the curriculum too often. The school needs to take a panoramic view of what they are doing for these pupils.

(Headteacher)

The curriculum in England has a problem with ethnic minorities. When we are looking at education and race, sometimes the curriculum feels narrow.

(Headteacher)

We need to diversify the curriculum in all subject areas to reflect the much wider communities the school serves.

(Headteacher)

There is a lack of representation of black and ethnic minority pupils in the curriculum resources currently found in the classroom. It was a hindrance to learning to read.' 'The books and resources in the classroom need to be audited to check for diversity. SAT papers and teaching materials need to reflect different communities.

(Headteacher)

The history curriculum is not relevant for black pupils. It does not look at the achievement of early Black civilizations, pre-colonial Black presence in Britain, migration patterns in Britain, ethnic and cultural diversity in Britain, the role of Blak and Asian peoples, and the colonies in both the Second World War.

(Headteacher)

The curriculum is not relevant for black and ethnic minority pupils, and there is a need to diversify and use the current curriculum, which adds to the growing pride of being black and Asian pupils in multicultural Britain.

(Teacher)

The above comments are also supported by research into curriculum barriers. Researchers on the issues of the British curriculum argued that the school curriculum has contributed to the underachievement of pupils and does not meet the needs of the community schools serve. The English curriculum that is taught in schools is biassed towards the majority ethnic group and marginalises minority ethnic groups. White British culture is the main subject of the curriculum. The national curriculum fails to sufficiently represent the need for a multi-ethnic society, and British history is taught from a European perspective, even positive-shaping colonialism (MacPherson, 1999; Gillborn, 2002; Demie and Mclean, 2017). There is a convincing argument in literature and this study that Black children are underachieving in schools because they feel that the curriculum does not relate to them.

School exclusions

Another key factor responsible for barriers to learning and the underachievement of children is school exclusion. This affects the learning opportunities of the children. Research suggests that Black Caribbean children are most likely to be excluded from school and represent the most excluded group of pupils in British schools (Demie 2022a; Gillborn and Youdell 2000; EHRC 2015; DfE 2000; the Runnymede Trust 2012; DfE 2000). DfE statistics on exclusion show that Black Caribbean pupils are over-represented in both permanent and fixed-term exclusions. Nationally in 2017/2018, the figures for Black Caribbean pupils were 0.28% permanent and 10.46% fixed term exclusions. This is significantly high when compared to the national average of 0.10% permanent and 5.08% fixed exclusions for all pupils (see Demie 2022a). The previous research by the Department for Education and Skills (DfES, 2006a:63) also suggests some other reasons why Black pupils are disproportionately excluded. The report argued that:

> Black pupils encounter both conscious and unconscious prejudice from teachers; for example, research has found that throughout their education, black pupils are disciplined more (both in terms of frequency and severity) and often for milder offences than those leading to their white peers being punished.
>
> *(DfES, 2006a:63)*

The research related to ability grouping found that Black Caribbean students were less likely to be put into higher sets than their White peers (see Demie, 2019; Gillborn, 2008). Steve Strand (2012). Other UK research also shows teachers' low expectations and allocation bias:

> Black pupils were more than 2.5 times more likely than white pupils to be allocated to a lower group than predicted. On the other hand, boys were more likely than girls to be assigned to higher sets than projected, and white students were more likely than black or Asian students to be assigned to higher sets than expected. This evidence suggests that there is an effect of stereotypes in the allocation of pupils to sets.
>
> *(Taylor 2019:1)*

Black students who question what they believe to be racism on the part of teachers are frequently excluded. Overall evidence suggests that schools perceive and respond to the behaviour of Black children more harshly than to other ethnic groups.

Racism

Another factor that was raised in the survey and literature about the reasons for the underachievement of pupils and barriers to learning is institutional racism. These are racialised practices, unfair policies, or discriminatory treatments that go beyond prejudice and provide Whites with an unfair advantage over people of colour (MacPherson, 1999). Much research has highlighted how racism has played a key role in the underachievement of Black and ethnic minority students. Racism extends to all groups but affects more Black Caribbean pupils compared to their Black African, Pakistani, White, and Bangladeshi classmates (Demie, 2019; 2022a,b,c; 2023,b; Demie and Mclean, 2017; Gershenson et al., 2016; Maylor et al., 2009; Strand, 2012; Race, 2024).

Institutional racism affects ethnic minority students in British schools, severely impacting their chances of academic performance (MacPherson 1999; DfES 2006a; Demie and Mclean 2017). The response of the headteachers to the questions shows institutional racism is an important factor.

> Absolutely! How many black police officers have we got, or how many black teachers have we got?
> *(Headteacher, Demie 22:44)*

> Institutional racism is still an issue in society. There is a lot of scaremongering in the press, vilifying young black men; they read the headlines, and though there has been a fall in knife crime, they will take one aspect and go on about that.
> *(Headteacher, Demie 22:44)*

> Getting a job is more difficult for black men. They are disregarded even when their qualifications are identical to those of a white counterpart.
> *(Headteacher)*

> Racism is a key factor in school exclusion.
> *(Headteacher, SP1)*

> Racism and lack of strong school leadership are issues in schools.
> *(Headteacher, SP1)*

The overall consensus among researchers in the field suggests that racism and the 'colour blind' approach are some of the factors that have put the raising of the achievement of ethnic minority pupils at a disadvantage in the English school system (see also Demie 2022c; Gillborn 2008; Demie and Mclean 2007; DfES 2006a; MacPherson 1999). This view of institutional racism and 'colour blindness' was supported by the government (DfEE, 2000) and pointed out:

> A colourblind approach can mean that factors important to the education of minority group pupils are overlooked.
>
> *(DfEE 2000:24)*

Overall, most recent research also concurs that Black and ethnic minority pupils are being subjected to institutional racism in British schools, and this is a barrier to learning and has affected pupils' chances of academic success (Macpherson, 1999; Parekh, 2000; DfES, 2006b; Demie 2022a,b,c; 2023, 2023b; Race, 2024). This is particularly revealed, for example, in teachers' differential treatment of Black children in terms of school exclusion and low teacher expectations and assessments made about the abilities of Black Caribbean pupils. Achievement gaps have been linked to teachers' perceptions and expectations of Black children's behaviour, according to research (Gillborn and Youdell, 2000; Strand, 2012). Black children are often placed in lower sets based on their ability and are not represented in entry to higher tiers compared to their White British peers. Research has shown that institutional racism and low expectations by teachers are two of the reasons why students are not entering top-tier exams. Moreover, it has been argued that teachers' sometimes 'conscious or unconscious stereotypes and assumptions about minority groups can impact negatively on pupils' achievements' (Maylor et al., 2009).

Teachers low expectations

In comparison to White British and Asian pupils, a number of additional research findings also support white teachers' low expectations of Black students (see Demie 2022a,b,c; Gillborn and Youdell, 2000; Demie and Mclean, 2017; Villegas & Irvine, 2010; McKown and Weinstein, 2008; Demie 2019). Researchers have highlighted that many White teachers are not aware of the negative impact of unconscious prejudice and stereotypes. Sometimes, 'conscious or unconscious stereotypes and assumptions about minority groups have negatively impacted students' achievements in the classroom,' according to teachers (Maylor et al., 2009; Milliard et al., 2018; Demie, 2019; Demie and Mclean, 2017). Recent research also shows some evidence in schools that suggests negative experiences for Black and ethnic minority pupils. These were highlighted by the parents we interviewed (see 2022a,b,c: 82).

> My British White teachers had a low expectation of me as a mixed-race child when I was in school. A-C or D grade estimate was the norm with all white British teachers, but I got an A* in all subjects when I took my A level. The same was true throughout my primary and secondary GCSE education. I am always assessed in teacher assessments about 2-4 levels below what I get when I take tests. Of greater interest is the fact that, in spite of the low expectations set by my primary and secondary school teachers, I attended the top university and obtained distinctions for both my undergraduate and graduate degrees.
> *(Parent, Demie 2022a:82)*

> Teachers' tends to underestimate the academic abilities of students of colour. Therefore, black students anticipate that their teachers will hold them in lower regard.
> *(Parent Governor, Demie 2022a:82)*

This parent view is supported by previous research confirming that White teachers hold low expectations of Black or mixed-race children compared to White British and Asian students (see Demie 2022a, b, and c; Demie and Mclean, 2017; Gillborn and Youdell, 2000; Villegas & Irvine, 2010; McKown and Weinstein, 2008).

Other factors

There are some other factors highlighted in the survey, including low ability grouping and social class issues contributing to barriers to learning, but no comments were made by respondents in our open questions. The survey and previous research suggest that Black children represent the most excluded group of pupils in British schools Demie (2022a,b,c; Gillborn and Youdell 2000; EHRC 2015; DfE 2000), and Black and ethnic minority students are less likely to be put into higher sets and are less likely to be entered for higher-tier exams than their White peers (see Demie, 2019; Gillborn, 2008). Steve Strand (2012). Parents' social class is also highlighted in the survey. In Britain, there is a strong class system, particularly with White British, and social mobility is considered poor. A lot of White British teachers have a middle-class background, which plays a big barrier to White working-class children's education. The class background remains a barrier to learning and accessing opportunities in later life. There is evidence from research that suggests middle-class children are classed as able and working-class pupils are labelled as less able by placing them into lower sets and denying access to parts of the school curriculum (Demie and Lewis 2010; Steve Strand 2012).

Conclusions

This chapter explored the key barriers to learning. It asks research questions about the factors that contribute to barriers to learning and underachievement. Two methodological approaches were used in the research, including reviewing literature and a survey of barriers to learning in schools for disadvantaged children and ethnic minority pupils. The results of the survey provide useful data on barriers to learning in schools and a clear picture of the views of the respondents.

The findings of the survey identified the main barriers to learning factors such as lack of funding, socioeconomic poverty, lack of parental engagement in schooling, low literacy level, language barriers, lack of family support, attracting and retaining good teaching staff, lack of parental aspirations, pupil aspiration, social class issues, parental negative attitudes towards education, and attracting and retaining good support staff. Other factors, such as curriculum barriers, lack of positive role models, setting in lower stream ability groups, teacher training and professional development opportunities, school exclusions, lack of diversity in the school workforce, racism, and a lack of sufficient tracking and monitoring systems, are also important in the view of the survey respondent but contributed less in the view of respondents.

All the above factors can perpetuate low attainment, and the body of available research suggests a worrying picture of a failure to address underachievement and barriers to learning in British schools. Researchers now agree that the biggest obstacles to raising achievement are institutional racism, the 'colour blind' approach, which has put ethnic minority groups at a disadvantage, and the failure of the national curriculum to adequately reflect the needs of a diverse, multi-ethnic society (Demie 2023,2023b; Gillborn 2002; MacPherson 1999; Race, 2024). The above evidence on the factors related to barriers to learning reinforces the findings of previous research, which identified serious concerns about the extent to which the education system and schools were meeting the needs of ethnic minority and disadvantaged pupils (Gillborn and Mirza 2000; Rampton 1981a,b; Swann 1985; Gillborn and Gipps 1996; Demie 2003 and 2005). These concerns persist. Increasing our knowledge of the factors behind barriers to learning and the causes of academic underperformance in schools is necessary.

The overall conclusion from the study is that all the above factors are barriers to learning for Black and ethnic minority disadvantaged pupils in English schools, and this has perpetuated low attainment. To address the issue, action must be taken. There is no research that shows that some schools are particularly successful in addressing barriers to learning to close the achievement gap (see Demie 2023,2023b; 2019; Ofsted 2009; Demie and Lewis 2010; Mongon and Chapman 2008). We can learn a great deal from these examples, but they are not yet well-researched and widely used.

Closer examinations of their work and further research into successful schools' impact will help create an evidence base that can tell us more about the approaches that might work elsewhere. Based on what we know from this and existing research, this study recommends that policymakers and school practitioners use effective strategies in successful schools to tackle the barriers to learning and raise achievement. The next chapters explore in detail key strategies used by schools to raise achievement and close the gaps for Black and ethnic minority children.

References

Demie, F. (2019) *Educational Inequality: Closing the Gap*. London: UCL IOE Press, July. https://www.ucl-ioe-press.com/books/social-justice-equality-and-human-rights/educational-inequality/

Demie, F. (2022a) *Understanding the Causes and Consequences of School Exclusions: Teachers, Parents and Schools' Perspectives*. London: Routledge.

Demie, F. (2022b) 'Tackling teachers' low expectations of Black Caribbean students in English schools. *Equity in Education and Society Journal*. https://doi.org/10.1177/27526461211068511

Demie, F. (2022c) Black pupils and school exclusions in England: What does research tell us? *Sociological Review* 31(3). Hodder Education.

Demie, F. (2023) *Raising the Achievement of Black Caribbean pupils: Barriers and Good Practice in Schools*. London: Lambeth School Research and Statistics Service.

Demie, F. (2024) *A Survey of Barriers to Learning, Success Factors, and Intervention Strategy in London Schools to Raise Achievement and Tackle Educational Inequality*. London: Lambeth Schools Research and Statistics Unit. April draft.

Demie, F. & Lewis, K. (2010) *White Working Class Achievement: An Ethnographic Study of Barriers to Learning in Schools*. https://doi.org/10.1080/03055698.2010.506341

Demie, F. & Mclean, C. (2017) *Black Caribbean Underachievement in Schools in England*. Lambeth LA. London: Schools Research and Statistics Unit.

DfE. (2000) *Removing the barriers: Raising Achievement Levels for Minority Ethnic Pupils*. London: Department for Education.

DfES. (2006a) *Exclusion of Black Pupils Priority Review: Getting it, getting it right*. London: Department for Education and Skills.

EHRC. (2015) *Is Britain Fairer? The State of Equality and Human Rights*. Equality and Human Rights Commission. https://www.gov.uk/government/publications/is-britain-fairer-the-state-ofequality-and-human-rights-2015

EHRC. (2016) *Healing a Divided Britain: The Need for a Comprehensive Race Equality Strategy*. London: Equality and Human Rights Commission. https://www.equalityhumanrights.com/sites/default/files/healing_a_divided_britain__the_need_for_a_comprehensive_race_equality_strategy_final.pdf

Gillborn, D. (1995) *Racism and Antiracism in Real Schools: Theory, Policy, and Practice*. Buckingham: Open University Press.

Gillborn, D. (2002) *Education and Institutional Racism, Inaugural Professorial Lecture*. Institute of Education, University of London.

Gillborn, D. (2008) Coincidence or conspiracy? Whiteness, policy, and the persistence of the Black/White achievement Gao. *Educational Review* 60(3): 229–248.

Gillborn, D. & Mirza, H.S. (2000) *Educational Inequality: Mapping Race, Class and Gender*. Ofsted.

Gillborn, D. & Youdell, D. (2000) *Rationing Education: Policy, Practice, Reform and Equity*. Buckingham: Open University Press.

Gillborn, D. & Gipps, C. (1996) *Recent Research on the Achievement of Ethnic Minority Pupils*. London: Ofsted Reviews of Research, HMSO.

Hornby, G. & Ian Blackwell, I. (2018) Barriers to parental involvement in education: An update. *Educational Review* 70(1): 109–119, DOI: 10.1080/00131911.2018.1388612

Macpherson, W. (1999) *The Stephen Lawrence Inquiry*. London: the Stationery Office, CM 4262-I.

Maylor, U., Smart, S., Kuyok, K.A. & Ross, A. (2009) *Black Childrens' Achievement Programme Evaluation*. London: Department for Children and Schools.

McDermott, P. & Rothenberg, J.J. (2000) Why urban parents resist involvement in their children's elementary education. *The Qualitative Report* 5(3): 1–16. https://doi.org/10.46743/2160-3715/2000.1947

McKown, C. & Weinstein, R.S. (2008) Teacher expectations, classroom context, and the achievement gap. *Journal of School Psychology* 46: 235–261.

Milliard, W., Brown-Viner, K., Baars, S., Tretheway, A. & Menzi, L. (2018) *Boys on Track Improving Support for Black Caribbean and Free School Meal Eligible White Boys in London A research report*. London: Greater London Authority (GLA).

Parekh, B. (2000) *Rethinking multiculturalism: cultural diversity and political theory*, Palgrave Macmillan Publihser.

Rampton, A. (1981a) *West Indian Children in Our Schools*. London: HMSO.

Mongon, D. & Chapman, C. (2008) *Successful Leadership in Promoting the Achievement of White Working-Class Pupils*. National College of School Leadership.

Rampton, A. (1981b) *West Indian Children in Our Schools*. Cmnd 8273. London: HMSO.

Strand, S. (2012) The White British-Black Caribbean achievement gap: tests, tiers, and teacher expectations. *British Educational Research Journal* 38(1): 75–101.

Swann, L. (1985) *Education for All: Final Report of the Committee of Inquiry into the Education of Children from Ethnic Minority Groups*, Cmnd 9453. London: HMSO.

Taylor, B. (2019) *The Evidence on Grouping by Attainment: Supporting More Equitable Practice in Schools*. https://blogs.ucl.ac.uk/grouping-students/2019/03/18/the-evidence-on-grouping-byattainment-supporting-more-equitable-practice-in-schools/

Villegas, A.M. & Irvine, J.J. (2010) Diversifying the teaching force: An examination of major arguments. *Urban Review* 42(3): 175–192.

Barton, A.C., Drake, C., Perez, J.G., St. Louis, K. & George, M. (2004) Ecologies of parental engagement in urban education. *Educational Researcher* 33(4): 3–12. doi: 10.3102/0013189X033004003. S2CID 144012401

Cooper, C.E., Crosnoe, Suizzom, Pituch (2010) Poverty race and parental involvement during the transition to elementary school. *Journal of Family Issues* 31(7): 859–883. doi:10.1177/0192513X09351515. S2CID 145197192

DCSF. (2008) *The Extra Mile: How schools succeed in raising aspiration in deprived communities*. London: Department for Children, Schools and Families. https://bit.ly/3CSBw31

Demie, F. (2003) Raising the achievement of Black Caribbean pupils in british schools: unacknowledged problems and challenges for policy makers. *London Review of Education* 1(3): 229–248.

Demie, F. (2005) Achievement of Black Caribbean pupils: good practice in Lambeth schools. *British Educational Research Journal* 31(4): 481–508.

Demie, F. (2023b) Tackling educational inequality: Lessons from London schools. *Equity in Education & Society*. https://doi.org/10.1177/27526461231161775

Demie, F. & Mclean, C. (2007) Raising the achievement of African heritage pupils: a case study of good practice in British schools. *Educational Studies* 33(4): 415–434.

DfEE (2000) *Removing the barriers: Raising Achievement Levels for Minority Ethnic Pupils*. London: DfEE.

DfES (2006b) *Exclusion of Black Pupils Priority Review: Getting it, getting it right*. London: Department for Education and Skills.

Gershenson, S., Holt, S. & Papageorge, N. (2016) Who believes in me? The effect of student–teacher demographic match on teacher expectations. *Economics of Education Review* 52: 209–224.

Hill, N.E. & Tyson, D.F. (2009) Parental involvement in middle school: a meta-analytic assessment of the strategies that promote achievement. *Developmental Psychology* 45 (3): 740–763. https://doi.org/10.1037/a0015362

Jeynes, W. (2012) A meta-analysis of the efficacy of different types of parental involvement programmes for urban students. *Urban Education* 47(4): 706–742. https://doi.org/10.1177/0042085912445643

Lambert, M.C., Duppong Hurley, K., January, S.-A., & Huscroft D'Angelo, J. (2022) The role of parental involvement in narrowing the academic achievement gap for high school students with elevated emotional and behavioral risks. *Journal of Emotional and Behavioral Disorders* 30(1): 54–66. https://doi.org/10.1177/10634266211020256

Ofsted. (2009) *Twenty outstanding primary schools: Excelling against the odds*. http://dera.ioe.ac.uk/11216/1/Twenty%20outstanding%20primary%20schools.pdf

Race, R. (2024) *Multiculturalism and Education*. London: Open University Press.

PART II

The Experience of Raising the Achievement of Black and Ethnic Minority Students in Schools

4
SUCCESS FACTORS IN IMPROVING LEADERSHIP AND TEACHING TO RAISE ACHIEVEMENT

Introduction

The previous research explored the empirical evidence and the barriers to learning. We would argue here that no book exploring underachievement in school would be complete without examining what previous research has contributed to our knowledge about what works in schools and exploring some of the factors that make schools effective.

This chapter discusses in detail 'what works' in schools in tackling educational inequalities and closing the achievement gap for Black and ethnic minority students. It asks two key questions: What are the reasons for such success in schools? 'What targeted intervention strategies does your school use to raise achievement and close the gap for Black and ethnic minority students?'

Success factors and intervention strategies used in schools

The body of research into how to make schools more effective in raising attainment has offered a valuable background and useful insights for driving school improvement and tackling inequality in schools. Several researchers in the field of school effectiveness and improvement attempted to study schools that were successful in educating students of all backgrounds, regardless of the student's socioeconomic background (see Demie, 2019; Edmonds, 1982; Hopkins et al., 1994; Sammons, Hillman, and Mortimore, 1995; Reynolds et al., 1996; Mortimore, 1999; Rutter et al., 1979; Stoll and Fink, 1994; Muijis et al., 2004; Blair and Bourne, 1998; Demie, 2003;Demie and Lewis, 2013; Stoll and Fink 1996). Others looked at the ethnic and social background of successful schools with a focus on Black Caribbean, Black African, Somali, mixed-race, Bangladeshi, disadvantaged pupils who are free school meals, and the White working-class (Demie, 2019; Mongon and Chapman, 2008; Ofsted, 2009a; 2009b Demie and Lewis, 2010a,b,c; Demie and McLean, 2015a,b, 2016a,b, 2017a,b).

Building on past research, this chapter explores how schools defy the association between poverty and low achievement through targeted interventions that close the gap between the attainment of disadvantaged pupils, ethnic minorities, English as an Additional Language (EAL), and their peers.

To investigate success factors and intervention strategies used by schools, we asked headteachers and senior management teams in schools to complete a survey (see Demie 2024). We wanted to establish whether issues covered in our literature reviews were also raised as key factors by the school staff. The survey asked the respondents how much they felt each of the factors and targeted intervention strategies used contributed to raising the achievement and closing the achievement gap of ethnic minority and disadvantaged pupils in schools, using a 7-point scale that was then grouped into 'strongly disagree, disagree, agree, strongly agree.' We also asked them to elaborate on the main reasons they believed had led to learning barriers and underachievement in response to more open-ended questions.

The survey also asked respondents to list and comment on other success factors and target intervention strategies that contributed to raising achievement and closing the gap. The survey was undertaken in all London schools between December 2023 and March 2024 (Demie 2024). There were several success factors that the survey respondents added and commented on. The survey's main findings indicate which factors the respondents rated as having the greatest impact on raising the achievement of Black, ethnic minority, and disadvantaged pupils. Figure 4.1 shows the factors that respondents rated as contributing to improving Black and ethnic minority attainment in the survey.

The factors that respondents agreed and strongly agreed in the survey as having the most contribution to improving ethnic minority and disadvantaged pupils' achievement were:

Factors that contributed to improvement	*Agree/strongly agree*
• High-quality teaching and learning	96%
• High expectations for all pupils	95%
• Effective leadership team	93%
• Effective headteachers	89%
• Effective use of data	89%
• Support for disadvantaged pupils	88%
• Assessment and progress monitoring	85%
• Parental engagement	85%
• Support for ethnic minority pupils	83%
• Celebrating cultural diversity and inclusion	80%

(*Continued*)

Success Factors in Improving Leadership and Teaching 65

Factors that contributed to improvement	Agree/strongly agree
• Use of trained teaching assistants	79%
• Support for EAL pupils	79%
• Specific targeted interventions programme	79%
• Effective self-evaluation	78%
• Community engagement	76%
• Pupil tracking in schools	73%
• Target setting at school and pupil level	70%
• Diversifying the curriculum	70%
• Effective governing body	63%
• Diversity in the school workforce	59%

Source: Demie, 2024.

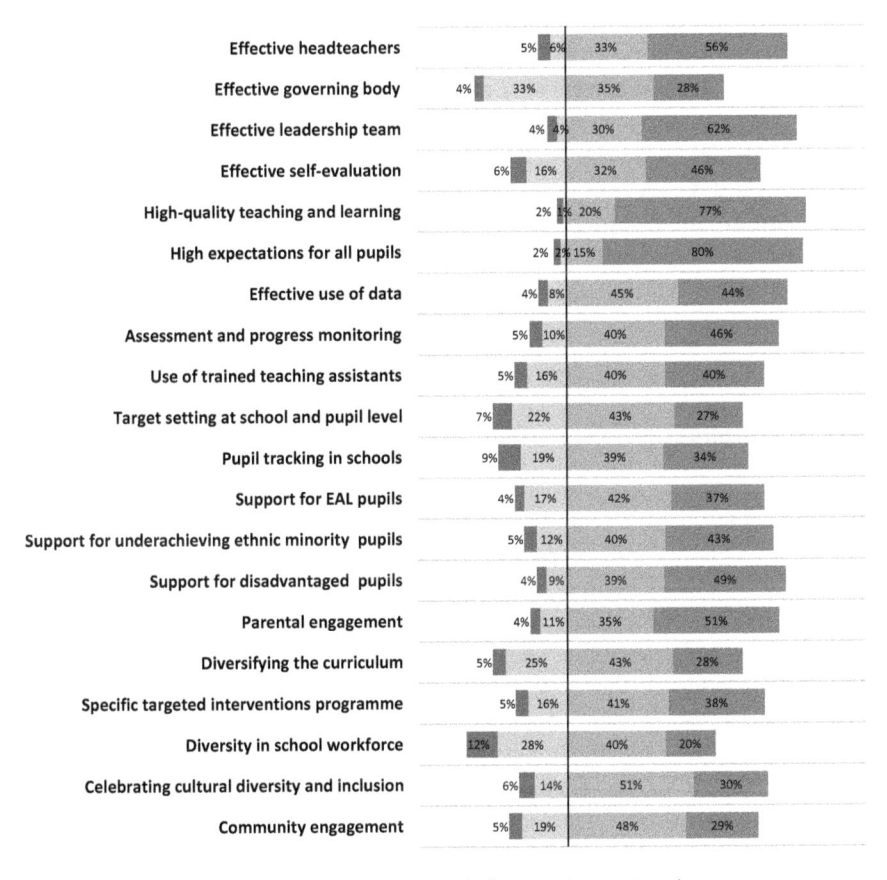

Factor	Disagree	Strongly disagree	Agree	Strongly agree
Effective headteachers	5%	6%	33%	56%
Effective governing body	4%	33%	35%	28%
Effective leadership team	4%	4%	30%	62%
Effective self-evaluation	6%	16%	32%	46%
High-quality teaching and learning	2%	1%	20%	77%
High expectations for all pupils	2%	2%	15%	80%
Effective use of data	4%	8%	45%	44%
Assessment and progress monitoring	5%	10%	40%	46%
Use of trained teaching assistants	5%	16%	40%	40%
Target setting at school and pupil level	7%	22%	43%	27%
Pupil tracking in schools	9%	19%	39%	34%
Support for EAL pupils	4%	17%	42%	37%
Support for underachieving ethnic minority pupils	5%	12%	40%	43%
Support for disadvantaged pupils	4%	9%	39%	49%
Parental engagement	4%	11%	35%	51%
Diversifying the curriculum	5%	25%	43%	28%
Specific targeted interventions programme	5%	16%	41%	38%
Diversity in school workforce	12%	28%	40%	20%
Celebrating cultural diversity and inclusion	6%	14%	51%	30%
Community engagement	5%	19%	48%	29%

FIGURE 4.1 A survey of the factors that contributed to improving ethnic minority and disadvantaged pupils' achievement.

Source: Demie (2024).

These findings are similar to previous surveys by Demie (2023) and several other studies (Demie and Mclean 2017a,b; Demie 2005; DfES 2003; Ofsted 2002a,b; Blair and Bourne 1998).

In addition to the above survey, a case study approach was carried out in 13 selected schools to study the strategies used to raise achievement and narrow the gap. The school was selected based on criteria such as the high achievement of ethnic minority and disadvantaged pupils, a high proportion of pupils eligible for free school meals, and good General Certificate for Secondary Education (GCSE) and KS2 results. To improve our understanding of the issues, we conducted a series of in-depth, semi-structured interviews with headteachers, deputy heads, and classroom teachers, where appropriate. Headteachers in the selected schools were asked to select at random the respondents who have closely worked in the schools on targeted interventions. What is also an advantage of the research is that the researcher has worked for over 20 years with the case study schools, has appropriate contact across a range of settings, and has varying experiences in teaching and leadership.

The survey research and case study interviews identified outstanding school leadership, effective teaching and learning, effective use of data, inclusive curriculum, support for ethnic minorities, EAL, and disadvantaged pupils, and targeted support and intervention as key factors to raise achievement and challenge poverty and inequality in schools. Some of these factors and good practices that emerged from the interviews of headteachers and teachers and the survey and literature review are explored below and in the next chapters.

Providing strong school leadership

The single factor that is critical to success in raising the achievement of disadvantaged and ethnic minority pupils is the excellence of their leadership in promoting equality and diversity in schools. There is a general recognition that the role of leadership is central to improving schools (Day et al., 2009). Harris and Chapman (2001) further stated that leadership in schools is critical and has a powerful influence on the achievement of students and effectiveness. Other research that has been undertaken on school effectiveness and improvement also shows that school leadership is vital to school improvement and has a significant impact on pupils' learning and performance (see Sammons, 1999; Sammons et al., 1995; Edmonds, 1982; Demie, 2019). This is further supported by Harris and Chapman (2002), who confirmed that strong leadership is one of the strongest explanations for the success of schools in high-poverty settings. Day et al. (2009) argued that effective school leaders actively set direction, develop people, and engage in an organisational redesign. Gillborn and Mirza (2000:37) have also highlighted strong leadership on equal opportunities and social justice from the teacher.

Another review carried out by Robinson et al. (2009) also identified eight dimensions of leadership practices and activities linked to student outcomes. Of all the activities identified, headteachers' leading and actively participating in professional learning and development had the largest impact on student outcomes, with an effect size twice that of the next most important contributory factor: planning, coordinating, and evaluating teaching and the curriculum.

Ofsted's (2002a,b) case research report into the good practices of Black Caribbean pupils that focussed on curriculum, the quality of teaching and learning, the way successful schools monitored pupil attainment, and the school's links with parents and comments suggests that:

> These are popular schools with strong leadership and strong systems. They have a culture of achievement. Central to their work are high expectations and the provision of intensive support so that the pupils meet them. A particular strength of the schools is their communication with parents.
>
> *(Ofsted 2002a:29)*

Many of the previous researchers highlighted some of the common characteristics of the leadership of school leaders in successful schools, including:

> Highly ambitious for each child to acquire the particular skills they need to reach their potential and lead successful lives.
>
> Able to remove barriers to pupils' learning and provide a culture of achievement with a positive can-do attitude.
>
> The diversity of pupils' backgrounds and circumstances is celebrated.
>
> They monitor pupils' progress by background, including ethnicity and disadvantaged factors. Leaders also monitor pupils' work, marking, record-keeping, teacher assessment, the quality of teaching and learning, and the progress made by individual pupils.
>
> Pupil tracking is rigorous.
>
> Leaders regard parental engagement as vital to the school's drive to raise achievement. They have developed genuine partnerships to encourage parental support for learning.
>
> *(Demie 2019:39)*

Similarly, many case study school leaders have successfully turned around schools deemed inadequate or requiring 'special measures' and later judged by Ofsted as 'outstanding.' Other case study schools, while always being recognised as 'good' schools, have been continuously improving to become outstanding in all areas. All schools in our study demonstrate 'outstanding' leadership by the headteacher and senior management teams. A committed

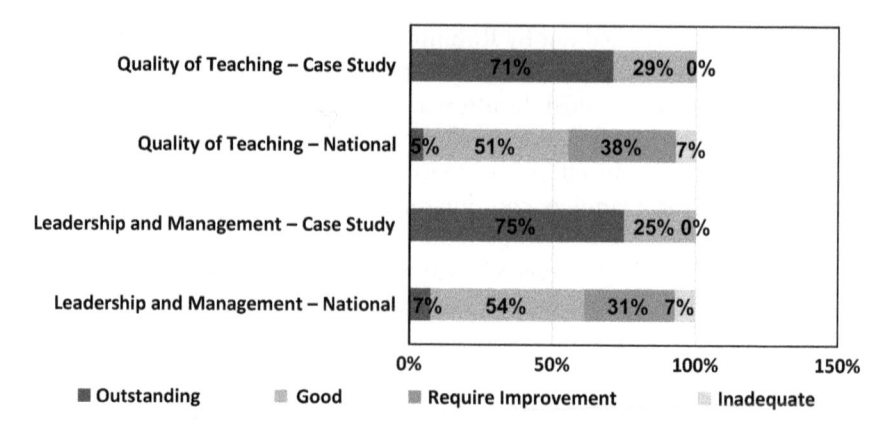

68 Black and Ethnic Minority Achievement in Schools

	Outstanding	Good	Require Improvement	Inadequate
Quality of Teaching – Case Study	71%	29%	0%	
Quality of Teaching – National	5%	51%	38%	7%
Leadership and Management – Case Study	75%	25%	0%	
Leadership and Management – National	7%	54%	31%	7%

FIGURE 4.2 Ofsted judgements about teaching and leadership quality in the schools.

Source: Demie, 2023:36.

team of teachers supports each other. Leaders are described as 'inspirational' and 'visionary' with a strong moral drive for pupils to succeed (Figure 4.2).

This is further confirmed by Ofsted inspection data that graded all school leadership and teaching as 'good and outstanding.' The Ofsted data in Figure 4.3 suggests that the leadership of the case study schools was judged 'good or outstanding' in 89% of schools (79% nationally). Overall, 85% of teaching was judged 'good or outstanding' (72% nationally).

Leaders in each school set high expectations for their staff teams with a relentless focus on improvement, particularly in the quality of teaching and learning, effective use of data, and higher achievement by students.

This is also confirmed by a selection of Ofsted inspection reports on the case study schools, which suggested that leadership in schools is critical and has a powerful influence on the achievement of students.

> Inspirational leaders and managers are determined to ensure pupils receive a "World Class Education." They are highly ambitious for each child to acquire the particular skills they need to reach their potential and lead successful lives.
>
> *(Ofsted, School V)*

> The headteacher and senior leaders and managers provide outstanding leadership. Leaders and managers very well support them at all levels, as do members of the cohesive staff team. There have been quick and long-lasting gains in curriculum, teaching behaviour, attendance, achievement, and other areas thanks to an ambitious vision and accurate assessment.
>
> *(School H, Ofsted)*

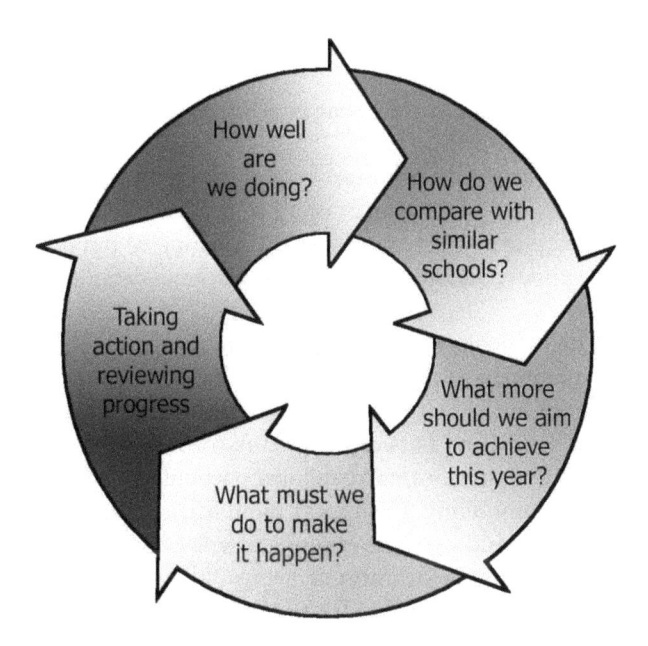

FIGURE 4.3 Five stages of the school improvement cycle.
Source: Demie (2013:6) Using Data to Raise Achievement.

> The headteacher is focused on improvement. This is driven by his passionate belief that all students, irrespective of their circumstances, are entitled to the best possible education.
>
> *(Ofsted, School A)*

> The headteacher has created a very strong team of staff who share her high expectations and aspirations. Together with governors, they have established a vibrant learning community in which all pupils thrive and flourish, academically and personally.
>
> *(Ofsted, School E)*

> Evaluation of the school is rigorous and accurate. They monitor teaching regularly and accurately, and there are many training opportunities for teachers to improve their expertise.
>
> *(Ofsted, School O)*

Similarly, the Institute of Education's (IOE) review of schools' leadership and management by Wood et al. (2013) and Morrison (2013) suggests that successful schools that are effective in driving school improvement and tackling inequality share some common characteristics, including

They have consistent, high expectations and are very ambitious for the success of their pupils.

They constantly demonstrate that disadvantage need not be a barrier to achievement.

They focus relentlessly on improving teaching and learning with very effective professional development of all staff.

They are experts at assessment and the tracking of pupil progress with appropriate support and intervention based upon a detailed knowledge of individual pupils.

They are highly inclusive, having complete regard for the progress and personal development of every pupil.

They develop individual students by promoting rich opportunities for learning both within and outside of the classroom.

They cultivate a range of partnerships, particularly with parents, businesses, and the community, to support pupil learning and progress.

They are robust and rigorous in terms of self-evaluation and data analysis, with clear strategies for improvement.

(Wood et al. 2013: 26; Morrison 2013:1)

The findings of the researchers at the IOE that identified the quality of leadership as one of the key factors driving the transformation are not surprising, as they are in line with many previous studies into school improvement (Demie 2019). Leithwood and Seashore Lewis (2012:3) sum up the case:

> To date, we have not found a single documented case of a school improving its student achievement record in the absence of talented leadership.

Such fundamentals are also highlighted in the case study comments by Ofsted and headteachers about the common threads in leadership and management that have the power to transform schools.

> The headteachers, together with senior leaders and managers, provide outstanding leadership.
>
> *(Ofsted, School B)*

> The leadership and the management are outstanding in all areas. Leaders have used data for school elevation and have accurately analysed all the assessment information. They have also put effective strategies in place to accelerate student progress at every key stage.
>
> *(Ofsted, School J)*

> Leaders monitor teaching regularly, and there are many CPDs for teachers to improve their professional expertise.
>
> *(Ofsted, School A)*

> The headteacher's school self-evaluation is rigorous and accurately reflects the school performance and the standards of teaching.
>
> *(Ofsted, School G)*

> The head teachers are excellent role models and have clear visions for raising standards and effective monitoring of the curriculum at all levels.
>
> *(Ofsted, School E)*

> As school leaders, we have to be flexible, look at our population – know who is in the population – and connect with the community. If the kids don't buy into the agenda, they won't do it. We constantly reflect with the children's voice.
>
> *(headteacher, H)*

> Anybody who says children from around here can't achieve is badly letting down local children and communities. We challenge stereotypes about the area served by the school by asking questions. Why can't children in the area have their dreams?
>
> *(Headteacher, School F)*

Clarity of roles and responsibilities in leadership teams is evident at every level in each school. One deputy head attributes the dramatic improvement in his school over the last decade to the promotion of a dynamic and decentralised approach to leadership which has given staff genuine authority but supported them in developing the best possible way of going forward. School leaders have high expectations for their staff teams with a relentless focus on improvement. This is particularly true in the quality of teaching and learning, effective use of data, and higher achievement by students.

> It is about staff taking responsibility for outcomes... everyone is clear about their roles and everyone is supported!
>
> *(Deputy Principal, School F)*

> We are constantly reviewing ourselves, reflecting on why we are here, our vision, our ethos.
>
> *(Headteacher, School A)*

> We teach them to the highest possible expectation.
>
> *(Headteacher, School R)*

Headteachers use school self-evaluation effectively, which is particularly incisive at the senior management level. It is underpinned by a drive to get the best possible outcomes for each child. Leaders also appeared to be very much focussed on rigorous monitoring and evaluation as a basis for improvement, as can be seen from a review of Ofsted comments about their school:

> In successful schools, headteachers take the views of pupils, parents, and students regularly. They are much valued and are used to inform worthwhile changes in the schools.
> *(Ofsted, School H)*

> There are very strong systems to monitor and evaluate the effectiveness of provision so that leaders and managers are fully aware of strengths and weaknesses and can plan better for improvement.
> *(Ofsted, School B)*

> The monitoring and evaluation of the quality of teaching and learning are systematic and robust. Careful use of data, rigorous monitoring in lessons, and regular tracking ensure that any variance in progress is tackled quickly.
> *(Headteacher, School B)*

> The school has excellent practice about self-evaluation. Every year, there is a thorough review of the whole school, including parental feedback and pupil voice, which feed into the school development plan and school self-evaluation.
> *(Headteacher, School O)*

> Teachers make effective use of data to evaluate the quality of provision and to identify and support differentiated groups of pupils.
> *(Head of School, School C)*

> There are excellent systems for monitoring the work of the pupils, identifying those who need additional help or extra challenge, and then providing them with appropriate additional support.
> *(Deputy Headteacher, School H)*

What is clear from our research is that the schools have very strong leadership. The headteachers and leadership team were committed to creating a school ethos that stresses high achievement, equal opportunities, and values cultural diversity. They want everybody to succeed, whatever the background of the children, to ensure the cultural and linguistic heritage of pupils is not left at the door of the schools but welcomed and valued within the curriculum (see also Ofsted 2009a,b).

High-quality teaching and learning

Good teaching is another key factor in tackling education inequality and raising attainment in successful schools (see Figure 4.3). Several researchers also argued that teachers' quality is the most important factor for pupil attainment and learning (Sammons, 1999; Day et al., 2009; Atherton, 2011; Hattie, 2009). Good teaching is another key factor in tackling education inequality and raising attainment in successful schools. Several researchers also argued that teachers' quality is the most important factor for pupil attainment and learning (Sammons, 1999; Atherton, 2011; Hattie, 2009), more than non-teacher factors such as class size and school organisation.

Sammons (2007) has also drawn attention to the centrality of teaching and learning. She observes (p. 29), 'It has been argued that the quality of teaching and expectations have the most significant role to play in fostering students' learning and progress, and she identifies several characteristics of effective teachers:

- '*They teach the class as a whole*;
- *They present information or skills clearly and animatedly.*
- *They keep the teaching sessions task-orientated.*
- *They are non-evaluative and keep instruction relaxed.*
- *They have high expectations for achievement (give more homework, pace lessons faster, and create alertness).*
- *They relate comfortably to students (reducing behaviour problems).*
- *In addition, effective teachers*:
- *Emphasise academic goals.*
- *Make goals explicit and expect students to be able to master the curriculum.*
- *Organise and sequence the curriculum carefully.*
- *Use clear explanations and illustrate what students are to learn.*
- *Ask direct and specific questions to monitor students' progress and check their understanding.*
- *Provide students with ample opportunities to practice.*
- *Give prompts and feedback to ensure success.*
- *Correct mistakes and allow students to use a skill until it is overlearned and automatic.*
- *Review work regularly and hold students accountable for their work.*'

(Sammons, 2007:29)

The McKinsey report on education systems further supports this. It claims,

> There is no more important empirical determinant of student outcomes than good teaching.
>
> (Barber and Mourshed, 2007:27)

Our research also shows how the quality of teaching and teachers' expectations play a key role in schools. Excellent teaching and learning are provided in schools that actively work to guarantee that all students, regardless of background, have access to the curriculum. There is evidence from Ofsted inspection data of the case study schools that about 85% of the quality of teaching is outstanding compared to 73% nationally (see Figure 4.3). The successful schools in our study have teachers with passion and the belief that they can make a difference for all pupils, whatever their background. They do not use disadvantage as an excuse for underachievement. A review of the sample of Ofsted inspections of the schools involved suggests that schools achieved outstanding grades for teaching and learning. The following Ofsted and Headteacher's comments about the case study summarise some of the statements on the quality of teaching in successful schools:

> High-quality teaching has had a significant impact on the impressive rise in pupils' achievements in school.
> *(Headteacher, School A)*

> Teachers have consistently high expectations of all pupils, whatever their background.
> *(Headteacher, School J)*

Effective use of data

The literature review clearly shows the importance of using data to improve teaching and learning in education. There is now a consensus in the literature that effective use of data is vital to driving school improvement and tackling educational inequality. Recent research in England (Demie, 2013; Kirkup et al., 2005) supports this line of argument, suggesting that the effective use of data can promote better teaching.

There has been a revolution in the use of data in support of school education in the English education system since the early 1990s. There is currently an incredibly rich collection of data on every student in the English school system (Rudd and Davies, 2002). The revolution has been brought about by the increase in available national curriculum assessment data at the pupil level. Add to that the pupil data from the School Census (SC) and School Workforce Census, and we have much more sophisticated information about how different groups of pupils progress at different key stages. Schools also collect an increasing amount of information about their students. They use optional CAT tests, individual pupil targets, and results from their assessment and monitoring.

The government attaches great importance to the use of data to raise standards. High-quality data is key to monitoring performance in OFSTED inspections of schools and allows schools and governors to ask important benchmarking questions as a means of identifying areas for improvement. Senior management and governors use data to ask questions such as:

- What does the data tell us about underperforming groups of pupils?
- What does the pupil progress data tell us about pupil value added?
- What are the overall strong points and areas for improvement?
- What can be done to improve?

The continued effective use of school data can promote the effective use of teaching and learning in schools by:

- Identifying pupils' attainment and informing target-setting
- Supporting the allocation of staffing and resources
- Supporting school self-evaluation
- Tracking pupils' performance and progress
- Identifying underachieving groups
- Narrowing the achievement gaps
- Celebrating good news

Additionally, it will strengthen a school's ability to advance and pose important queries like:

- How well are we doing?
- How do we compare with similar schools? How well should we be doing?
- What more can we aim to achieve?
- What must we do to improve?

Figure 4.3 provides the DfE five-stage cycle for school improvement using data. This chart sets pupil achievement and use of data at the heart of school improvement. The DfE recognises that school self-evaluation is informed by effective monitoring and pupil tracking across subjects, year groups, and key stages. It is argued that schools should also use contextual factors such as gender, ethnicity, free school meals, and types of special educational needs to track the progress and performance of individual cohorts of pupils. In addition, the schools need to use comparative performance data.

Many researchers highlighted that at the core of every good school policy, improvement is the effective use of data in self-evaluation and planning for improved outcomes for pupils and for setting high expectations. They argued data is used to identify underachievement and intervention, to make informed decisions on resource allocation, and to monitor benchmark performance (Rudd and Davies, 2002; Demie, 2004; Ofsted, 2010).

Schools in England operate in a data-rich environment where students are assessed using key stage assessments, Cognitive Abilities Tests (CATs), and GCSE public examinations at ages 7, 11, 12, 13, 14, and 15. These assessments generate data for the schools. Spreadsheets and school management software are used by schools to maintain meticulous records of each student.

The school data now allows foundation stage profiles and tests on entry, FSP, KS1, KS2, KS3, and GCSE by any combination of ethnic origin, gender, free school meal status, mobility rate, EAL stage, SEN stage, years in the school, term of birth, which teachers classes had been attended, previous school, number of schools attended, date of admission, and pupils addresses and postcodes. Schools produce their own internal teacher assessment that is widely used by senior managers, assessment coordinators, heads of year, heads of department, and classroom teachers.

One of the core elements of the case study schools' success in raising achievement is a robust focus on tracking and monitoring individual student's progress and achievement in the widest sense of the term. The case study schools have a wealth of data, ranging from KS2 and optional assessments and tests to GCSE examination data, to pinpoint areas that need improvement. Schools have good systems for assessing and mapping the progress of all pupils, including ethnic and bilingual pupils, at individual and group levels.

Every school follows best practices when it comes to using data. Evidence from the case study and school survey attests to the following:

- Key stage data is collected as early as feasible and thoroughly examined based on gender, ethnicity, and mobility; additional assessments, such as those in verbal reasoning, mathematics, and English, are included.
- The school extensively uses KS2 to GCSE value-added data to improve the attainment of individual pupils in addition to monitoring the standards of year groups or the whole school.
- Teachers make effective use of data to identify and provide support for differentiated groups of pupils.

(Demie, 2013,2019,2023; Demie and Mclean 2016a,b)

The most common types of interventions employed in the schools, where data analysis had highlighted issues to be addressed, were providing additional support, including one-to-one support or booster groups, and making changes to the teaching programme or curriculum, such as more personalised or differentiated teaching to meet the needs of EAL pupils, SEN pupils, or pupils in targeted initiatives to improve performance. The school also makes good use of data to evaluate student environments and teaching groups, which has raised achievement (Demie and Mclean (2016b).

The following comments summarise the views of headteachers and teachers on the use of data from the survey and case study evidence:

> The monitoring and evaluation of the quality of teaching and learning are systematic and robust. Careful use of data, rigorous monitoring in lessons, and regular tracking ensure that any variance in progress is tackled quickly.
> *(Headteacher, School J)*

The school has excellent practice about self-evaluation. Every year, there is a thorough review of the whole school, including parental feedback and pupil voice, which feed into the school development plan and school self-evaluation.

(Headteacher, School D)

Teachers make effective use of data to evaluate the quality of provision and to identify and support differentiated groups of pupils.

(head of school, School D)

There are excellent systems for monitoring the work of the pupils, identifying those who need additional help or extra challenge, and then providing them with appropriate additional support.

(Deputy Headteacher, School Y)

The school is good at assessing all pupils, and teachers look at data carefully.

(Deputy Headteacher, School O)

We use data incredibly well for personalised learning, and we have a well-developed tracking system with detailed assessment data and background information, including ethnic background, languages, EAL, SEN stage, data of admission, mobility rate, years in school, attendance data, type of support, and postcode data that is used for tracking pupil progress.

(Deputy Headteacher, School F)

Teachers use the data to review pupil performance, to have reflections and good conversations, and to produce class profiles. This has been useful for the assessment of learning and tracking individual pupils' performance. You cannot do without data.

(Assistant Headteacher, School F)

Teachers interviewed also acknowledged the effectiveness of the data and commented that:

Use of data raised the expectations of staff and pupils and helped us focus on what children were learning.

(Teacher, School O)

The data provided by the school helps you target groups of children for specific types of help.

(Teacher, School C)

The school is very successful in identifying and tackling barriers to learning and providing well-targeted guidance and support.
(Teacher, School R)

To conclude, one common feature of strategies for raising achievement in all schools is the intelligent use of assessment data, progress tracking, target setting, and support for students slipping behind with targeted interventions. The use of data involves all staff and governors. Headteachers, senior administrators, teachers, and teaching assistants use data efficiently to track students' development and create goals by asking and answering questions about existing standards, trends over time, and individual student achievement.

Conclusions

This chapter looked at the school's key factors in raising the achievement of Black and ethnic minorities. In particular, it explored in detail the success factors behind outstanding achievement in successful schools to close the achievement gap. The conclusion from this study is that successful schools outperform schools in the rest of England in both examination results and Ofsted inspection grades. The lessons from the successful schools' case study and the school survey also suggest that it is possible to tackle the link between poverty and underachievement. The findings also suggest that disadvantaged and ethnic backgrounds need not always be barriers to achievement. There is evidence that schools were using various highly effective strategies for raising the achievement of disadvantaged and Black and ethnic minority pupils. Pupils of all ethnic backgrounds and with all kinds of learning needs are treated as potential achievers. Teachers have high expectations of all pupils, which is reflected in the curriculum and teaching styles. Key success factors and effective strategies include:

- Providing strong leadership
- High-quality teaching
- Effective use of data
- Effective use of a diverse, multi-ethnic workforce

The research confirms beyond doubt key success in raising achievement and tackling inequality due to the outstanding leadership of the headteachers and the senior management teams (see also Ofsted 2002a,b, 2009a,b). Leaders are described as 'inspirational' and 'visionary.' Schools have a culture of high expectations, strong collaboration with colleagues, and close links with families and the community. There is an exceptional sense of teamwork across each school, which is reflected in the consistent and committed way managers at all levels work towards the schools' aims of raising achievement.

The high achievement is also due to outstanding teaching (Demie 2019; Ofsted 2002a,b and 2009a,b; EEF, 2019). The staff holds high expectations for what pupils can achieve. They deliver stimulating and enthusiastic teaching that interests, excites, and motivates pupils and accelerates their learning, as well as well-planned lessons that meet the differing needs of pupils. Teaching assistants are well-trained and highly skilled. Effective marking and assessment ensure that all pupils' learning is closely checked. Rigorous and consistent characterise the schools. The inexperienced teachers are paired with outstanding teachers or work with parallel-year groups of colleagues across a federation to plan optimally effective lessons. Collaborative planning, supervising, and marking pupils' work offers support and challenge to the teachers too. Pupils are motivated in lessons because tasks and explanations are matched to their needs. Teachers capture the pupils' enthusiasm and make them want to succeed by showing how much they enjoy teaching them.

Effective use of data is also the strength of the schools. Evidence indicates the excellent ways in which teachers and school leaders were amassing and applying forensic data to drive school improvement and identify underachieving groups. Many schools in the survey and study kept careful records by ethnic background and found systematic and detailed ethnic monitoring using data as an effective method of raising achievement levels. Through ethnic monitoring, it is possible to observe the performance of different groups and to consider possible explanations and strategies for action. All use detailed, relevant, and constantly updated assessment procedures and feed the findings back to the staff. Every school monitored each pupil's progress all through their school life and connected the test and assessment data with the data on the child's ethnic background, language spoken, level of fluency in English, date of admission, attendance rate, eligibility for free school meals, EAL stage of fluency, SEN stage, mobility rate, years in school, which teacher's classes they attended, attendance rate, and types of support. This data was used to set challenging targets. Early intervention and a wide range of support mechanisms – booster groups, one-to-one, tailoring teaching levels, and mentoring – helped the pupils achieve. Systems for monitoring the work of the pupils identify those who need additional help or extra challenge and give them appropriately. This also helped the school to question why ethnic groups achieved well in some subjects while others underachieved.

In addition to the success factors discussed above, the school also uses other strategies such as effective targeted intervention, inclusive curriculum, parental engagement, and support for pupils with EAL as a means of driving school improvement and closing the achievement gap (Demie, 2019). Significantly, these schools are all effective at targeting intervention and support.

All use outstanding teachers to teach English and math and provide tailored support for individuals in the classroom, one-to-one support, and booster classes delivered by the class teacher. Small groups are put in the hands of expert teachers who can focus on overcoming the gaps in their learning. Enrichment activities and funded school trips enhance the children's experiences and support their learning. Parental involvement and the use of well-trained TA to support Black and Minority Ethnic (BAME) are also other common strategies identified in the study. The funding available from pupil premium money is targeted at disadvantaged pupils, EALs, and underachieving Black and ethnic minority pupils, and this has made a dramatically large contribution to closing the achievement gap. This good practice will be discussed in detail in the next chapters.

References

Atherton, J. S. (2011) *Teaching and Learning; What works best*. https://www.learningandteaching.info/teaching/what_works.htm

Barber, M. & Mourshed, M. (2007) *How the World's Best Performing School Systems Came Out on Top*. London: McKinsey and Company.

Blair, M. & Bourne, J. (1998) *Making the Difference: Teaching And Learning Strategies in Successful Multi-Ethnic Schools*. London: Department for Education and Employment Publication Research Report RR59.

Day, C., Sammons, P., Hopkins, D., Harris, A., Leithwood, K., Gu, Q., Brown, E., et al. (2009) *The Impact of School Leadership on Pupil Outcomes*. London: DCSF.

Demie, F. (2003) Using value-added data for school self-evaluation: A Case Study of Practice in Inner City Schools. *School Leadership and Management* 23(4): 445–467.

Demie, F. (2004) Examples of good and innovative practice in the effective use of data in Lambeth schools. In Bird and Fowler (eds.) *School Improvement: Making Data Work*. DfES and TEN publications, p. 22–28 & p. 60–62.

Demie, F. (2005) Achievement of Black Caribbean pupils: Good practice in Lambeth schools. *British Educational Research Journal* 31(4): 481–508.

Demie, F. (2013) *Using Data to Raise Achievement*. London: Lambeth Research and Statistics Unit.

Demie, F. (2019) *Educational Inequality: Closing the gap*. London: UCL IOE press. July. https://www.uci-ioe-press.com/books/social

Demie, F. (2023) Tackling educational inequality: Lessons from London schools. *Equity in Education & Society*. https://doi.org/10.1177/27526461231161775

Demie, F. (2024) *A Survey of Barriers to Learning, Success Factors, And Intervention Strategy in London Schools to Raise Achievement and Tackle Educational Inequality*. London: Lambeth Schools Research and Statistics Unit, April draft.

Demie, F. & Lewis, K. (2010a) *Outstanding Secondary Schools: Good Practice*. London: Lambeth Research and Statistics Unit.

Demie, F. & Lewis, K. (2010b) Raising the Achievement of Portuguese pupils in British Schools: a case study of Good Practice. *Educational Studies* 36(1): 95–109.

Demie, F. & Lewis, K. (2010c) *White Working Class Achievement: An Ethnographic Study of Barriers to Learning in Schools*. https://doi.org/10.1080/03055698.2010.506341

Demie, F. & Lewis, K. (2013) *Outstanding Secondary Schools: A Study of Successful Practice*. https://www.lambeth.gov.uk/sites/default/files/2021-06/Outstanding_Secondary_Schools_Executive_Summary_2010.pdf

Demie, F. & Mclean, C. (2015a) *Outstanding Primary Schools: Good Practice*. London: Lambeth Research and Statistics Unit.

Demie, F. and Mclean, C. (2015b) *Narrowing the Achievement Gap: Good Practice in Schools*. London: Lambeth Research and Statistics Unit

Demie, F. & Mclean, C. (2016a) Tackling disadvantage: what works in narrowing the achievement gap in schools. *Review of Education* 3(2): 138–174. https://doi.org/10.1002/rev3.30

Demie, F. & Mclean, C. (2016b) *What Works in School Improvement: Examples of Good Practice*. Lambeth LA: Lambeth Research and Statistics Unit.

Demie, F. & Mclean, C. (2017a) *Black Caribbean Underachievement in Schools in England*. Lambeth LA: Lambeth Research and Statistics Unit.

Demie, F. & Mclean, C. (2017b) *The Achievement of Black Caribbean Pupils: Good Practice*. London: Lambeth Research and Statistics Unit.

DfES. (2003) *Aiming High: Raising the Achievement of Minority Ethnic Pupils*. London: DfES Consultation.

Edmonds, R. (1982) Programmes of school improvement: An overview. *Educational Leadership* 40(3): 8–11.

EEF. (2019) *Teaching and Learning Tool Kit*. London: Education Endowment Foundation. https://educationendowmentfoundation.org.uk/evidencesummaries/teaching-learning-toolkit/

Gillborn, D. & Mirza, H.S. (2000) *Educational Inequality: Mapping Race, Class and Gender*. London: Ofsted.

Harris, A. & Chapman, C. (2001) *Leadership in school facing challenging circumstances*, Department for Education and Skills, London.

Harris, A. & Chapman, C. (2002) Democratic leadership for school improvement in challenging contexts. *International Electronic Journal for Leadership in Learning* 6 (9).

Hattie, J. (2009) *Visible Learning; A Synthesis of Over 800 Meta-analyses Relating to Achievement*. London: Routledge.

Hopkins, D., Ainscow, M. & West, M. (1994) *School Improvement in an Era of Change*. London: Cassell.

Kirkup, C., Sizmur, J., Sturman, L. & Lewis, K. (2005) *Schools' Use of Data in Teaching and Learning*. DfES Research Report 671. London: DFES.

Leithwood, K. and Seashore Lewis, K. (2012) *Linking Leadership to Student Learning*. New York, NY: Wallace Foundation.

Mongon, D. & Chapman, C. (2008) *Successful Leadership for Promoting the Achievement of White Working Class Pupils*. National College for School Leadership (NCSL).

Morrison, N. (2013) *The Eight Characteristics of Effective School Leaders*. https://www.forbes.com/sites/nickmorrison/2013/12/30/the-eight-characteristics-of-effective-school-leaders/

Mortimore, P. (1999) *The Road to Improvement: Reflections on School Effectiveness*. London: Taylor & Francis.

Muijis, D., Harris, A., Chapman, C., Stoll, L. & Russ, J. (2004) Improving Schools in Socioeconomically Disadvantage Areas- A review of research evidence. *School Effectiveness and School Improvement* 15(2): 149–175.

Ofsted. (2002a) *Achievement of Black Caribbean Pupils: Good Practice in Secondary Schools*. London: Ofsted Publications HMI 448, April.

Ofsted. (2002b) *Achievement of Black Caribbean Pupils: Three Successful Primary Schools*. London: Ofsted Publications HMI 447, April.

Ofsted. (2009a) *Twelve Outstanding Secondary Schools: Excelling Against The Odds*. London: Ofsted. http://www.lampton.org.uk/wpcontent/uploads/2012/03/Twelve_outstanding_secondary_schools1.pdf

Ofsted. (2009b) *Twenty Outstanding Primary Schools: Excelling Against The Odds*. London: Ofsted. http://dera.ioe.ac.uk/11216/1/Twenty%20outstanding%20primary%20schools.pdf

Ofsted. (2010) *London Challenge*. https://webarchive.nationalarchives.gov.uk/ukgwa/20141107033128/http://www.ofsted.gov.uk/resources/london-challenge

Reynolds, D., Sammons, P. et al. (1996) School effectiveness and school improvement in the UK. *School Effectiveness and School Improvement* 7(2): 133–158.

Robinson, V., Hohepa, M. & Llyod. (2009) *School Leadership and Student Outcomes: Identifying What Works and Why: Summary of The Best Evidence Synthesis*. The University of Auckland.

Rudd, P. & Davies, D. (2002) *A Revolution in The Use of Data: The LEA Role in Data Collection, Analysis and Use and Its Impact on Pupil Performance*. LGA Research Report 29, NFER.

Rutter, M., Maughan, B., Mortimore, P. & Ouston, J. (1979) *Fifteen Thousand Hours: Secondary Schools and Their Effect on Children*. London: Open Books.

Sammons, P. (1999) *School Effectiveness: Coming of Age in the 21st Century*. Abingdon: Swets and Zeitlinge.

Sammons, P. (2007) *School Effectiveness and Equity: Making Connections- A Review School Effectiveness and Improvement Research-Its Implications for Practitioners and Policymakers*. Reding: CFBT Education Trust.

Sammons, P., Hillman, J. & Mortimore, P. (1995) *Key Characteristics of Effective Schools: A Review School Effectiveness Research*. London: Ofsted.

Stoll, L. & Fink, D. (1994) Views from the field: linking school effectiveness and school improvement. *School Effectiveness and School Improvement*, 5 (2): 149–177.

Stoll, L. & Fink, D. (1996) *Changing Our Schools*. Open University Press.

Wood, C., Husband, C. & Brown, C. (2013) *Transforming Education for All: The Tower Hamlet Story*. https://www.researchgate.net/publication/320242317_Transforming_Education_for_All_the_Tower_Hamlets_Story

5
TARGETED INTERVENTION STRATEGY TO RAISE ACHIEVEMENT

Introduction

Another approach that is successfully used to tackle inequality and close the achievement gap is targeted intervention and support. In the previous chapter, we identified key success factors used in schools to raise the achievement of ethnic minority and disadvantaged pupils, including providing strong leadership, high-quality teaching and learning, effective use of data, and parental engagement. In this chapter, drawing lessons learned from recent school survey findings and the London Challenge and Education Endowment Fund (EEF) research, we explore the targeted interventions and strategies used in schools to support ethnic minorities and disadvantaged children. The chapter hopes to answer two research questions: What are the targeted intervention strategies to close the achievement gap? What are the implications for policy and practice?

Intervention strategies are employed for a targeted teaching programme in schools. Research shows that carefully targeted interventions and support have significantly impacted closing the gap between the achievement of ethnic minority and disadvantaged pupils and their peers (Demie 2019b, 2023; EEF 2019). It is unarguable from the research evidence available in this area that poverty is the biggest single indicator of low educational achievement (Demie 2020), which is faced by policymakers, teachers, and school leaders. However, previous school effectiveness and improvement research has shown that schools can make a difference through the use of targeted interventions and support, including one-to-one support, booster classes, small group tuition, personal tutoring, booster classes, pastoral care, enrichment programmes (e.g., trips), effective support for English as an additional language

DOI: 10.4324/9781003499633-7

pupils to improve English proficiency, and parental support (see Demie 2019a, 2020; Demie and Mclean 2016; Baars et al. 2014; Mongon and Chapman 2008; Ofsted 2009; Sammons et al. 1995). There is no doubt such intervention strategies enabled ethnic minorities and disadvantaged pupils to make faster progress to catch up with their peers and close the gap in successful schools (Baars et al., 2014; Demie, 2019a, 2023; 2024).

The school survey evidence on effective intervention strategies in schools

A recent survey by Demie (2024) of headteachers in London schools, which investigated the barriers and good practices in raising achievement, also investigated the targeted interventions used by schools to raise achievement and tackle inequality among disadvantaged and ethnic minority pupils. The findings of the survey suggest that schools use many targeted interventions. Figure 5.1 looks at the strategies used by the headteachers responding to the survey.

The survey's main findings show many targeted interventions to raise achievement and tackle educational inequality in their schools. A significant number of respondents agree and strongly agree on using effective teaching and learning strategies (99%), literacy and reading (98%), addressing attendance (95%), feedback between teachers and pupils (94%), metacognition and self-regulation (92%), raising aspiration (91%), early interventions (89%), oral language interventions (87%), parental involvement (84%), use of data (82%), and small group tuition (80%). In addition, 24% to 77% of respondents reported using mastery learning (77%), teaching assistant (TA) support (77%), English as an Additional Language (EAL) support (77%), small class sizes (77%), one-to-one tuition (65%), offering higher salaries to attract teachers (65%), investing in digital technology (60%), and peer tutoring (53%) and homework (24%) (see Demie, 2024).

The survey respondents were also asked to comment on any other strategies and interventions used in schools. Many targeted interventions and support were mentioned by respondents to the survey and the headteacher we interviewed. For example, one headteacher reported the use of a range of targeted interventions to raise achievement and close the gap, including small group additional teaching, one-to-one tuition, the use of the strongest teachers to teach English and math intervention classes, the use of well-trained TAs, parental involvement, booster classes, and enrichment programme, for example, trips to cultural venues. The small group tutoring involved five pupils each, based on their learning gaps. This headteacher argued in addition to strategies and interventions used in schools. Many targeted interventions and support were mentioned by respondents to the survey and the headteacher we interviewed. This headteacher argued in addition

Targeted Intervention Strategy to Raise Achievement 85

Strategy	Disagree	Strongly disagree	Agree	Strongly agree
One-to-one tuition	7%	28%	37%	28%
Feedback between teachers and pupils	1%	5%	40%	54%
Meta-cognition and self-regulation	1%	6%	51%	42%
Homework	31%	45%	21%	4%
Small group tuition	1%	18%	52%	28%
Mastery learning	4%	19%	52%	25%
Oral language intervention	1%	12%	44%	43%
Literacy and reading	1%	1%	31%	67%
Peer tutoring	13%	34%	49%	4%
Parental involvement	1%	15%	51%	33%
Effective teaching and learning		1%	20%	79%
Use of data to identify underachieving groups	5%	13%	46%	37%
Use of well-trained teaching assistants	7%	16%	39%	38%
Early interventions scheme	3%	9%	42%	47%
Smaller class sizes	12%	17%	40%	31%
Investing in digital technology	12%	28%	47%	13%
Offering higher salaries to attract higher-quality teachers	10%	25%	30%	34%
Addressing attendance	1%	4%	31%	64%
Raising aspiration	3%	5%	34%	58%
EAL support	4%	20%	44%	32%

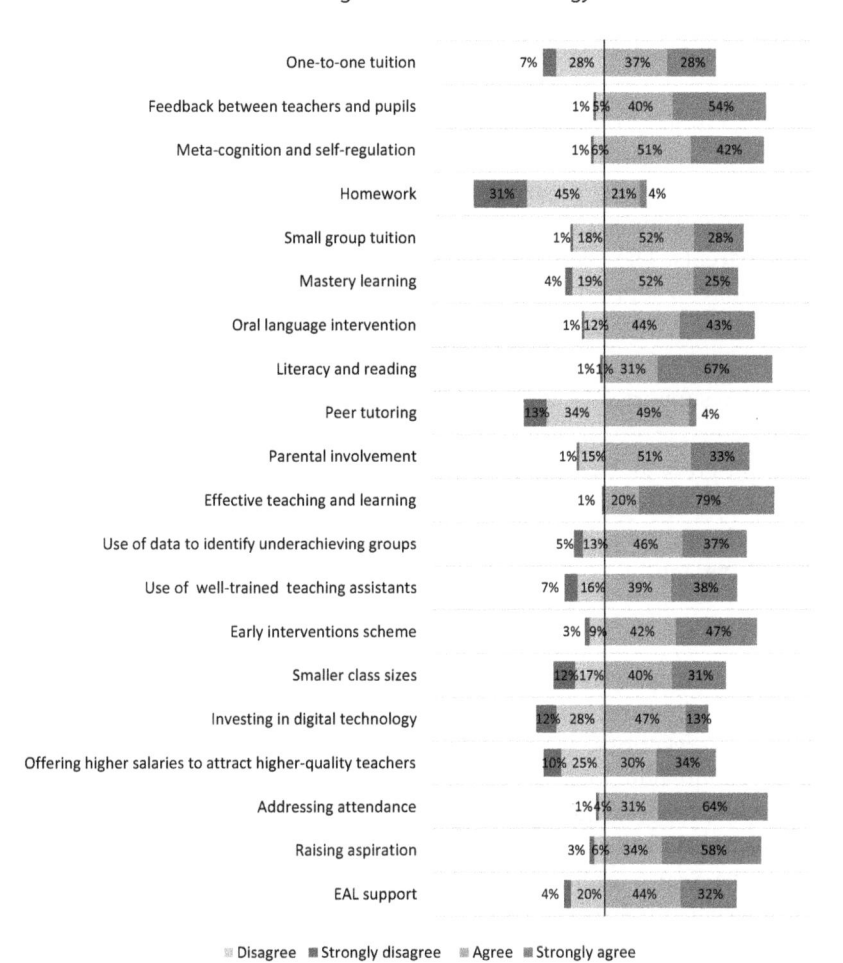

FIGURE 5.1 A survey of the targeted intervention strategies used by schools to raise attainment.

Source: Demie (2024).

> I took my strongest teachers out of class in each phase team, Year 1 and 2, Year 3 and 4, and Year 5 and 6, and each picking up intervention groups. Headteacher, 'School Y'
>
> *(Demie 2023)*

He further confirmed that:

> Use of best teachers has helped SEN, Black Caribbean, and other disadvantaged pupils in the intervention groups who were level 3 or below to achieve the expected standard and higher level at the end of KS2.
>
> *(Headteacher, School Y; Demie and Mclean 2016, 2023)*

Another headteacher highlighted

> We offer a range of interventions and support to vulnerable children: support with the transfer of KS2 to KS3, a pupil mentor, helping with forming friendships, helping to ensure entitlement to free school meals, encouraging participation in extracurricular activities, and regular communications with parents. The school has a strong support system in place and goes the extra mile to support children and ensure their needs are met.
>
> *(Headteacher, School D)*

This is also supported by another headteacher, who commented that

> The progress and attainment of our disadvantaged pupils have always been key priorities. One-to-one tutoring, additional tutoring before and after school, and mentoring of pupils by a senior staff member have all had a positive impact.
>
> *(Headteacher, School O)*

Numerous examples were also given of intervention strategies used by school headteachers and teachers in the case study 'School V,' for example, 'early morning interventions, in class in a small group with a TA or 1:1 support tailored to individual needs, Assessments at the end of Year 5 cover Year 6 SAT papers, tailored questions, and gap analysis to identify pupils needing further booster classes after school and a summer school led by an Assistant Head and a Year 6 teacher for Year 5 pupils.'

In a recent 2024 survey, there were also many additional comments on several factors reported by respondents. Teachers and headteachers also mentioned again the targeted intervention and support they used in their schools:

> High-quality teaching that has been highly trained and built relationships with the community for several years.
>
> *(Headteacher, SP36)*

> Team approach support: We have a culture in the school that focusses on every child achieving and the leadership team giving support so that teachers can analyse the reasons for underperformance, and then a team approach supports the development needed, e.g., interventions, tuition, curriculum change. For the most complex children, e.g., those with behaviour needs because of trauma or attachment disorder, social care support and a team around the family make a huge difference.
>
> *(Headteacher, SP36)*

Targeted Intervention Strategy to Raise Achievement **87**

We use early reading support – daily supported reading – devised from reading recovery, which is very successful at our school in getting year 1 children to read with confidence and fluency.

(Headteacher, SP11)

Storytelling approach to writing – so children understand the structure of stories – lots of talking, drama, etc. Headteacher, SP11)

We are running a new project to identify the lowest 20% of children at the end of reception class. Senior leaders have met with parents to discuss any barriers to learning at home and school. We have identified key adults to monitor and check in with these children regularly. The Head of School is researching how this could be used in Year 2, and all teachers have a research project regarding teaching and learning.

(Headteacher, SP18)

Supporting children with complex SEN – e.g., ASC or ADHD – in an environment that does not create overstimulation and anxiety is ideal.

(Headteacher, SP36)

Positives have been focussing on attendance, engagement at school, and effective use of local authority support, parent training, and social services.

(Assistant Headteacher, SP37)

Most schools know exactly what to do to help disadvantaged pupils catch up or attain the same as their peers. Targeted interventions, additional EAL support, securing and training high-quality staff (teachers and support staff), etc.

(Headteacher, SP44)

As part of our school-targeted intervention strategy and support, we run 'parent workshops,' 'parenting classes,' and 'EAL support' in our school.

(Headteacher, SP68)

The tuition is hard; during the school day, they miss other vital curriculum areas, and after school, they can be too tired.

(Headteacher, SP56)

Setting targets: Strategies to raise attainment have to start with setting appropriate targets that do not bake in the previous underachievement and maintain the disadvantaged gap. Also, school leaders and teachers should note that closing the gap would require additional support for disadvantaged students in terms of resources as well as additional teacher interactions over and above that provided for other non-disadvantaged students.

(Headteacher, SP44)

Option classes in KS4 just for EAL students and not mixing EAL students with SEND students has helped greatly. EAL coordinator raises awareness of EAL students' needs regularly and works closely with teachers.

(EAL coordinator and teacher, SP72)

Effective training: We have invested in metacognition training for schools over the last six years to help schools close disadvantage gaps. The training is always invigorating, but I am not convinced there is a deep understanding of what this looks like in the classroom. It's my opinion that metacognition, along with AfL, should seep deeply into all teacher training, CPD, and practice.

(Headteacher, SP83)

Training school staff to value teamwork, including good communication, accepting feedback from colleagues, and not making assumptions about other ethnicities...

(Headteacher, SP32)

Targeting disadvantaged children made a difference. Our disadvantaged gap has closed from –0.85 to –0.12 over the past 4 years. At first, it was identifying those Pupi Premium students most at risk of underachieving and tracking progress and intervention as well as regular mentoring.

(Assistant Headteacher, SP39)

There was also evidence that almost all schools use pupil premium money for targeted intervention and support, as can be seen from the comments below:

We use a pupil premium grant to support a pupil literacy programme, a reduction in class size, extracurricular activities, a numeracy programme, small group tuition, and behaviour interventions.

(Headteacher, School V)

We use PP money for CPD.

(Headteacher, School A)

The PP money is used to pay for additional teachers and teaching assistants to deliver one-to-one and small group support with a focus on English and mathematics.

(Headteacher, School V)

The evidence from the school survey and case study interview outlined above also suggests that the continuing assessment in detail of pupils' progress is also an important factor in schools' success, as mentioned by headteachers and teachers. The schools draw on a wide range of data to track the progress of individual pupils and groups. Half-termly pupil progress meetings are held, usually involving a senior leader, SENDCo, and class teacher, to discuss the progress of each pupil and the next steps required. Both teachers and pupils know their targets, can measure pupils' learning and attainment regularly and objectively, and can review the effectiveness of any intervention. Assessment for learning, reflective marking, and feedback are among the practices that help accelerate children's progress. The schools use assessment and feedback very productively to plan and adapt the curriculum and promote individual learning. It helps pupils aim towards what they need to do to improve.

Every opportunity is taken to fit in an extra bit of support for those pupils who need to deepen their understanding; for example, during assemblies, TAs take pupils for particular interventions, or a class teacher or assistant head will take a group to give them very in-depth pre-teaching prior to the lesson. Teaching assistants are very well-trained and equipped to teach phonics and early math. Learning mentors work with children and parents (e.g., when children enter the school as a result of 'managed moves' or those new to the area) to settle them into school. They support pupils with a range of challenges, such as those who are LAC, bereaved, and those needing EAL or SEND support.

Pastoral care is provided through a lot of emotional or practical support, such as by arranging visits to universities and colleges to build pupils' aspirations or by discreetly providing for pupils' physical needs for food and clothing. The schools are inclusive of students with different strengths and offer unstinting support to their families. Schools demonstrate great empathy with the challenges pupils face, such as coming from families facing eviction or visa concerns, poverty, and mental health and social care issues.

There is a willingness among the teaching staff to go the extra mile to support groups of students to achieve their very best, and staff give generously of their time. Many booster classes for mathsa and English run during the spring half-term break, Easter holidays, and May half-term.

Teachers volunteer to run them.

The schools do more than monitor pupils' academic progress. Staff throughout these schools have a sense of mission and are committed to pupils' welfare and personal development through strong pastoral systems to promote this. They allow pupils to achieve in a wide range of activities. There is an extensive range of enrichment activities on offer to build social and cultural capital, especially for pupils who wouldn't otherwise have these opportunities.

The London Challenge evidence on effective intervention strategies in schools

England has had several major successful school-targeted initiatives in recent years, such as the national strategies, the London Challenge, the Raising the Achievement of Ethnic Minorities Children, and pupil premium projects. The main aims of these projects were to raise standards in the poorest performing schools, to narrow the attainment gap, and to create better and outstanding schools (Kidson and Norris, 2015; DfE, 2013). It also adopted 'beyond the school gate' initiatives to tackle the achievement of ethnic minorities and disadvantages in the communities (Baars et al. 2014; Demie 2019a, 2023, 2024). The London Challenge was on the front line in the attempt to break the link between deprivation and underperformance and underachievement of ethnic minority pupils through targeted interventions. In all of these projects, underachieving ethnic minority groups and disadvantaged pupils were supported with a range of targeted interventions, including using successful headteachers to lead the strategy of raising the achievement of ethnic minority pupils, small group tuition, personal tutoring, booster classes, pastoral care, and enrichment programmes, for example, trips (Baars et al. 2014; Demie 2019a, 2023, 2024).

The London Challenge initiatives also invested heavily in school leadership to support leaders of struggling schools and worked with key boroughs to ensure robust local planning and support for school improvement (Hutchings et al. 2012). The London Challenge was responsible for a number of initiatives and support to London schools as can be seen from Figure 5.2.

Data support formed a core part of the innovation and was used to determine where support was required and to monitor whether interventions were successful. As a result of the initiatives, London schools improved rapidly between 2003 and 2013, with primary and secondary schools now outperforming the rest of the country. During the period, local authorities in inner London also went from the worst performing to some of the best performing nationally. All the evaluations confirm that it made a huge improvement in London schools (Hutchings et al. 2012).

The positive impact of the London Challenge and national strategies has been further explored in several research studies (see Hutchings et al. 2012 and Baars et al. 2014). For example, Hutchings et al. (2012) and Baars et al. (2014) also evaluated the Challenge programme and associated it with gains in attainment in London, with a narrowing of the attainment gap between pupils eligible for free school meals (FSM) and those not eligible (Hutchings et al., 2012). Further studies show that those gains in attainment in London were sustained through the high levels of change that have continued to characterise the school system in England since 2013, including changes to the

Mapping the London Challenge

Key elements surrounding the LONDON CHALLENGE:
- Shared vision, purpose, and objectives
- Challenge and support to key to success schools
- Effective partnership and networking
- Close attention to narrowing the gaps
- Making full use of data
- Strong accountability
- Systems leadership and school to school support
- A relentless focus on teaching and learning

FIGURE 5.2 Mapping the London challenge.

Source: Drawn by the author based on evidence by Wood, D., and Brighouse, T. (2017). The Story of the London Challenge.

primary curriculum and the national assessment frameworks in both primary and secondary phases.

Similarly, the evaluation of the Aiming High: Raising the Achievement of Minority Ethnic Pupils project (DfES 2003; Tikly et al. 2006) also confirmed that schools that were in the project were strongly committed to the ethos that stressed high achievement, equal opportunities, the valuing of cultural diversity, partnership with parents and communities, and effective use of assessment data for tracking and target setting for individual pupils and groups (Ofsted 2009; Tikly et al. 2006). What is particularly significant is that successful schools use effective intervention strategies such as effective feedback, one-to-one support, booster classes, small group tuition, effective support for English as an additional language pupils to improve English proficiency to access the curriculum, and parental support. Overall, there were excellent systems for monitoring the work of the pupils, identifying those who needed additional or extra challenges, and then providing them with additional support (Tikly et al., 2006; Demie, 2023).

92 Black and Ethnic Minority Achievement in Schools

Educational attainment in London by ethnic background also confirms and shows the impact of the London Challenge in closing the Black and minority ethnic achievement gap in London compared to White British (see Figure 5.3 and Figure 5.4). In 2006, white British pupils's attainment of 47% gaining five passes was compared to that found in London overall (45%). However, by 2019, they were still on par with London but had higher levels of achievement than nationally, with a gap of five percentage points (65% vs. 60% nationally).

Figure 5.3 and Figure 5.4 also show the impact of target intervention by ethnic background. For example, since 2003, the relative attainment of Black African pupils in London schools has improved, and they were two percentage points below the London average by 2019. The data also shows three percentage points above the national average, improving at a faster rate than Black African pupils nationally. In 2003, their attainment was the same, with both groups having 44% meet the expected standard. However, the gap had widened to three percentage points by 2019, with 63% of Black African pupils in London and 60% nationally getting five passes, including English and math.

Similarly, while other pupils in London schools had attainment rates a few percentage points below the corresponding White British attainment levels, by 2019, it was two percentage points below. The data also show Whites were 63% above the national average of 60%.

Between 2003 and 2017, Indian pupils had the highest levels of attainment of any ethnic group in London. In 2017, 79% of Indian pupils met the

Ethnicity	2006	2011	2012	2014	2016	2017	2018	2019	Diff 2006-2012	Diff 2014-2019
Bangladeshi	42%	66%	68%	65%	65%	70%	70%	71%	26%	6%
Black African	38%	61%	64%	59%	59%	64%	64%	63%	26%	4%
Black Caribbean	30%	51%	54%	49%	46%	50%	45%	45%	24%	-4%
Black Other	32%	52%	58%	53%	53%	55%	54%	53%	26%	0%
Indian	64%	75%	77%	75%	73%	79%	78%	77%	13%	2%
Mixed White/Black African	44%	61%	66%	61%	60%	64%	62%	63%	22%	2%
Mixed White/Black Caribbean	37%	55%	59%	54%	52%	55%	53%	52%	22%	-2%
Pakistani	48%	66%	66%	63%	62%	69%	68%	70%	18%	7%
White British	47%	62%	64%	61%	61%	65%	64%	65%	17%	4%
White Irish	53%	68%	73%	70%	71%	76%	74%	75%	20%	5%
White Other	43%	59%	63%	57%	59%	63%	61%	63%	20%	6%
London	45%	62%	65%	60%	61%	65%	64%	65%	20%	5%
National state-funded	44%	59%	61%	57%	58%	61%	60%	60%	17%	3%

← London Challenge Period | No National strategy →

FIGURE 5.3 The impact of the London challenge in closing the ethnic minority gap.

Source: DfE NPD, 2006–2019; Demie 2019a and 2022.

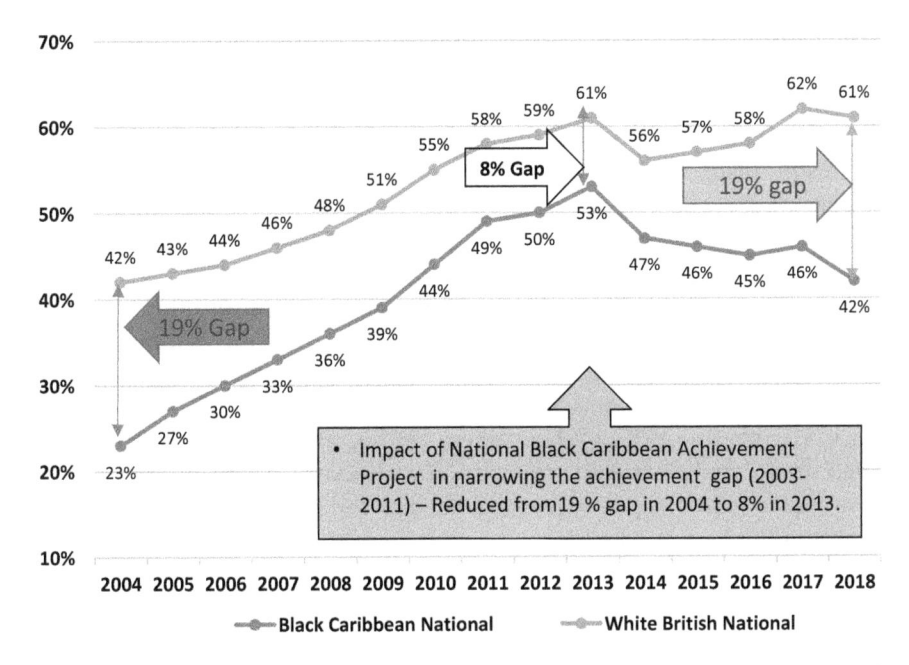

FIGURE 5.4 GCSE Black Caribbean and White British achievement gap in England (5+A*-C incl. English and Maths).

required standard, which was 14 percentage points higher than White British pupils or London pupils overall. Similarly, the attainment of Pakistani and Bangladeshi pupils is consistently higher than that found overall in London or nationally; by 2019, Pakistani pupils in London outperformed White British pupils by 5 percentage points.

Black Caribbean pupils have made a huge improvement during the London challenge period. The research evaluation found that targeted interventions have improved the attainment of Black Caribbean pupils attending Aiming High Schools compared to those not attending Aiming High Schools (see Tikly et al., 2006). At the national level, there is also statistical evidence that shows the positive impact of the project. Black Caribbean students reduced the achievement gap at the GCSE level from 19 percentage points in 2004 to 8 points in 2013 as a result of the interventions (Demie 2019a; Demie and Mclean 2017; Demie 2023).

There were several reasons for the improvement of all ethnic groups. Ethnic minority achievement grants (EMAG) and the Black Caribbean Project were used to tackle the underachievement of ethnic minority pupils (Tikly et al., 2006). The government invested £219 million per year through the EMAG to tackle the underachievement of ethnic minority pupils, and with another Black Caribbean Project in 30 successful schools with £16,000 to support leadership and £10,000 per year for each school involved in the project, it has made a difference (see Tikly et al., 2006). There are other reasons for the success story of Black Caribbean pupils, particularly during the London Challenge period. They were supported by strategies such as using successful Black headteachers, small group support, personal tutoring, booster classes, pastoral care, and training teachers, as well as teaching assistants and learning mentors funded by raising the achievement of Black Caribbean grantees (Tikly et al., 2006; Demie, 2019a).

EMAG funding has also helped with the improvement of other minority ethnic groups in London. As a result of EMAG and the National Black Caribbean Achievement Project, all main ethnic groups made a huge improvement, with Bangladeshi and Black Africans improving by 26%, followed by Black Caribbean (24%), White others (20%), and White British (17%). There is no doubt national strategies, the London Challenge, and EMAG have had a huge impact on closing the gap for all underachieving ethnic groups in England and London.

The EEF evidence on effective intervention strategies in school

Recently, the EEF research project into 'what worked and what failed' in school improvement in schools also revealed several effective interventions that have made an impact (EEF 2019, 2023). Figure 5.4 provides the EEF Teaching and Learning Toolkit evidence that summarises the effectiveness of a range of strategies used commonly in schools. This is based on existing evidence from the UK and internationally.

The focus of EEF research was on disadvantaged pupils, which also applies to Black and ethnic minority pupils. The EEF evidence in Figure 5.4 shows that the use of effective feedback, metacognition and self-regulation, and reading comprehension as intervention strategies will deliver an additional 6–8 months of progress for disadvantaged children. For delivering an additional 4–5 months of progress, the EEF research recommends using small group additional teaching, peer tutoring, early intervention, one-to-one tutoring, homework (secondary), mastery learning, phonics and parental engagement, attendance and behaviour interventions in secondary, collaborative learning, oral language interventions, and EAL support (see Figure 5.5). These strategies are now widely recommended by the EEF**. The lessons learned in the EEF's research also suggest that 'targeted small group and one-to-one interventions have the potential for the largest immediate impact on attainment (EEF 2020:1).'

These are the most effective intervention strategies now recommended by the EEF and Ofsted to be used in English in primary and secondary schools. However, it is important to note that to achieve success in learning interventions, schools need to understand the importance of thorough identification of

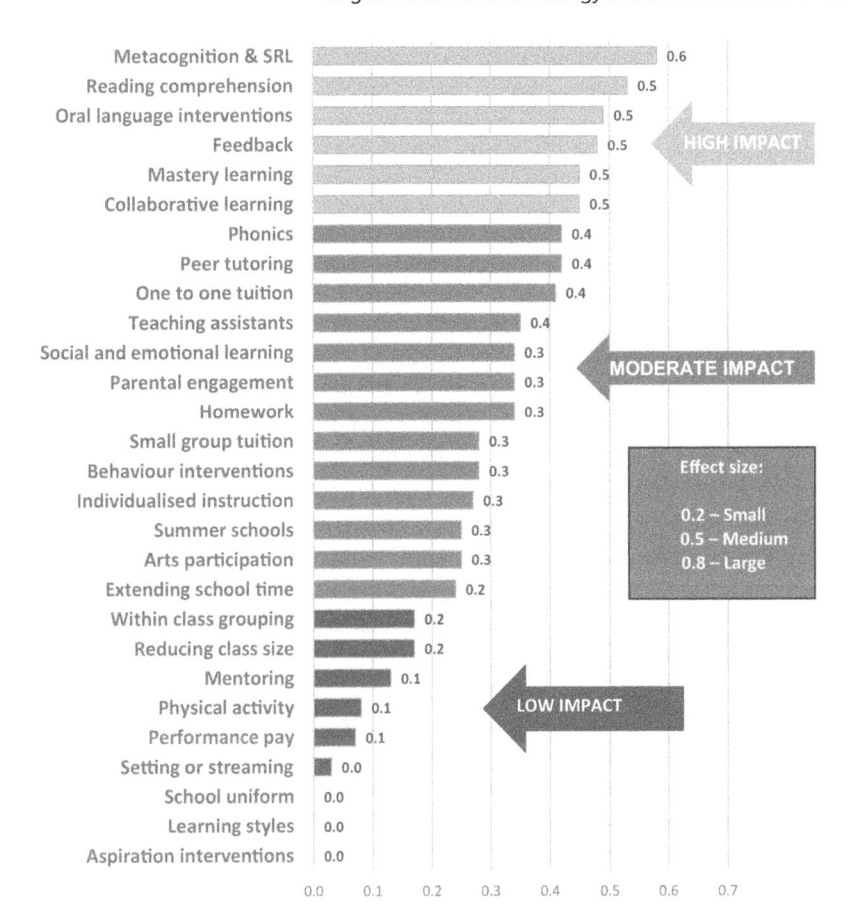

FIGURE 5.5 Interventions strategies to close the achievement gap of disadvantaged pupils.

Source: EEF, 2023.

pupils' needs through the effective use of data. Researchers and school improvement practitioners (Demie 2019a; EEF 2019) suggest starting with the usual types of formative and summative assessments to identify the pupils who would greatly benefit from extra support or risk underachieving, including:

- Pupils not meeting the expected standard in the national curriculum.
- Any ethnic groups, boys, EAL, FSM, summer-born, and SEN pupils that are at risk of underachieving.
- Pupils with low attainment due to exclusions and poor attendance.
- Any pupils receiving pupil premium or EAL needs.
- EAL pupils who are left behind because of a lack of English proficiency cannot access the national curriculum.

Monitoring and tracking quickly identify the children who drop below the expected level or appear to be at risk of falling behind, and their needs are targeted through additional targeted interventions.

Similarly, a review and meta-analysis of 53 studies at the international level also suggested targeted *'interventions are moderately effective in improving achievement and outcomes'* for underachieving students (see Snyder et al. 2019:1).

The DfE (2015) school survey also shows how targeted intervention and support are used in schools to make a difference. The DfE asked schools to select the strategies they had used to raise the attainment of disadvantaged pupils and close the gaps. The strategies included in the survey were based on those included in the Sutton Trust/EEF Teaching and Learning Toolkit. The survey revealed that schools were using a large number of strategies to improve disadvantaged pupils' attainment. Schools had used a range of different types of strategies, most of which focussed on teaching and learning. The most common strategies were paired or small group additional teaching, improved feedback between teachers and pupils, and one-to-one tuition. In addition, trips to cultural venues, additional teachers, and social and emotional strategies were also used by most schools. On the whole, the strategies adopted by the largest number of schools are also those identified as most effective in the EEF Teaching and Learning Toolkit. Metacognition and collaborative learning, which are highly rated, were less popular among the schools surveyed for this research.

However, a majority of schools used a few strategies (especially trips to cultural venues, extra-curricular clubs, and strategies to improve behaviour). Still, it was identified by less than 1% as their most effective strategy (DfE 2015).

Conclusions

This chapter explored the effective targeted support and intervention strategies used by schools in raising attainment and closing the achievement gap for Black and ethnic minorities. The evidence from England (Demie 2019a, 2023; Demie and Mclean 2016; Baars et al. 2014; Mongon and Chapman 2008; Ofsted 2009; EEF 2019, 2020; DfE 2015) is based on what works research and has helped many schools use targeted interventions to close the achievement gap between disadvantaged pupils and their peers. The findings provide important and original insights into schools' intervention strategies to support ethnic minority and disadvantaged pupils. It also suggests that schools use a range of targeted interventions, including early intervention, small group additional teaching, one-to-one tuition, peer tutoring, parental involvement, booster classes, mastery learning, pastoral care, improving behaviour and attendance, and enrichment programmes.

We would argue that there is a wealth of evidence that targeted interventions work well in school. The findings of our study are also in line with recent EEF (2019) research that suggested using peer tutoring, early intervention, one-to-one tutoring, small group tuition, homework (secondary), mastery learning, and phonics as effective intervention strategies. These intervention strategies can deliver about 4–5 months of additional child progress (see EEF 2019). These intervention strategies are very popular in the case study schools and are used effectively to raise achievement and close the gap between disadvantaged pupils and their peers.

There is also a lesson schools and policymakers can learn from research into raising the achievement of Black and ethnic minority disadvantaged students through effective targeted interventions and support. The lessons from successful schools both here and elsewhere suggest that it is possible to tackle the link between poverty and underachievement and raise the achievement of ethnic minority students. The key strategies are ensuring access to additional support for ethnic minorities through targeted intervention (DfE 2020a,b; Demie 2019a, 2020; Baars et al. 2014; Demie and Mclean 2016; Mongon and Chapman 2008; Ofsted 2009; Sammons et al. 1995). Several teachers and school leaders are now using targeted intervention to raise achievement and tackle inequality both in England and elsewhere. The overall conclusion from the lesson learned from the research on targeted interventions has relevance for practice and offers a worthwhile example of a success story that is worth learning from schools.

However, we would argue that the choice of which intervention strategies to use will depend on the context of the school. All these intervention strategies, while highly effective in delivering additional progress for Black and ethnic minority and disadvantaged children, are likely to need strong leadership, effective use of data for tracking pupils' attainment and progress, and whole school implementation. Where these strategies are effectively implemented, underachieving ethnic minority and disadvantaged children are likely to show gains in progress, leading to higher attainment and ultimately improved educational outcomes (EEF 2019; Snyder et al. 2019; Demie 2020; Ofsted, 2010).

The overall conclusion of this chapter is that intervention strategies used in successful schools can make a difference in the achievement of Black and ethnic minority pupils and close the gap.

Notes

** For a guide and definitions of the terminology of the intervention strategies used in schools, see EEF (2023) Teaching and Learning Toolkit, https://educationendowmentfoundation.org.uk/education-evidence/teaching-learning-toolkit

This website is a handy place to check to see what the evidence says. Each strategy has an overview section and information on how effective it is. It is also important to note that the following strategies have a particularly high impact and are worth reading:

- *Metacognition and self-regulation: The teaching methods of metacognition and self-regulation encourage students to consider their learning more critically, frequently by imparting to them particular techniques for organising, observing, and assessing their learning.*
- *Mastery learning is a collection of individualised and group-based teaching and learning strategies built on the idea that, given enough time, students may attain a high degree of comprehension in a particular subject. Topics in mastery learning are divided into units or blocks with predefined goals and outcomes.*
- *Oral language interventions, sometimes referred to as 'oracy' or 'speaking and listening interventions,' are methods that highlight the value of verbal communication and engagement in the classroom.*
- *Peer tutoring* encompasses a variety of methods where students collaborate in pairs or small groups to give specific educational support to one another.

References

Baars, S., Bernardes, E., Elwick, A., Malortie, A., McAleavy, T., McInerney, L., Menzies, L. & Riggall, A. (2014) *Lessons from London Schools*. London: CfBT and Centre for London. Available: https://www.cfbt.com/enGB/Research/Research-library/2014/r-london-schools-2014

Demie, F. (2019a) *Educational Inequality: Closing the gap*. UCL IOE press. July. https://www.ucl-ioe-press.com/books/social-justice-equality-and-human-rights/educational-inequality/

Demie, F. (2019b) Raising the achievement of black Caribbean pupils: good practice for developing leadership capacity and workforce diversity in schools. *School Leadership and Management*, 39(1): 5–25.

Demie, F. (2020) *What Works in Driving School Improvement?* London: Lambeth School Research and Statistics Unit. https://bit.ly/3o4G8wT

Demie, F. (2023) *Raising the Achievement of Black Caribbean pupils: Barriers and Good Practice in Schools*. London: Lambeth Research and Statistics Unit. https://www.lambeth.gov.uk/sites/default/files/2023-05/Raising_Achievement_of_Black_Caribbean_Pupils_-_Barriers_and_Good_Practice.pdf

Demie, F. (2024) *A Survey of Barriers to Learning, Success Factors, And Intervention Strategy in London Schools to Raise Achievement and Tackle Educational Inequality*. London: Lambeth Schools Research and Statistics Unit, April draft.

Demie, F. & Mclean. (2016) Tackling disadvantage: what works in narrowing the achievement gap in schools. *Review of Education*, 3(2): 138–174.

Demie, F., & Mclean, C. (2017) *Black Caribbean Underachievement in Schools in England*. Lambeth LA: Lambeth Research and Statistics Unit.

Department for Education. (2015) *Supporting the Attainment of Disadvantaged Pupils: Articulating Success and Good Practice Research Report.* London: Department for Education. https://bit.ly/3bLxCNq

DfE. (2006) *Raising the Achievement of Bilingual Learners in Primary Schools: Evaluation of the Pilot/Programme.* Nottingham: Department for Education and Skills Publications. https://www.nfer.ac.uk/publications/ABL03/ABL03.pdf

DfE. (2013) *History Programme of Study: Key Stages 1 And 2. National Curriculum in England.* London: Department for Education.

DfE. (2020a) *School Teacher Workforce.* https://www.ethnicity-facts-figures.service.gov.uk/workforce-and-business/workforce-diversity/school-teacher-workforce/latest

DfE. (2020b) *English Proficiency of Pupils with English as an Additional Language.* Ad Hoc Notice February 2020. Available at: https://www.gov.uk/government/publications/english-proficiency-pupils-with-english-as-additional-language

DfES. (2003) *Aiming High: Raising the Achievement of Minority Ethnic Pupils.* London: DfES Consultation.

EEF. (2019) *Teaching and Learning Tool Kit.* London: Education Endowment Foundation. https://educationendowmentfoundation.org.uk/evidencesummaries/teaching-learning-toolkit/

EEF. (2020) *Teaching and Learning Tool Kit.* London: Education Endowment Foundation. https://educationendowmentfoundation.org.uk/evidencesummaries/teaching-learning-toolkit/

EEF. (2023) *Teaching and Learning Tool Kit.* London: Education Endowment Foundation. https://educationendowmentfoundation.org.uk/evidencesummaries/teaching-learning-toolkit/https://educationendowmentfoundation.org.uk/education-evidence/teaching-learning-toolkit

Hutchings, M., Greenwood, C., Hollingworth, S., Mansaray, A., Rose, A. & Glass, K. (2012) *Evaluation of the City Challenge Programme.* https://www.semanticscholar.org/paper/Evaluation-of-the-City-Challenge-programmeme-Hutchings-Greenwood/d4324a2e696e40c84e4d4267b93b58688a19db3d

Kidson, M. & Norris, E. (2015) Implementing the London Challenge. https://www.instituteforgovernment.org.uk/sites/default/files/publications/Implementing%20the%20London%20Challenge%20-%20final_0.pdf

Mongon, D. & Chapman, C. (2008) *Successful Leadership for Promoting the Achievement of White Working Class Pupils.* National College for School Leadership (NCSL).

Ofsted. (2009) *Twelve Outstanding Secondary Schools: Excelling Against The Odds.* London: Office for Standards in Education, HMI: 080240. https://dera.ioe.ac.uk/id/eprint/11232/2/Twelve.pdf

Ofsted. (2010) London Challenge. https://webarchive.nationalarchives.gov.uk/ukgwa/20141107033128/http://www.ofsted.gov.uk/resources/london-challenge

Sammons, P., Hillman, J. & Mortimore, P. (1995) *Key Characteristics of Effective Schools: Review School Effectiveness Research.* London: Ofsted.

Snyder, K., Fong, C., Paintwer, K., Pittard, C. Barr, S. & Patall, E. (2019) Interventions for academically underachieving students: A systematic review and meta-analysis. https://www.sciencedirect.com/science/article/abs/pii/S1747938X18306316?via%3Dihub

Tikly, L., Haynes, J., Caballero, C., Hill, J. & Gillborn, D. (2006) *Evaluation of Aiming High: African Caribbean Achievement Project.* Bristol. https://research-information.bris.ac.uk/ws/portalfiles/portal/128456398/RR801.pdf

Wood, D. & Brighouse, T. (2017) *The Story of London Challenge.* London: London Leadership Strategy.

6
STRATEGIES AND SUCCESS FACTORS TO RAISE PUPILS WITH ENGLISH AS AN ADDITIONAL LANGUAGE ACHIEVEMENT

Introduction

English as an Additional Language (EAL) attracts much interest among educationists and policymakers, yet little is known about what works to raise EAL pupils' achievement in schools. This chapter explores how pupils with EAL are supported by answering some research questions, including: What does research tell us? How are pupils with EAL assessed? 'What does the data tell us about the achievement of children with English as an Additional Language (EAL)?', and 'What are the school strategies for raising the achievement gap of EAL pupils?' These research questions are the subject of much discussion and interest in England (Demie, 2013; Demie & Strand, 2006; Strand, Malmberg & Hall, 2015). Yet there are relatively few studies that have examined EAL attainment and language diversity, the relationships between EAL learners' English proficiency and their attainment in schools in England (Demie, 2013; Demie & Strand, 2006; and Strand, Malmberg & Hall, 2015), and the targeted intervention strategies to support EAL in the classroom. This issue is increasingly important for EAL policy development, given the prevalence and growth of the EAL population in England. English as a second language students in England have likewise seen a sharp rise over time, rising from 499,000 in 1997 to 1,715,912 in 2023 (DfE 2023). There are now more than 1.7 million pupils between 5 and 18 years old in England's primary, secondary, and special schools and Pupil Referral Units speaking over 360 languages between them and who are at varying stages in their learning of EAL, from newcomers to English to those that are fully fluent. In 2023, about 20.2% of the school population in England and Wales spoke English as an Additional Language (DfE 2023). This is a huge increase, and

DOI: 10.4324/9781003499633-8

there is a need for research on how to support the growing EAL school population in schools.

It is also important to note that using EAL status alone is not necessarily an accurate marker for studying the attainment of pupils with EAL. EAL is a very heterogeneous group, made up of pupils from many different ethnic and cultural backgrounds, and likely to show a wide variation in achievement. We need to be cautious and recognise that:

> EAL is not a precise measure of language proficiency at the pupil level. "First language", which is used here, is the language to which a child was initially exposed during early development and continues to be exposed in the home or the community. It does not mean that pupils are necessarily fluent in a language other than English or that they cannot speak English fluently. Pupils can therefore be identified in the census as EAL when they are bilingual and have no specific need for support to access mainstream education in English.
>
> *(see DfE 2016:27)*

Researchers have now recognised the weaknesses of using such national data in EAL achievement studies and have argued that it is unhelpful information that does not differentiate a pupil's performance by their proficiency in English (Demie 2013, 2015; Demie and Strand 2006). There is a need for more research on the relationship between fluency in English and attainment to improve our knowledge about EAL pupils' academic performance in schools.

A review of the previous literature has shown that the attainment of pupils with EAL varies considerably based on a range of factors such as language background, social background, length of schooling in England for people who come from abroad, proficiency in English, and gender (Strand et al. 2015). For example, Strand et al. (2015) and Demie (2016) research have shown that pupils with EAL on free school meals (FSM) perform much lower than their relatively more affluent peers. Demie (2016) research into language diversity and attainment in schools found language spoken at home is useful for attainment analysis for pupils with EAL. The findings of his study using language at home suggest that:

> Of the Black African language groups, Manding, Lingala, Wolof, Portuguese, Italian, and Fula/Fulfulde-Pulaar speakers were the lowest-achieving groups, while the Igbo, Zulu, Yoruba, Amharic, Ewe, and Ga-speaking Black African pupils achieved better than White British and the national average.
>
> *Demie (2016:19)*

In addition, previous studies also confirm that English language proficiency is the major factor influencing the performance of pupils with English as an Additional Language. With English being the language of instruction for pupils to access the curriculum fully and effectively, it is clear that they need to be fluent in English. Several other studies also carried out research into the factors affecting EAL pupils' achievement and attributed the root of EAL pupils' underachievement to various factors, including difficulties in speaking English and other factors such as poverty and recent entry to the country (Strand et al., 2015). However, the language barrier is a significant factor affecting the academic performance of EAL students. In order for EAL students to fully participate in the curriculum, they must speak English fluently. Many studies have now been conducted on EAL students' assessment methods, English language competency, and the connection between English proficiency and attainment levels. In particular, there is research evidence from England showing that a pupil's fluency in English is a key predictor of their achievement in national tests at age 11 and public examinations at age 16 (e.g., Demie, 2017a,b 2016, and 2013; Demie & Strand, 2006). Previous data also shows that there is a strong relationship between the stages of fluency in English and educational attainment (Demie 2016). The empirical evidence shows that the performance level of EAL pupils increases as fluency in English increases. We would contend that the government's failure to distinguish EAL students by levels of fluency in English and languages spoken at home has hidden the alarmingly low achievement of EAL students who do not speak the language fluently. The relationship between language variety, EAL attainment, and proficiency in English is further examined in the part that follows, including data from the local authority case study.

The achievement of pupils with EAL in schools by language diversity

It is possible to unpick EAL and ethnic and first-language backgrounds. Doing so clearly shows that there are significant differences in attainment within the larger EAL classification related to ethnic and first language background. Table 6.1 presents the attainment at KS2 (percentage reaching the expected standard in reading, writing, and math) and GCSE (percentage achieving grades 4 to 9 in English and math), broken down by the most commonly spoken first languages in the LA. The largest language group is speakers of English only, followed in descending order of total number of speakers by Portuguese, Spanish, Somali, French, Yoruba, Arabic, Twi-Fante, Polish, Bengali, Tigrinya, Italian, Ibo, Urdu, Chinese, Lingala, Amharic, and Krio. Numbers for languages with fewer than 10 speakers are not included, as they are considered too small for reliable statistical analysis.

TABLE 6.1 Attainment by main languages spoken in the LA at end of KS2 and GCSE, 2023

Home Language	Main Ethnic Group(s)	KS2 Cohort	RWM%	GCSE Cohort	9–4 EM%
English	White British, Black Caribbean	1454	63%	1287	59%
Spanish	White Other, Any Other Group	159	55%	199	59%
Portuguese	White Other	160	59%	170	54%
Somali	Black African	118	63%	99	67%
Polish	White Other	111	84%	65	85%
French	White Other, Black African	90	68%	86	63%
Arabic	Any Other Group	83	67%	63	76%
Yoruba	Black African	70	71%	49	80%
Akan/Twi-Fante	Black African	44	64%	39	59%
Bengali	Bangladeshi	31	71%	32	69%
Romanian	White Other	13	77%	20	95%
Tigrinya	Black African	31	65%	23	78%
Italian	White Other	41	78%	26	69%
Turkish	Turkish	X	X	22	73%
Urdu	Pakistani	53	68%	13	92%
Amharic	Black African	37	73%	13	85%
Vietnamese	Vietnamese	X	X	11	91%
Albanian/Shqip	White Other	22	64%	11	73%
Tagalog/Filipino	Any Other Group	10	70%	12	67%
Lingala	Black African	X	X	14	50%
Chinese	Chinese	14	86%	X	X
Igbo	Black African	18	89%	X	X
Krio	Black African	13	38%	X	X
Pashto/Pakhto	Asian Other	12	67%	X	X
All Pupils		2876	64%	2438	63%
National (state-funded)		n/a	60%	n/a	61%

N.B.: Afrikaans, Balochi, Bulgarian, Caribbean Creole French, Czech, Danish, Dutch/Flemish, Edo/Bini, Esan/Ishan, Estonian, Ewe, Finnish, Fon, Ga, German, Greek, Gujarati, Hausa, Hebrew, Hindi, Hungarian, Icelandic, Itsekiri, Japanese, Katchi, Kurdish, Latvian, Lithuanian, Luganda, Luo (Kenya/Tanzania), Macedonian, Malayalam, Manding/Malinke, Mauritian/Seychelles Creole, Norwegian, Pahari, Panjabi, Pashto/Pakhto, Persian/Farsi, Russian, Serbian/Croatian/Bosnian, Slovak, Slovenian, Sundanese, Swahili/Kiswahili, Swedish, Tamil, Thai, Ukrainian, Venda, and Wolof.

These data reveal interesting and pedagogically important information about the relative attainment of pupils with EAL from different ethnic and linguistic backgrounds. For example, 95% of Romanians and 92% of Urdu speakers gained a pass in the English and Maths GCSE, more than twice the proportion of Lingala speakers (50%). The top four performing groups at GCSE were speakers of African and Asian languages: Urdu (92%), Vietnamese (91%), Polish (85%), Amharic (85%), and Tigrinya (78%). Of the language groups that performed better than the national figure, only two European languages were represented: Polish (85%), Romanian (95%), and Albanian and Turkish (73%). Moreover, speakers of other European languages are among the lowest performers: Spanish (59%), French (63%), Portuguese (54%), and those who speak only English at home (59%).

Similar patterns of achievement are also evident at KS2. Whereas these data present a generally more positive picture, attainment nonetheless varies between language groups quite considerably. The two largest language groups after English are Spanish and Portuguese, They are the lowest performers with Spanish attaining 55% and Portuguese 59% at KS2. The highest-attaining group were speakers of Ibo (89%) and Polish (85%).

This evidence shows that ethnolinguistic background based on home language may be associated with other important characteristics that affect educational chances, such as socioeconomic status, educational experiences before arriving in the UK, community support and cohesion, and so on. Data analysis of the kind presented here allows teachers to identify at-risk groups from within their cohorts and plan support accordingly (Strand et al., 2015).

The achievement of pupils with EAL in schools by stages of English proficiency

EAL professionals have long recognised the factors affecting EAL performance. They used proficiency in English measures to determine the levels of needs for EAL. Five stages are used in monitoring and tracking English proficiency in case schools and nationally (DfE: 2020). These include:

- **Stage A (*new to English*)**: May use their first language for learning and others. May remain completely silent in the classroom. May be copying or repeating some words or phrases. May understand some everyday expressions in English but may have minimal or no literacy in English. Needs a **considerable amount of EAL support.**
- **Stage B (*early acquisition*)**: May follow day-to-day social communication in English and participate in learning activities, beginning to use spoken English for social purposes. May understand simple instructions and can follow narratives or accounts with visual support. I may have developed some skills in reading and writing. May have become familiar with some

subject-specific vocabulary. Still needs a **significant amount of EAL support** to access the curriculum.
- **Stage C (*Developing Competence*):** May participate in learning activities with increasing independence. I am able to express myself orally in English, but structural inaccuracies are still apparent. Literacy will require ongoing support, particularly for understanding text and May be able to follow abstract concepts and more complex written English. Requires ongoing EAL support to access the curriculum fully.
- **Stage D (*competent*):** Oral English will be developing well, enabling successful engagement in activities across the Can read and understand a wide variety of texts. Written English may lack complexity and contain occasional evidence of errors in structure. Needs some support to access subtle nuances of meaning, refine English usage, and develop an abstract vocabulary. Needs **some or occasional EAL support** to access complex curriculum material and tasks.
- **Stage E (*fluent*):** 'Can operate across the curriculum to a level of competence equivalent to that of a pupil who uses English as his or her first language **without EAL support** across the curriculum.'

(DfE 2020:5)

In this chapter, pupils at Stages A–E are classified as 'EAL.' Stage A is classified as 'beginners' in English, and those at Stage E are classified as 'fully fluent.'

For pupils to have access to the curriculum, it is clear they need to be proficient in the language of instruction, which is English. When educators have reliable information about the English proficiency of the children in their care, they can identify areas where support is needed and target their resources appropriately through data-informed policy and practice.

National testing and assessment provide a comprehensive account of the attainment of EAL pupils at various key stages of the national curriculum, and as fluency in English improves, average outcomes correspondingly increase. Our case study LA shows that attainment at KS2 and GCSE varies considerably by proficiency in English (see Tables 6.2 and 6.3).

At the end of primary education, the KS2 results show fully fluent bilingual speakers had the highest levels of attainment, with 85% meeting the expected standard in reading, writing, and maths (RWM) combined. This compares with 62% of English-only speakers and 70% of bilingual competent speakers. All groups improved between 2022 and 2023, but the improvement was lowest for English-only speakers, up one percentage point, compared to an improvement of six percentage points for Stage D – competent bilingual speakers.

Similarly, at the end of secondary education at GCSE, the achievement of pupils with EAL confirmed that fully fluent bilingual speakers had the highest

TABLE 6.2 – English proficiency stage and EAL attainment at KS2 (% reaching expected standard)

Stages of English proficiency	2022				2023				RWM[a] change 2022–2023
	Reading	Maths	Writing	RWM	Reading	Maths	Writing	RWM	
Stage A–C (not fluent)	55	58	42	35	53	63	48	40	+5
Stage D – Competent	81	84	77	64	83	87	81	70	+6
Stage E – Fluent	92	89	91	82	91	91	92	85	+3
English speaker	79	72	74	61	77	73	73	62	+1

a RWM-Reading, Writing, and Maths.

TABLE 6.3 English proficiency and EAL attainment at GCSE

Stages of English proficiency	2022 Attainment 8	Progress 8	E+M4–9 (%)	Cohort	2023 Attainment 8	Progress 8	E+M4–9 (%)	Cohort
Stage A-C non fluent	31.5	-0.4	35	100	43.8	0.71	53	119
Stage D – Competent	41.1	-0.2	59	150	47.4	0.39	63	180
Stage E – Fluent	52.0	0.2	78	441	49.7	0.31	73	512
English Only	42.6	-0.5	60	745	42.1	-0.30	59	877

attainment in each of the three key GCSE indicators and were the only group to have made positive progress in both years. It should be remembered that pupils at the earliest stages of English fluency often comprise small cohorts, especially at the secondary level. At each key stage, their improvement rate was much lower than that found in the borough overall, and the gap is widening with their more fluent peers. This may not be surprising, as until they have an adequate grasp of English to access the curriculum effectively, it is a bar to attainment and improvement. What is notable is that fully fluent bilingual learners outperform English-only speakers by a considerable margin.

In the GCSE data, we see that at Stages A and C (not fluent), 53% achieved grades 4 to 9 in English and math, compared to 63% at Stage D (competent) and 73% at Stage E (fluent). Only 63% of EAL pupils in Stages A to C achieved grades 4 to 9 at GCSE, suggesting this group to be one of the more underachieving in LA. The achievement of EAL pupils who are fluent in English continues to be high, at one percentage point above English first language pupils.

Overall, the findings of both sets of data confirm that there is a strong relationship between proficiency in English and educational attainment at the end of primary and secondary education.

Success factors and school strategies in raising the achievement of EAL pupils

This section examines the success factors behind the increased achievement of pupils with EAL and what works to close the achievement gaps. The body of available literature suggests that there is a paucity of research on what works in raising the achievement of EAL pupils in schools (DfE 2016; Demie 2013). However, recent research identified the reasons behind schools' success in raising achievement, which included the quality of teaching and learning, effective leadership at all levels, an inclusive curriculum, the use of data, and targeted support for pupils with EAL (see Demie 2015, 2017a, 2017b). The key challenge for this study is therefore to find out which strategies schools can use to make a difference in the achievement of pupils with EAL.

There are various reasons for the vast improvement in the achievement of EAL pupils in the case study schools compared to the local authority and nationally in England. Therefore, the key question for research is, 'What is the reason for such achievement in the case study schools?' As part of the interviews, headteachers and teachers were asked, 'What strategies does your school use to raise the achievement of EAL pupils?' Our good practice research identified a range of common factors that supported pupils with EAL to achieve well at school. These included effective EAL teaching and learning, an understanding of pedagogy that best supported pupils with EAL, targeted support towards their progress, an inclusive curriculum, and the use of data for pupils' progress and achievement. These good practices are discussed below.

Strong leadership in school that supports pupils with EAL

One of the main reasons for the excellent performance of pupils for whom English is an Additional Language and the huge improvement in the schools as a whole over time was strong leadership on equality and diversity. The head teachers set high expectations for the senior team and the staff as a whole. There was a relentless focus on improvement, particularly in the quality of teaching and learning, effective use of data, and higher achievement by students. The headteachers were very well supported by effective senior teams that understood EAL pedagogy. The leadership team placed great importance on staff members' social and academic accomplishments, and the schools were closely linked to the community they served. This was evident in the steadfast and dedicated manner in which management at every level contributed to the school's efforts to improve student accomplishment.

One headteacher asserted that such a service is 'critical for schools with large numbers of pupils with EAL,' while the other headteachers were proud of their schools' focus on expanding the EAL Department. All staff were trained in specific techniques in the EAL programme, including techniques related to speaking and listening, use of the first language, talk partners, pre-teaching, and application of these techniques across the curriculum. These were supported by scrutiny and analyses of students' performance data to appropriately target resources towards specific individuals or groups. The outcomes of such interventions were evaluated candidly and informed future planning. This can be seen from the headteachers' interviews in 'School D' about what works, which are summarised below:

> All pupils are allowed to succeed, whatever their backgrounds.
> *(Headteacher)*

> We are very good at using data and monitoring progress, and this has been useful in identifying pupils with EAL who are underachieving.
> *(Headteacher)*

The care and concern for every student were of the utmost importance, and there was a strong commitment to making sure that students with EAL were included in all activities.

Every employee who took part in the interview thought that upper management provided them with good support and that they knew who to turn to when they needed assistance. Staff members met on a regular basis to discuss strategies for addressing concerns brought up regarding individual students. The high standards for everyone and the excellent performance of EAL students were clear indicators of their influence.

The schools pride themselves on their diversity. The staff has high expectations of their pupils and understands the value of bilingualism in raising achievement. Two teachers who were interviewed talked about their school and the achievement of pupils with EAL at Schools A and B.

- Teacher A: Teacher A was impressed by the sense of community that pervades the school, to which she felt welcomed. She feels the headteacher is a community leader and has made a big improvement to this school. Teacher A enjoys the diversity of the school population and has blossomed into the aspiring culture of the school community. (EAL Teacher, School A)
- Teacher B: Teacher B works as a teacher of EAL and English and has head of EAL for the past seven years. She is well-qualified, experienced, and knowledgeable, and her work was highly praised by Ofsted in previous inspections. She feels the headteacher in our school is a community leader, is inspirational, and ensures that the school has high aspirations for all its pupils, regardless of their ability or background.

I am the first person to be seen by pupils with EAL because of my role as head of EAL. One of my main roles is helping their parents, as they can have difficulty with the English language. I am the first point of contact for parents with EAL when they are new to the school. Parents see how having a diverse workforce has made a big difference for their children, and they are confident that they get the help they need. A lot of this changed with the current headteacher, and the school is now outstanding. Parents and the community appreciate and value the diversity of the schools and the school EAL initiatives and programmes. I enjoy teaching in the school and supporting all pupils.

(EAL Teacher, School B)

Effective EAL teaching and learning in the classroom

One of the main reasons for the excellent performance of pupils for whom English is an Additional Language and the huge improvement in the schools as a whole over time is strong leadership on equality and diversity and effective teaching and learning in the classroom. The senior team and the entire staff are held to high standards by the headteachers. A headteacher asserted that such a service is 'critical for schools with large numbers of pupils with EAL.' The headteachers are proud of their schools' focus on expanding the EAL Department. The staff members we spoke with and the observations we made indicated that the schools have exceptional proficiency in helping kids learn English as a second language. Every employee received specialised training on methods such as scheduled speaking and listening sessions, using one's native tongue, and conversation partners. These support components were developed by carefully examining and analysing student performance data in order to provide resources to the right people or groups. The outcomes of such interventions were evaluated candidly and informed future planning.

Overall, in these schools, there is a strong culture of self-evaluation pervading all areas. The views of pupils, parents, and students have been sought regularly and are highly valued; they are used to inform worthwhile changes. This can be seen from the headteachers' interviews in 'School R' about what works, which are summarised below:

> The cultural and linguistic heritages of pupils are valued within the school curriculum.
>
> We are very good at using data and monitoring progress, and this has been useful in identifying pupils with EAL who are underachieving.

The care and concern for every student were of the utmost importance, and there was a strong commitment to making sure that students with EAL were included in all activities. Every employee who took part in the interview thought that upper management provided them with good support and that they knew who to turn to when they needed assistance. Overall, there was a clear emphasis on collective responsibility in the school, which ensured that senior and middle leaders were fully accountable for their areas of responsibility and for pupil progress. There were regular meetings with staff to discuss various strategies to address any issues raised about specific pupils. The impact of these strategies was apparent in the good performance of pupils with EAL and the very high standards achieved by all pupils.

Most importantly, in the words of the school head teacher,

> The schools pride themselves on their diversity, and the school has ensured that all groups of pupils achieve equally well. Staff worked successfully to remove barriers to learning faced by large numbers of pupils.

It was also evident that all staff in the schools, including senior managers and the teaching assistants, were responsible for the achievement of EAL pupils and understood how high-quality teaching was for all pupils, and the same was true for EAL learners. In the school, everything was done from the EAL perspective.

All EAL students underwent an English language assessment upon entering the school, utilising national curriculum descriptors and the stages of English. To make sure that instruction was pitched at the right cognitive level, students' reading and numeracy abilities were evaluated in their native tongue in addition to in English.

All staff adopted a holistic approach that incorporated a range of strategies known to be effective for learners with EAL. These included collaborative learning, a focus on talk and vocabulary development throughout the curriculum, an experiential curriculum, and the promotion of pupils' first languages in the classroom as a tool for learning. These assessments have been useful for target setting and additional interventions such as EAL talk sessions for small groups of pupils, one-to-one support, booster sessions, and mentoring of pupils by bilingual teaching assistants.

Schools recognised that the most successful way of introducing a first language in the classroom was through the use of 'talk partners' or 'talk buddies.' Talk partner is a strategy used in most settings and is a key part of helping all children feel more involved in their learning. In each school, there was a focus on talk partners and talk frames. In this approach, pupils were paired up and given planned opportunities to talk with one another in English or their first language. Several schools were using talk partners more frequently and noted their benefits, including:

> Children were encouraged to talk more constructively, which keeps them "on task."
>
> More articulate responses were elicited, often from pupils who were reluctant to contribute.
>
> Children were more confident talking one-on-one with another child in their first language and less embarrassed than if it were to the whole class.
>
> *(teacher)*

The role of collaborative learning in both cognitive and language development was emphasised by all teachers, as was their awareness of their roles in providing good role models for the English language. Teachers use good practice pairings and groupings of pupils to encourage pupils to use their home languages. This has provided good scaffolding for the EAL learners to learn the English language. One pupil concurred, suggesting,

> When I say a word wrong, he corrects me and says try again, and every day I learn a couple more words.
>
> *(pupil)*

'Talk partners' were often employed to allow students to practice and discuss language, and talk frames were utilised to scaffold students' language as they moved towards the written form. All learning was supported by scheduled talk times, to the extent that a new student made a comment as soon as they arrived.

Everyone was talking so I could learn the word from them.

(pupil)

Grammar is recognised as important, and issues in grammar were identified and addressed. People were supported with sentence structures orally, requiring pupils to respond in full sentences. In one school, an EAL coordinator stated:

I encourage the teaching of language structures through talk partners, with a focus on response.

(EAL co-ordinator)

In the early years, pupils learn English through carefully planned opportunities to hear and use English in meaningful activities and experiences. Teachers scaffolded pupils' learning through role play, songs and rhymes, and circle activities.

Teachers in KS1 and KS2 also highlighted how they focused on vocabulary development when teaching reading. The teacher described how they were repeating it throughout the day and through deliberate choices of texts so that pupils met academic language in texts. Before a new text, vocabulary is identified, displayed, modelled, and referred to. One child explained,

The teacher explains clearly to us, and if we don't understand, they give us examples. The teacher constantly reads faces for understanding; repeat, pair, and group pupils so they can listen and understand.

Home languages were considered key in supporting EAL pupils and were given priority in classrooms as a tool for learning. Through talk partners, theatre, and Talk for Writing, students who spoke the same language were encouraged to assist one another in the classroom and to use their first language. Pupils were encouraged to maintain and develop their home languages so that the skills learned in their first languages were transferred to English. Our observation during the research suggests there was evidence in all the schools that children were happy to use their first languages in the classroom. They were using their first language in a range of learning and social contexts, and this good practice and approach is valued and appreciated by school leadership, teachers, and parents.

The discussion above summarises some of the key strategies used by teachers to support pupils with EAL, including oracy in the classroom. It confirms that talking is a vital key to language acquisition. We would further argue that encouraging EAL pupils to develop skills and versatility in speaking and listening is vital for understanding ideas. More importantly, expressiveness, narrative, strong talking, and writing are also important links to learning for EAL pupils.

Another strategy identified above is also the use of home language. For EAL pupils, the opportunity to use their first language at school is key to supporting their learning. Many EAL pupils, like Somali, come from a culture with strong oral traditions. For these reasons, in school, pupils' home languages are valued, recognised, and well-used.

Another good practice in teaching EAL pupils that we observed and identified above is active and collaborative learning in small groups. Pupils working cooperatively on task groups share skills and support each other.

Targeted support for EAL pupils

To enhance teaching and learning, schools employ EAL support workers, many of whom are multilingual, in addition to designated EAL instructors. Schools use termly learning assessment meetings to identify the needs of individual pupils and their EAL targets. The stages of English assessments were discussed in detail with headteachers, deputy headteachers, inclusion managers, and EAL staff in the termly meeting, with a focus on individual pupils. Interventions are also put into place. This is monitored regularly for effectiveness. Schools have drawn sufficiently flexible timetables to meet the changing needs of the school. For example, in one school, bilingual teaching assistants were placed in the Early Years Foundation Stage and Year 1 to help pupils build EAL pupils' confidence. Teachers argued that this encouraged them to develop their first language and supported their English. Schools use multilingual teaching assistants, and this has helped build partnerships with parents, as multilingual teaching assistants are often able to communicate with parents. It has also helped parents engage in their children's learning.

In almost all the case studies, schools implement change and improvement through clear induction processes, targeted interventions to improve EAL proficiency in English and attainment, one-to-one support, and interventions in English and math. The extent to which EAL pupils make progress is evident in several discussions we had with an assistant headteacher (Inclusion), various teachers, teaching assistants, learning mentors, and the leadership team in one case study school. The impact of targeted support in raising achievement can be seen from the examples of outstanding school practices outlined above from one of the case study schools. The school provided the following targeted support that was effective in raising achievement:

- *'Induction support: The school has a clear induction process for new arrivals, which incorporates assessments of both English literacy and numeracy skills in their first language.*

- *The policy on new arrivals is also adhered to during the settling phase and learning mentor support.*
- *In-class EAL support programmes and resourcing, such as dual language dictionaries*
- *Monitoring by the Senior Management Team (SMT) of the differentiation from class teachers*
- *Teachers are working with inclusion managers to develop differentiated resources and plan to support learning.*
- *Visual resources to support learning*
- *Talk about writing and math.*
- *Clear tracking of progress and monitoring via provision mapping.'*

(Demie 2019:180–181)

Overall, our interviews and observations in this school demonstrate teachers' knowledge and understanding of EAL pedagogy and strategies. We noted that EAL teaching principles inform classroom pedagogy and are incorporated into lessons. These consist of speaking frames, discussion partners, sentence openers, cooperative working techniques, etc.

Evidence from our examination of the progress of individual EAL students in school A also points to an impressive accomplishment in terms of advancement in English proficiency levels and attainment at the conclusion of critical phases. For instance, we saw that a Portuguese-speaking student who entered the school in Year 1 and was evaluated as a Stage 1 (beginning in English) had significantly improved. By the time she started sixth grade, she had progressed from the beginner stage to full fluency with the additional support mentioned above. More importantly, her KS2 grades verify that she attained mathematical proficiency levels 5 and 4 as well. As an EAL student who knew no English when she started school, we would argue that this is a fantastic accomplishment. The efficacious targeted help offered to EAL students in this case study school is further demonstrated by this research.

Schools emphasised the importance of distinguishing between EAL and special educational needs (SEN) and described how progress through the stages of English is carefully monitored and unpicked to identify any learning difficulty. Where there is concern, an assessment of and through the first language using mother tongue materials is carried out, and interpreters are employed for meetings and assessments with outside agencies, demonstrating that there are clear protocols to differentiate between needs arising from learning EAL and those related to SEN and how this informs choice of provision.

Targeted support from EAL coordinators and EAL teachers

There is evidence that many of the schools in the case study had a dedicated EAL coordinator. These coordinators had oversight of EAL provision throughout the school and also worked as class teachers or assistant heads, who had oversight of EAL provision throughout the school. In one of the case study schools, where 20% of its school population was Portuguese-speaking, the coordinator herself was of Portuguese origin and had come to the school originally as a Portuguese support teacher. As a senior manager within the school senior management team, she enabled Portuguese parents to see how their culture and heritage were valued by the school. She was also able to raise their profile at a strategic level and brought to the school a detailed understanding of the needs of the Portuguese community, the changing nature of the community surrounding the school, and how all these issues affect the pupils and their parents. This EAL good practice helped the EAL coordinator develop an action plan that empowered Portuguese pupils, parents, and staff in their effort to raise the achievement of not only the Portuguese pupils but all EAL pupils in the school.

The evidence from the interview also shows that the EAL coordinators regularly observed class teachers with an EAL focus and discussed targets with teachers and teaching assistants to improve their future practice. This also helped in updating EAL registers and overseeing target setting for individual pupils. Many subject coordinators also managed teaching assistants who worked under the EAL coordinators' and class teachers' direction. They held assistants accountable for their capacity to improve the learning of students with EAL and trained them in particular tactics for EAL learners.

To enhance teaching and learning, schools employ EAL support workers, many of whom are multilingual, in addition to designated EAL instructors. There is teamwork in successful schools to support pupils with EAL needs. Schools use term learning assessment meetings to identify the needs of individual pupils and their EAL targets. The stages of English assessments were discussed in detail with headteachers, deputy headteachers, inclusion managers, and EAL staff in the termly meeting, with a focus on individual pupils. Interventions are also put into place. This is monitored regularly for effectiveness. Schools have drawn sufficiently flexible timetables to meet the changing needs of the school. For example, in one school, bilingual teaching assistants were placed in the Early Years Foundation Stage and Year 1 to help pupils build EAL pupils' confidence. Teachers argued that this encouraged them to develop their first language and supported their English. Since multilingual teaching assistants could frequently contact parents, placing them here also aided in the development of long-lasting relationships with parents. It has also helped parents engage in their children's learning.

In almost all the case studies, schools implement change and improvement through clear induction processes, targeted interventions to improve EAL proficiency in English and attainment, one-to-one support, and interventions in English and math. The extent to which EAL pupils make progress is evident in several discussions we had with an assistant headteacher (Inclusion), various teachers, teaching assistants, learning mentors, and the leadership team in one case study school. The above examples of excellent school practices demonstrate the clear impact that focused help has on boosting success.

Overall, our interviews and observations in this school demonstrate teachers' knowledge and understanding of EAL pedagogy and strategies. We noted that EAL teaching principles inform classroom pedagogy and are incorporated into lessons. These consist of speaking frames, discussion partners, sentence openers, cooperative working techniques, etc.

In addition to advising students on how to go through the English language learning stages and stressing the importance of differentiating between SEN and EAL needs, schools also closely monitor and analyse each student's performance to identify any challenges. When there is cause for concern, a first language assessment is conducted using materials from the mother tongue, and interpreters are hired for meetings and assessments with external agencies. This shows that there are established procedures to distinguish between needs associated with special education needs and those arising from learning English as a second language and how this influences the selection of services.

The data analysis at the school guided the work of the EAL teachers in all the schools. Using EAL data, the EAL instructor attended planning meetings and determined new vocabulary and areas of difficulty for EAL students in the focus classes. One coordinator 'located objects for the teacher to use when introducing the story' and 'identified unfamiliar vocabulary for the new story, Traction Man.' In order to advance students from Stage 2 to Stage D of the LA Stages of English fluency, she also determined the language requirements of the class and established language targets. Throughout the lessons, these language targets were discussed with all staff members, class teachers, and students. The EAL coordinators' and teachers' methods of operation had been embedded throughout. This way of working patterns by EAL teachers and coordinators had become ingrained across the schools and shared as good practice with other schools. Our observation of classroom teaching also shows that in the afternoon, EAL teachers often worked with new arrivals in small groups of no more than three, especially those at an early stage of learning English.

Targeted support from EAL support staff

An important factor in the educational achievement of students with EAL in schools was adult support. All EAL support staff received the teacher's specific training in routine practices and specific interventions to raise the achievement of pupils. These include encouraging children to use their first language, talking with partners, pre-teaching specific concepts, and then applying these techniques across the curriculum. One other good practice is that teachers and support staff plan and deliver lessons together. The teacher led the lesson. The support staff modelled the English language for pupils using visuals. They supported the pupils with EAL in drama activities, using activities such as hot seating.

Pupils might move quite quickly from Stage A, being new to English, to Early Acquisition (Stage B), becoming familiar with English. However, the evidence shows that they often needed additional support to develop a more demanding language for learning to operate successfully in written activities. In one instance, a teacher and teaching assistant were talking about how Stage A students lacked confidence in class discussions but were 'chatty' on the playground. Teachers and support staff planned together a series of short, regular slots centred on group work for four pupils using pictures. This talk is supported by adult modelling, sentence starters, and then supported writing. The teachers and the staff encouraged pupils to use this learning in the classroom context.

Similarly, teaching assistants led a 'Talking Maths' programme, which developed the use and understanding of language in mathematics and was closely linked to class work when pupils were supported to use their learning in a whole class setting. Small groups of EAL students with grammatical problems received assistance from teaching assistants. Sessions are focused on what children might need in their whole class sessions. Teaching assistants also monitored and recorded pupils' progress to show how group work developed pupils' oral confidence.

Key adults, often teaching assistants, who were described as 'buddies,' were assigned to newly arrived pupils who did not know English, especially when they shared the same language. In one school, brand-new students were frequently handed a set of visual cue keys to help them communicate during their initial days there. 'The magic words, please, thank you, hello, I'm sorry,' was how one young child put it. In addition to teaching their mother tongue as a foreign language, many teaching assistants also led language clubs and offered interpretation services when required. The Spanish TA served newcomers with EAL needs, taught Spanish as a Modern Foreign Language to Year 3, and offered Spanish after-school clubs twice a week.

Effective use of assessment data for monitoring EAL pupils

The use and analysis of EAL data was one of the good practices used by schools to raise achievement and narrow the gaps. There is strong evidence that individual teachers within the classroom used data to:

- inform teaching and learning, including lesson planning;
- inform targets for students by gender and ethnic groups;
- arrange groupings for teaching and learning; and
- track the progress of pupils and set high expectations.

As part of the research, we asked the question, 'How effective is the school in using EAL data for improving the quality of teaching and learning?' To what extent is the English proficiency assessment data used for tracking the progress of pupils with EAL to identify support needs and target interventions? The teacher interviewed responded to the questions as follows:

> The school has a good system for assessing and mapping the progress of pupils with EAL at individual and group levels. Gender, English proficiency, and ethnicity are taken into consideration while analysing a large amount of data on National Curriculum levels and English proficiency. It is used by the school to determine who requires support and which EAL students are underachieving.
>
> *(Deputy Headteacher, School C)*

> Targeted interventions can be initiated via the school assessment monitoring system by identifying students who meet certain thresholds. Grades for the GCSE or National Curriculum levels are tied to the points that teachers use to track students' progress. It is helpful to have conversations with parents about the tracking spreadsheet, which is simple to understand and uses the colours red, amber, and green to represent 'actual' versus 'expected' levels of growth and attainment.
>
> *(Manager of Data, School H)*

> Ensuring that no student with English as an Additional Language (EAL) falls behind in their studies is a top priority. Students with EAL who perform below expectations or are in danger of falling behind are promptly identified, and their unique requirements are addressed thanks to thorough monitoring and tracking. The LA levels of fluency in English are meticulously used to evaluate each student to make sure they are receiving the right support and moving forward as needed.
>
> *(School H's Head of the EAL Department)*

Similar findings in other case study schools were also supported by this research, which also showed that the schools had well-developed, efficient student tracking and monitoring information systems. Every teacher had student monitoring papers that listed the students' favourite topics, prior school, and sources of support. Specifically, the EAL Department's sheet contained comprehensive background information to monitor each student's progress, including date of birth, place of birth, arrival date in the UK, ethnic background, home language, English proficiency level, date of admission, attendance rate, eligibility for FSMs, SEN stage, mobility rate, and years in school.

Overall, the information gathered from our case studies, interviews, and observations revealed that teachers in these schools effectively use data to assess the quality of their instruction and to pinpoint and support children in differentiated learning groups. When it comes to tracking the success of specific groups, such as boys, pupils with SEN, those receiving FSM, or those learning English as a second language, the schools are especially 'forensic.' The school implemented interventions to address concerns identified by data analysis. These included one-on-one and additional support, as well as modifications to the differentiated or personalised teaching programme to better suit the requirements of students with EAL. Students with EAL advance quickly and accomplish.

Conclusions

This chapter examined the achievement pattern of EAL and the success factors behind their achievement in schools. The main finding from the empirical data revealed that EAL pupils overall do not perform as well as their non-EAL peers in English schooling because of language barriers. EAL pupils who are not fluent in English are underachieving, and their performance is significantly below the national average. The empirical evidence shows that there is a wide variation in performance and the achievement gap between EAL pupils who are not fluent in English and monolingual pupils.

The analysis by language spoken at home revealed that Black African language groups, Somali, Lingala, Ibo, and Krio speakers were the lowest-achieving groups, while Yoruba, Amharic, Twi-Fante, Tigrinya, and English-speaking Black African pupils achieved above the national average and their peers. There is a large variation in performance for White and other ethnic groups, depending on the languages spoken. The highest-achieving groups were European language speakers of Polish, Italian, and Albanian, who all outperformed pupils who had English as a first language. This contrasts with Spanish, French, and Portuguese-speaking pupils, where far fewer in these groups achieved the expected standard.

Analysis of the GCSE attainment data by proficiency in English stages showed that no child at Stages A and B (New to English and Early Acquisition) achieved grades 4 to 9 in English and Maths, compared to 43% at Stage C (Developing Competency), 62% at Stage D (Competent), and 67% at Stage E (Fluent). As a group, more EAL pupils who are competent or fluent in English performed better than did English first language speakers. Similar evidence also emerged from the analysis of KS2 results by stages of English proficiency, suggesting that there is a strong relationship between stages of proficiency in English and attainment.

The findings also confirm that English language proficiency is a major factor influencing the performance of pupils with EAL, both at KS2 and GCSE. The empirical evidence also suggests that EAL pupils in the early stages of English proficiency performed at low levels, while the achievement of EAL pupils who were fully fluent in English was better than that of White British, for whom English is a mother tongue. The results suggest that the percentage of pupils attaining expected outcomes at KS2 and GCSE increased as the stage of proficiency in English improved.

One of the key success factors in the case study schools in closing the achievement gap is providing effective, targeted support to improve EAL pupils' language skills to access the national curriculum. In these schools, teaching and learning were also of high quality and informed by assessment, and the schools provided effective, targeted support for EAL pupils at whatever stage of English proficiency. The level of expertise within the schools to support pupils with EAL was very good. The EAL coordinators, teachers, and staff work as a team to support EAL pupils. All staff were also well aware of the needs of those learners who speak English as an Additional Language. Consequently, the EAL pupils' needs were met in lessons, and targets for their literacy needs were set regularly. These learners made very good progress during their time at school. The schools also use well-known, proven good practices in teaching pupils with EAL, including oracy in talk in the classroom, first language, active and collaborative learning in small groups, and partnership teaching.

There is evidence that the use of data for school improvement was also a strength of the schools. Each school also focused on tracking and monitoring EAL pupils' progress and achievement throughout their school life and collected test and assessment data, followed by background data. The data was used to track EAL performance and set challenging targets to close the achievement gap for EAL pupils.

We would argue that accurate and reliable disaggregated ethnic and language data are important to address educational inequalities. The recommendations from these findings are that data on language spoken at home and EAL English proficiency need to be collected to monitor the performance of all groups, identify groups that are underachieving, and inform teaching and learning in multicultural classrooms. Teachers need to assess EAL pupils using EAL proficiency stages to monitor EAL pupils' progress and attainment to inform teaching and learning, track pupils' performance and progress, identify underachieving groups, and target individual support appropriately for those at risk of falling behind.

References

Demie, F. (2019) English language proficiency and attainment of EAL (English as a second language) pupils in England. *Journal of Multilingual and Multicultural Development* 39(7): 641–653.

Demie, F. (2017a) *English as an Additional Language: Good Practice to Raise Achievement in Schools*. London: Lambeth Research and Statistics Unit.

Demie, F. (2017b) English as an Additional Language and Attainment in Primary Schools in England. *Journal of Multilingual and Multicultural Development*. Doi: 10.1080/01434632.2017.1348508

Demie, F. (2015) Language Diversity and Attainment in Schools: Implication for Policy and Practice. *Race Ethnicity and Education* 18(5): 723–737. Doi: 10.1080/13613324.2014.946493

Demie, F. (2016) EAL Stages of Proficiency: The Implication for National Data Collection. *EAL Journal, NALDIC*, 1(1), autumn.

Demie, F. (2013) English as an Additional Language: How long does it take to acquire English Fluency? *Language and Education*, 27(1): 59–69.

Demie, F. & Strand, S. (2006) English Language Acquisition and Educational Attainment at the End of Secondary School. *Educational Studies* 32(2): 215–231.

DfE. (2016) *National tables: SFR47/2016- Characteristics Summary*. Available at: https://www.gov.uk/government/statistics/national-curriculum-assessments-key-stage-2-2016-revised

DfE. (2020) *English proficiency of pupils with English as an additional language*. Ad Hoc Notice February 2020. Available at: https://www.gov.uk/government/publications/english-proficiency-pupils-with-english-as-additional-language

DfE (2023) *School Census 2023*. London: Départment foe Education.

Strand, S., Malmberg, L. & Hall, J. (2015) *English as an Additional Language (EAL) and Educational Achievement in England: An Analysis of the National Pupil Database*. London: Educational Endowment Fund. Available at: https://educationendowmentfoundation.org.uk/uploads/pdf/EAL_and_educational_achievement2.pdf

PART III

Good Practice in Parental Engagement, Use of Inclusive Curriculum, and School Exclusions

7
THE EXPERIENCE OF PARENTAL ENGAGEMENT

Teachers, Headteachers, Parents, and Pupils View

Introduction

One of the success factors of the schools is their good link with the community they serve and their good practice in engaging parents. Drawing on teachers' and headteachers, parents, and pupils' views on partnership with parents, this chapter explores the success factors behind raising the achievement of ethnic minority pupils in schools, particularly those of Black Caribbean and Black African, through effective use of parental engagement. It presents some of the major findings reported in local publications over the last 25 years (see Demie 2005, 2017; Demie and McLean, 2015, 2016a,b, 2017a, b; Demie 2023), which show the positive impact of parental engagement.

Considerable attention has been devoted to the underachievement of Black pupils in British schools and the role of parents. The main findings from previous research confirm that they are less likely than children of other backgrounds to achieve their full potential at school (Gillborn and Gipps, 1996; Gillborn and Mirza, 2000; Demie, 2001) and parental engagement in schools also plays a key role in closing the achievement gap in successful schools (Demie, 2019; Ofsted, 2002a, b).

International research has also shown that parental engagement has a positive impact on many indicators of student achievement. There is strong consensus that 'positive parental engagement can and does significantly influence student academic attainment (Lambert et al., 2022; Hornby and Blackwell, 2018; Jeynes, 2012, 2007, 2005, 2003).

Teachers and headteachers' views about partnerships with parents

Relationships with parents are of paramount importance, and there is evidence of a partnership between the schools and parents based on the case study schools and the school survey evidence. The schools encouraged and valued the active involvement of parents in their children's education, and communication between school and parents is a major strength. Schools sought imaginative ways to break down barriers, make parents welcome, and respond to parents' needs. The staff shared information with parents on achievement and development and disciplinary issues and established a high level of trust. The schools saw themselves as part of a community. Parents were overwhelmingly supportive of the school and appreciated what it did to provide an environment for learning. They applauded the schools' efforts to guide their children and give them a firm grounding, both academically and socially. They felt that each child was valued on their terms and encouraged to achieve their very best. One headteacher of the case study 'School A' said,

> child is held in higher regard with comparisons made one to another. Each child is recognised as an individual. The key is confidence.

Another commented,

> The school offers a nurturing, caring environment. Children are taught they can succeed regardless of their level without being singled out as better.

The school headteacher meets regularly with parents, whom they regard as key partners in the endeavour. He clearly stated:

> I want the parents of all pupils to feel we value and care for their children. Every Monday morning, when I meet with parents, I make an effort to make it clear. I try to make it clear that the school stands for fairness and high expectations for all.

Another headteacher of 'School B' said:

> Parental involvement in schools and child support are highly encouraged. Our working premise is that all parents desire the best for their kids. We work to create plans to keep that going. We make an effort to highlight the importance of flexibility in the provision of help. There are situations when it makes more sense for a youngster to read to their parents before school in the morning rather than at night when everyone is stressed. We attempt to take the initiative and pick up the slack.

The classroom teachers also recognised the importance of a positive dialogue with parents to help raise the achievement of Black and other ethnic minority pupils. A classroom teacher in a case study, 'School B,' said in the interview:

> The parents knew the schools were worried when pupils were underachieving, but they emphasised that something could and would be done. Individual logs of pupils' work and behaviour detailing the good and the disappointing were kept and shown to parents by pupils. I thought hard about the comments I made, as a stray negative comment could be destructive. Particularly good pieces of work were also copied so the children could take them home and keep them at home. Regular contact on the phone proved to be much better than sending notes. We could have just dwelt on our calls on the negative but decided instead to always try discussing positive developments.

Parental support was hard-won; however, when the school announced its plan to set up specific sessions for groups of five pupils to work with an external mentor, the headteacher of 'School B' reported:

> We had a meeting with the parents to discuss the proposal about the strategy that involved external intervention. After a lot of discussion, the parents agreed to let the sessions proceed. In the event, the group performed better in national tests than had been predicted and made a smoother transfer to secondary schools than had at one time been anticipated. Parents understood the bonus of having someone who could help their children. The mentoring offered to the pupils helped them prepare for and then cope with the transition to secondary school. We think that the work we conducted had an impact. The learning mentor made regular visits to secondary schools. He spoke with the staff and the pupils concerned. All the pupils are reported to have welcomed such continuing contact in the early stages of their transfer.

These successful schools take the time to listen to parents and understand their aspirations for their children. They recognise that parents care deeply about their children's education and want to know about their progress, the curriculum, and homework. They want information about what they can do to help. One positive response from the case study 'School B' is summarised by its head teacher:

> Listening to all parents is very important. We try to understand their aspirations for their children. We worked together, and I have learned the power of constant dialogue. Communication with parents, particularly by phone, is important.

The schools listened to and learned from pupils and their parents and tried to see things from the student's point of view. The schools regarded liaison with parents and the community as vital to their drive to raise standards.

Another case study, 'School V,' incorporates the Children's Centre and offers a range of services that support families through childcare, adult learning, parenting programmes, and helping to bring a range of service providers into the community. The school makes extraordinary efforts to enable parents to support their children's learning. This is especially important as most of the parents are unfamiliar with the British education system. The school understands that simply passing information to parents without enabling them to understand what it means in practice is unhelpful. The school has overcome this by inviting parents to come into the school and see first-hand how a phonics lesson is taught to groups of children in Years 1 and 2. They can see the materials used and can ask questions. Many ask to buy the resources they see being used in the lesson so they can use them at home. Similar demonstration lessons in mathematics are offered to parents. The Key Stage 1 coordinator told us, 'It is very powerful for parents to see a lesson. Staff keep encouraging parents to attend the workshops; we keep reminding them to come.'

This school also takes a whole-school approach to engaging parents and adopts an outward-facing strategy that uses information and expertise from others. The EYFS/KS1 phase leader explained the lengths the school goes to make sure that every parent is engaged:

> We had a lot programme for me to be more available to meet with parents. In the case of one PPG pupil who only sees her dad at weekends and can't come to school, I email him to make sure all the family members are engaged. Last year, the first year, we did everything possible to get parents into school.

Parents and carers in the case study 'School V' are pleased with how well the headteacher and staff know their children. This mirrors the teachers' view that knowing each child and building firm foundations for the relationship with home is key to the school's success. The pupils feel secure and valued, and so they grow academically and socially in a warm family atmosphere in which each is known for their characteristics. This generates great confidence in the pupils when they face new experiences, and it enables the school to rapidly pinpoint resources and actions to meet their needs. A 'parents' forum' has long been established to facilitate listening to and responding to the parents' views. It meets every half-term as a platform for parents to suggest improvements at the school, and staff take their views seriously.

A parent governor in the school recalled when the school was not doing well:

Parents had stopped believing in the place; it was not a school of choice. When the new management took over, a lot of teachers left and went on to describe the challenge the new leadership faced and how the new headteacher began to transform the school.

Upon assuming leadership, the headteacher attended to the details. It was evident from the beginning that she had a vision for the direction she wanted the institution to go. She also introduced the concept of instructors learning from other teachers and reward systems that inspired the kids to work hard, which in turn inspired the teachers to work even harder. She was quite active. She also wanted the parents to be part of the process. She returned for the following meeting and shared with them how she had addressed the issues they had raised. With parental participation, things began to improve little by little.

Ofsted inspectors affirmed the successful partnership that the school had developed with parents:

> Engagement with parents and carers is very effective. Almost all who responded to the questionnaire say that the school helps them support their children's learning. They attend music and mathematics workshops, parents' forums, and consultation days. Parents also effectively contribute to the curriculum provision of the school.

In another two case study schools, parental engagement with the school is outstanding, but these positive relationships did not happen overnight. It took perseverance and a genuine commitment to listen to parental concerns and address them.

One of the case studies, 'School G,' is noted to have a poor reputation in the community, and parents who were hostile and occasionally violent towards the staff have also made a huge improvement of the appointment with the headteacher, who worked hard with parental engagement. Ofsted judged relationships with parents to be 'poor.' The newly appointed headteacher (the executive headteacher, as he is now) put in place effective strategies to improve attendance and punctuality and to involve parents and the community in the process. He and his deputy would walk around the local streets before school started, encouraging parents and children to get into school before the morning bell rang. They also targeted local shops, enlisting the support of shopkeepers by asking them not to serve children if they were late for school. To encourage parents into the school and make them feel welcome, he provided a designated 'parents' room' with comfortable chairs. Parents were invited in for coffee mornings to meet the headteacher and hear what his plans were for the children. He urged them to attend school rallies and musical performances. The parents' confidence increased, and the school's reputation began to improve. It took genuine commitment and perseverance by the school leadership to make it happen. The headteacher of 'School G' reflected:

> We don't believe it is hard to reach parents in this school. How we engage with parents underpins pupil achievement and our ethos, which values all people regardless of their background. I have to model these messages as a school leader, respecting each other, and judging individuals as individuals. I have made a deliberate and conscious effort to form a relationship with these parents. I am not frightened to talk about issues; none of my staff hide behind people; it's important to get everything out on the table. We arrange a flexible time for parents. If people are unable to come, we make another arrangement with the help of the class. Parents are contacted regularly by the TA and teachers as required. If that doesn't work, the office will ring. I will also write a letter to my parents when needed. We do all we can to get the parents in.

In the case study, 'School V,' numeracy and literacy workshops are run with targeted groups of pupils in school to make games that they take home to play with their parents. This school is very good at engaging with parents. Curriculum evenings are also held annually for all-year groups with the parents, not the children. There are also parent-teacher consultation meetings and academic tutoring days. The headteacher said:

> We talk to parents about feeding their children properly, regular sleeping habits, and tips to support them with homework. We explore the target system with mid-term monitoring. We talk to them like we do the girls, about aspirations and the job market.

Another case study, 'School R,' noted for strong parents' involvement, found many parents were educated abroad and don't know much about the British system; the school has to work hard to keep them informed. It regularly surveys parents to find out their preferred means of communication and is constantly looking to improve matters.

> The weekly newsletter breaks down walls between home and school. We tell parents about school and local events. We consult with parents about, for example, the behaviour policy. We also survey parents regularly and get 95 percent feedback sometimes – there's a very strong sense of parental involvement. We invite parents in a lot. For instance, when they are new to the school, we have a Year 7 Mass for parents to bring them into our community. The parents are on board with us. They want their kids to do well. They appreciate that we are spending the extra time with them.
> *(Headteacher)*

The school does communicate successfully with parents about ways in which they can support their children. Consequently, the students told us that their parents were interested and fully involved in their learning at home.

The curriculum in this school reflects the diverse backgrounds of the students, and the parents contribute meaningfully by attending and taking part in the many religious and cultural celebrations. An Ofsted inspection quoted a parent:

> Choosing the school is one of the best decisions we have made as parents. We have never regretted it for a moment. This comment reflects the high level of parental support that exists for this popular and oversubscribed school. Harmonious relationships, excellent behaviour, and a strong desire to learn are features that make this an outstanding school where girls feel very happy and safe. They enjoy school because they know they are taught well and are supported to do their best.
>
> *(Ofsted)*

This school is rightly proud of its positive relationships with parents and carers. The school is committed to working closely with families so that their children can succeed in school.

> Parents are brought into the school to make the school the heart of the community. The purpose of their continuing education is threefold: to raise their aspirations, to support them to support their children, and to bring the community together.
>
> *(Community Education Coordinator)*

The school also works together with the Community Resource Centre and the nearest college, offering courses in English for speakers of other languages (ESOL), information and communications technology (ICT), advanced ICT, digital photography, and mathematics. The new school building provides an impressive venue for this Saturday's programme. Through business and enterprise specialisation, the school is launching a community project available to 60 participants. It will bring together a range of ethnicities, including Portuguese and Somali. Together, they will decide on their focus, learn how to get funding, and learn about working together. The school facilitates people getting into work as best it can. Parents and members of the local community who aspire to work in a school have the opportunity to come in for 12 weeks to shadow teachers and receive help with their CVs.

> We support parents and learning mentors to study for foundation degrees. We also have an international link with a school in Sierra Leone, we run a World Family Day, and we have Aids Awareness, Rights, and Responsibilities.
>
> *(Community Education Coordinator)*

The executive headteacher at another case study, 'School A,' described the school's work with parents to support the achievement of pupils as follows:

> There is a lot of engagement with parents. We do home visits: the inclusion manager and teacher, or teacher and TA, would meet with the family. We try to get children into reception within the first two weeks of the autumn term. The first week is home visits, and the second week, they enter on a staggered basis. The EY lead runs coffee mornings, speech and language sessions, or how to help your child with homework.
>
> Many parents bring in their difficulties, and they are increasing, for example, mental health, housing issues, domestic abuse – things they aren't coping with on their own. They need guidance on where to go for support. The inclusion manager is doing more to signpost them. She is now doing more about EAL courses, housing benefits, etc.

The school encourages and values the active involvement of parents in their children's education, and communication is a major strength. It has created imaginative ways to break down barriers, make parents feel welcome, and respond to their needs. It shares with parents information on their children's achievement and development as well as issues of discipline. The school's staff see themselves as part of a community. Parents are overwhelmingly supportive and know what the school does to provide an environment for learning. They appreciate the school's efforts to guide their children and give them both academic and social grounding. Parents feel that each child is valued on their own terms, and although children might perceive differences in standards, the school encourages them to do the best for themselves. Ofsted noted:

> One parent wrote that, "I am extremely grateful for all the encouragement, care, and support my daughter gets." Care, guidance, and support are outstanding.

Parents and carers are encouraged to be actively involved in their children's education, especially their homework. The school exemplifies its commitment by giving parents progress reports and having discussions with teachers on academic consultative evenings. Families are invited to share in those glorious moments when their children are singing, acting, playing an instrument, or receiving an award. These events celebrate the pupils' talents.

The schools engaged parents in a range of creative ways. They arranged meetings at convenient times for parents, implemented low-cost means of bringing home learning into school and school learning into the home, held international evenings to which parents brought food from their country of origin, and involved parents who were already engaged with the school as ambassadors for others in the community. Home visits by teachers or other staff are particularly important in building home-school links, and they offer staff insight into the child's background. The headteacher of the case studies, 'School A,' said:

> Members of staff make home visits, and then the parents and children are invited to visit the classroom before they start school. I do not know what the family story is, but there is a single parent; I have not seen Dad. The visit revealed a chaotic home. The staff were ushered up to a bedroom, and the discussion about the child took place sitting on a bed.

Parents view on the partnership with schools

The Black African parents who were interviewed valued education highly. Some have themselves received a good education and gained professional qualifications, although their jobs in the UK may not fully reflect this. The schools recognise that parents, even if they have low-status jobs, can build and support a culture of achievement at home to support their children's education. Many parents are themselves continuing their studies. One said,

> My child's father is Nigerian, and he is very focused on learning. He never says, "I haven't got anything to do." He is always improving his skill set. This is an African thing; it is like that in Jamaica too.

All the Black African parents interviewed in the case study 'School R' see a good education as the key to their children's future success:

> Africans invest in education because we need it. We do not have the same opportunities as these children back home. Education makes a way for you.
>
> *(Parent 1)*

> Education is important and key to getting a good job and salary. It is always good to push your children as much as you can to get a good education.
>
> *(Parent 2)*

> Behind many of the Black African students' achievements, you will find some of the most dedicated parents supporting their children to ensure their children are high achievers. It is not always the school you go to; it's how strong the parental support network is behind you.
>
> *(parent 3)*

These attitudes are the driving force behind the parents' support of their children and schools, and the teachers welcome the shared values and aspirations. A teacher in one case study, 'School C,' said:

> I like to teach at this school. I have the support of African parents, and they will take any advice I give them about their children's education. African parents already have this sense of the importance of education; we can work together. We know we have their backing, so there are no behaviour issues to be resolved.
>
> *(Teacher)*

Parents also have strong views on the importance of respect for teachers' authority. One parent told us that in Africa,

> The teacher is an authority figure in the classroom. There is a good tradition of respecting teachers. Students are standing up to greet the teacher at the start of the lessons. Pupils should respect the authority of the teacher.

When asked what parents expect their children to do at school, one parent replied,

> Hard work, respect, discipline, listening to the teacher, working together. What you feed them at home is what they bring to school; this is reinforced at school.

In short, they support the authority of teachers. A teacher with twenty years of experience in the case study 'School B' comments:

> Parents are respectful of teachers and adhere to their professionalism. Children's achievement is greatly influenced by their desire to discover how they might contribute. It is supported by results.

One of the most frequent ways in which parents support teachers and their children is by ensuring that they do their homework. At primary age, parents often help children with their homework. One said,

> I will meet teachers at the end of the day to ask for ideas about homework.

In the case study of secondary 'School D,' parents check homework diaries and follow up on comments made by teachers, ensuring that work is completed. The parent attendance rate is generally very high because parents value the opportunity to discuss their child's progress with teachers. In the school, teachers share performance data with parents and include them in discussions about target settings. Thus, parents feel well informed about the progress of their children, and children feel that parents know of their success. A Year 9 pupil at a school where tutors and teachers regularly telephone parents said,

> When I do well, they tell my parents. This reflects on me at home.

A Year 13 student at the same school commented on the parents' and teachers' efforts:

> Parents give strong motivation from day one... Our head of year pushes us – he's really behind a lot of students' success.

All the case study schools have strong links with their students' parents and communities. Each school's headteacher and senior management team have devoted substantial resources, time, and commitment to this end. These schools see parents' engagement as central to the school and consequently receive good support from the parents. Staff, in turn, support the parents. Partnership with parents is a key component of a school's success. Staff involve parents early in any lapses in behaviour, and the parents appreciate the school's commitment to keeping them informed. Two Black African parents confirmed this:

- Parent A is the father of a girl in Year 9. He is generally supportive of the school, although it was not his first choice, but he is supplementing his daughter's education with a home tutor. He also calls on his extended family. His eldest son is a graduate and is expected to help. The family takes regular trips home to Nigeria to maintain traditions and remind their children that they should fulfil their potential.
- Parent B is the father of three daughters, two of whom have already left the school. The third is in Year 10. He is very pleased with the work the school is doing for his children. He believes the school shares his expectations of his daughter and is respectful of his Sierra Leonean culture. Respect and responsibility are the cornerstones of the parenting philosophy he conveys to his daughters. However, he is of the view that sanctions should be applied if his daughters step out of order'; then it is a case of 'tough love.'

Both of these fathers feel that key features contributing to African achievement are maintaining African traditions at home and letting children know they are obligated to maximise the opportunities available in school. In the classroom, they are seeking to 'blend with the best of British society.'

They consciously protect their daughters from, as they perceive them, the worst, more permissive, anti-education elements. They argue that early intervention is essential to getting students back on track. Interestingly, both of these men are keen to continue their studies as well, which models a family commitment to education as a transformational tool.

The headteacher of another case study, 'School H,' is an active churchgoing parent herself and makes common cause with other Black parents trying to enable their children to achieve their potential. Schools know their parents well; leadership has encouraged and promoted the involvement of these parents, who are passionate about church-school education. Most of the students have two parents at home, and both parents, but especially the fathers, attend parents' evenings. Parents have high aspirations, and their first statement is often their first statement when children start school: they hope that their child can go to university after they finish school.

The school has a parent engagement programme as a key strategy to raise achievement. For example, one school used external consultants to teach study skills to Years 7 and 8 during the school day and offered it as a masterclass for parents after school too. The strong faith background of families is recognised and supported, and schools conform to African notions of a church school with its formality and sense of pride. The formality of school processes reflects notions of respect and courtesy towards teachers and between students; it includes smart uniforms, lining up before entry to lessons, formal introductions, and prayers before each lesson starts. This school's ethos, its niche market, is communicated and endorsed by Black African parents.

Parents' evenings at the beginning of the academic year encourage students and parents to review and evaluate the year that has passed and renew their commitment to targets for the coming year, echoing the symbolic ritual of renewal. Lots of social evenings are held at which parents and staff can interact. When the parent–school relationship does not work, it tends to be because the parent has not responded to the invitation to be part of the community and is too distant from key processes and interventions. But recovery is always available. The headteacher thanks parents for their support in writing when the school does well.

Overall, the headteacher's, teachers, and parents' comments on the education of Black African children confirm that the schools are making significant inroads in engaging Black African parents and other parents. Such possibilities and opportunities are reinforced by the displays in corridors and classrooms. The case study schools also make constant efforts to maintain good motivation and have good holistic and pastoral systems to support students and their families. The parent–school partnership is of great importance in establishing and maintaining high standards for Black African students. What makes this partnership so strong in counteracting 'street culture' is that parents, teachers, and students share the same aspirations and the same values.

The Black Caribbean parents interviewed also gave their stories about the partnership with schools. The evidence from our observation and research shows that Black Caribbean parents face numerous barriers to engagement, including costs, time, and transport. Some of them have low levels of literacy and numeracy and lack confidence in supporting their children's learning or engaging with the school. However, these schools place a premium on knowing all the students as individuals. If you ask students why their schools are so good, they will commonly reply, 'Because teachers care.'

Some students find it difficult to study at home, and their parents are not in a position to support them, so these schools invest additional time in teaching and learning. Staff are generous with their time, typically running sessions at lunchtime, after school, during weekends, and on their holidays. A headteacher said, 'It's a relentless struggle.' These students receive a good deal of individual help and attention. This reinforces the positive relationships that exist between students and staff because students see that teachers 'care.'

The staff of the LA schools were aware that they had to draw parents in for positive reasons and recognised that many had had negative experiences at school themselves. We asked what the key factor was in the successful and positive relationships that exist between staff and parents in your school between Black Caribbean parents and schools. A teacher in 'school A' replied:

> The personal touch is what makes it. Parents are invited; there is a partnership ethos. It's very warm. I know some of the parents by their first names. I care about their offspring as if they were my own, and then they feel it. Building trust is important; parents appreciate someone who understands children.

The deputy headteacher said:

> Our relationships with parents are key. If you have built good relationships, you are halfway there with the young people. If parents are on board with a plan of action, you will have success. We have a lot of young parents in our school. A majority would say that they can relate better to Black staff. A lot of parents take on what their parents went through. It pours down through generations. Many Black Caribbean students do perceive White authority figures negatively; their perception is a hybrid of rage and anxiety over injustice.

Schools that are committed to improving the academic performance of Black Caribbean students will go above and beyond to build a rapport based on trust with the parents.

A group of parents from the case study 'School C' reflected on the excellent links the school has made with parents and the local community over the years:

> My grandma and granddad came here in the 1950s from Jamaica. My daughter struggled with reading, but she gets more attention with phonics, and she gets taken out to focus in a small group.
>
> As the parent of a child with ADHD and anger problems, the school supports him by getting someone in every other week. I find it helpful to get him one-on-one. I went to my GP for help. He used to go to another local school before he joined the school.

A parent governor said:

> The school has a "diversity month" where pupils look at their family trees. There is also Black History Month. In Year 5, someone came in to do a drama about Caribbean history, and there were visits from the Black Cultural Archives. Parents come in to talk to the children about their heroes during Black History Month. In Year 3, the children got to dress up as their heroes. There are African arts and cultural displays everywhere in the school.

When we asked what the consequence would be if the school did not engage effectively with Black Caribbean parents, the headteacher of 'School A' responded:

> It would be them and us. It's a defense. You have to break down the barriers. In my previous school, we went about things the wrong way; we were on the phone with the parents the whole time about all the wrong things. Communication was poor. You have got to be brave if you do it little by little and have lots of positive things to say about children too, rather than just focussing on when the child is naughty.

Another case study, 'School G,' is also adept at engaging parents. One of the success factors of the school is its good links with the community it serves and its good practice in developing partnerships with parents. Researchers held a focus group discussion with the parents, who originally came from Poland and Somalia. The Polish parent we interviewed felt her children's education was of great importance; she was ambitious for her sons and daughters:

> Education is very important for us. I have completed university, and my husband also finished university. We both finished university in Poland but we did not speak when I came to England. The school worked closely with

parents, and they supported me in my English language development and socially. The school employed a Polish teaching assistant, and she helped Polish children and families with translation and settled in the area.

The Somali parent we interviewed in the case study school was also positive about the school and spoke warmly of the help given to Somali children and parents:

> Somali parents value education highly, and they have high expectations of their children and teachers, and the school meets their needs.

The school places a high value on children's culture and home language, and the pupils benefit from its active partnership with their parents and its support of their families.

Parents appreciated the work of all the staff at the school. They recognised the value of the focussed small groups that children across the ability range have access to. One parent observed, 'In the case of my child, she needed special needs support, which she got. The special needs staff supported her. They built up her confidence. They helped her to enjoy learning. They made it fun.' Another commented, 'The staff know the children and don't allow them to slip. The school reports on our children are very detailed. They know our children.'

The pupil's views on parental engagement

The pupils we interviewed in the case study schools also praised their schools' engagement and communication with parents and argued:

> Parents are invited to get feedback about our performance and to celebrate our achievement during award ceremonies.
> The school uses texts to send information to parents.
> They send parents information through leaflets and letters every time.
> They have prayer meetings for parents, and these are well attended and valued.
> Schools are good at sharing with parents about our achievements and progress.
> Our parents are confident to discuss and talk with teachers and headteachers.
> Parents see the school like a family.
> Our school is a community school and very inclusive.
> We are all like families.
> Parents value the school's stand against racism and high aspiration for all.

School is a multicultural school that values every culture, heritage, and religion.

The school is good at breaking up cultural differences and outstanding in community cohesion. They bring everyone together.

Celebration of cultural diversity

The case study schools are multicultural schools, where the diversity of ethnic origin, languages spoken, and cultural heritage brings real life to learning, values the cultural heritage of each child, and celebrates diversity through assemblies, the curriculum, International Day, International Links, and Black History Month.

Black History Month recognises and values inspirational individuals and events within the Black communities. It was introduced in the UK in 1987 and is celebrated annually. Every October, the schools explore different countries and celebrate a range of activities during and outside the school day. They organise heritage days, series of lessons, activities, and assemblies to focus on Black and minority achievement through the curriculum. In 'School O' headteacher's words:

> The school uses Black History Month to recognise and value the inspirational individuals and events that have shaped the Black generation. Throughout the month-long celebration of both the significant individuals from the past and the present who support and enhance our society, this takes precedence in the classroom.

A pupil at the case study 'School R' said that the school uses Black History Month as an opportunity to explore different countries and celebrate diversity:

> Every class studies a different country to give them a wealth of knowledge about the culture, the food, the language and people. Each class presents their country through an assembly – last year we learned about 12 countries, and this ingrains diversity in the children.

The events during Black History Month elicited praise from parents, teachers, and pupils. A parent governor observed:

> It helped our children to understand the Black history and heritage. Every culture and history are recognised and this is a great thing about this school.

Another case study, 'School O,' has an annual International Day for pupils, parents, and neighbours that celebrates cultures from across the globe at the school. In the words of the headteacher:

> All the colours, sights, and sounds of the world were brought to life at a buzzing International Day. The parents and pupils from different parts of Africa played colourful African dances and music in traditional dress from Ghana, Nigeria, Ethiopia, Somalia, and other African countries. A Scotsman played the bagpipes in traditional dress, while elsewhere a steel band played by pupils from the Caribbean world and there was African drumming by pupils from the African continent. Many parents and students performed traditional Portuguese dance and music.

Conclusions

Parental engagement is another important factor in raising achievement and closing the achievement gaps. Effective parental engagement sits at the heart of effective practice in schools. Black and ethnic minority parents in the case study schools value education highly. Parents at all schools expressed the need for their children to receive a good education while retaining their cultural identities. The teachers, headteachers, pupils, and parents interviewed highlighted that the support of parents and the engagement of the local community contributed to raising pupils' achievement levels in the case study schools. The case study evidence, the school survey, and the focus group research indicated that this was a particular strength of the case study schools. The engagement of parents enabled mutual trust and understanding to develop between the school and home and enabled the construction of a bridge between the schools and the local community. It also has a large and positive impact on children's learning. This is also supported by previous authoritative reviews of the evidence and research:

> Parental involvement in the form of 'at-home good parenting' has a significant positive effect on children's achievement and adjustment even after all other factors shaping attainment have been taken out of the equation. In the primary age range the impact caused by different levels of parental involvement is much bigger than differences associated with variations in the quality of schools. The scale of the impact is evident across all social classes and all ethnic groups.
>
> *(Desforges and Abouchaar 2003:4)*

Therefore, the recommendation from this study is that schools should make it a top priority to identify interventions that help parents become more active in their children's education, especially for those parents who don't participate much.

References

Demie, F. (2001) Ethnic and gender difference in educational achievement and implications for school improvement strategies. *Educational Research* 43(1): 91–106.

Demie, F. (2005) Achievement of Black Caribbean pupils: Good practice in Lambeth schools. *British Educational Research Journal* 31(4): 481–508.

Demie, F. (2017) *English as an Additional Language: Good Practice to Raise Achievement in Schools*. Lambeth LA: Lambeth School Research and Statistics Unit.

Demie, F. (2019) *Educational Inequality: Closing the gap*. London: UCL IOE Press, July. https://www.ucl-ioe-press.com/books/social-justice-equality-and-human-rights/educational-inequality/

Demie, F. (2023) *A School Survey of Barriers to Learning, Success Factors, And Effective Inclusive Curriculum That Contributed to Improving Black and Minority Ethnic (BAME) Pupils Attainment in Schools*. London: Lambeth Research and Statistics Unit.

Demie, F. & Mclean, C. (2015) *Narrowing the Achievement Gap: Good Practice in Schools*. London: Lambeth Research and Statistics Unit.

Demie, F. & Mclean, C. (2016a) Tackling disadvantage: what works in narrowing the achievement gap in schools. *Review of Education* 3(2): 138–174. https://doi.org/10.1002/rev3.30

Demie, F. & Mclean, C. (2016b) *What Works in School Improvement: Examples of Good Practice*. Lambeth LA: Lambeth Research and Statistics Unit.

Demie, F. & Mclean, C. (2017a) *Black Caribbean Underachievement in Schools in England*. Lambeth LA: Lambeth Research and Statistics Unit.

Demie, F. & Mclean, C. (2017b) *The Achievement of Black Caribbean Pupils: Good Practice*. London: Lambeth Research and Statistics Unit.

Desforges, C. & Abouchaar, A. (2003) *The Impact of Parental Involvement, Parental Support and Family Education on Pupil Achievement and Adjustment: A Literature Review*. London: Department of Education and Skills.

Gillborn, D. & Gipps, C. (1996) *Recent Research on the Achievement of Ethnic Minority Pupils*. London: OFSTED Reviews of Research, HMSO.

Gillborn, D. & Mirza, H.S. (2000) *Educational Inequality: Mapping Race and Class*. London: Office for Standards in Education.

Hornby, G. & Ian Blackwell, I. (2018) Barriers to parental involvement in education: an update. *Educational Review* 70(1): 109–119. DOI: 10.1080/00131911.2018.1388612

Jeynes, W. (2012) A meta-analysis of the efficacy of different types of parental involvement programmes for urban students. *Urban Education* 47(4): 706–742. https://doi.org/10.1177/0042085912445643

Jeynes, W.H. (2003) A meta-analysis: The effects of parental involvement on minority children's academic achievement. *Education & Urban Society* 35(2): 202–218. DOI:10.1177/0013124502239392. S2CID 145407192

Jeynes, W.H. (2005) A meta-analysis of the relation of parental involvement to urban elementary school student academic achievement. *Urban Education* 40(3): 237–269. https://doi.org/10.1177/0042085905274540

Jeynes, W.H. (2007) The relationship between parental involvement and urban secondary school student academic achievement: a meta-analysis. *Urban Education* 42(1): 82–110. https://doi.org/10.1177/0042085906293818

Lambert, M.C., Duppong Hurley, K., January, S.-A., & Huscroft D'Angelo, J. (2022) The role of parental involvement in narrowing the academic achievement gap for high school students with elevated emotional and behavioral risks. *Journal of Emotional and Behavioral Disorders* 30(1): 54–66. https://doi.org/10.1177/10634 266211020256

Ofsted. (2002a) *Achievement of Black Caribbean Pupils: Good Practice in Secondary Schools*. London: Office for Standards in Education, HMI 448.

Ofsted. (2002b) *Achievement of Black Caribbean Pupils: Good Practice in Primary Schools*. London: Office for Standards in Education, HMI 448. https://dera.ioe.ac.uk/id/eprint/10139/1/Achievement_of_black_caribbean_pupils_-_three_successful_primary_schools.pdf

8
INCLUSIVE CURRICULUM TO RAISE ACHIEVEMENT

Teachers and Headteachers' Perspectives

Introduction

Curriculum innovations are another success factor that makes a difference. This chapter explores the weaknesses of the current British curriculum and looks more in detail at the inclusive curriculum used to decolonise the curriculum in successful schools. Drawing on the views of headteachers, teachers, parents, governors, and students on Black and ethnic minority students' experiences with the British Curriculum, it looks to answer two key research questions: Why does curriculum diversity matter? What is the effective, inclusive curriculum that is used by schools to support Black and minority ethnic (BAME) pupils?

The first section looked at a literature review on why diversifying curriculum matters. The second section explores the evidence from case study schools in the effective inclusive curriculum to support BAME pupils. Section 3 provides evidence from school surveys about diversifying the curriculum. This is followed by Section 4, which discusses the key findings of the case study and the school survey. The final section considers recommendations and implications for policy, practice, and research.

Why does curriculum diversity matter?

This chapter explores the weaknesses of the current British curriculum. It looks more in detail at some of the good practices developed and used to decolonise the curriculum in successful London schools.

The need to diversify the British Curriculum has attracted great attention recently. There is a growing concern that students in the UK are not being

DOI: 10.4324/9781003499633-11

taught Black British History as part of the national curriculum, despite numerous findings demonstrating its importance (Demie 2019; Harris and Reynolds, 2018; Moncrieffe, 2018). The Macpherson (1999: 382) inquiry into the murder of Stephen Lawrence stated that:

> Consideration be given to the amendment of the National Curriculum aimed at valuing cultural diversity and preventing racism to better reflect the needs of a diverse society.

Unfortunately, national curriculum policymakers have continued to ignore the Macpherson (1999) recommendations by claiming that a national curriculum that covers British history is 'broad and balanced in aims and contents (Moncrieffe, 2022). This is not true. The National Curriculum is dominated by Eurocentric historical starting points (Moncrieffe, 2020), with a focus on 'Britain's settlement by Anglo-Saxons and Scots' and 'the Viking and Anglo-Saxon struggle for the Kingdom of England' (DfE, 2013:5). All evidence from research suggests that the English school curriculum focusses on British culture and ignores ethnic minorities in the curriculum (Demie and Mclean, 2017a; Moncrieffe, 2018, 2020). There has been increasing central government control over aspects of education since the Education Act of 1988, and the government has institutionalised a more restrictive curriculum (Harris, 2020:7). Students from minority backgrounds continue to face challenges in the schooling system concerning adequate representation, and their experiences are rarely reflected in the curriculum, while those from dominant sociocultural groups, that is, White and middle class, are often centralised and normalised in the school curriculum in England. The 'history curricula sideline in-depth examinations of Britain's imperial and colonial past, black histories, and the contribution of ethnic minorities to the making of modern Britain' (Stamou et al. 2020:1). At present, the evidence does not suggest that the BAME experience is used to enrich the curriculum in art, dance, music, geography, history, and technology or to foster a sense of pride in being Black in England (Demie 2019; Moncrieffe 2018, 2020).

The concern is that, despite various iterations of the national curriculum for history, little has changed, and BAME children are not receiving the quality of education they need to thrive in the English education system. The curriculum is restrictive, and there is no freedom for individual schools to innovate and interpret the curriculum as they wish. Despite this, teachers, school leaders, and BAME professionals have continued to champion the need to improve the existing curriculum by adding more BAME experience (see Leach et al. 2020). The lives of well-known BAME individuals in Britain, the accomplishments of ancient civilisations like Benin in West Africa and Cushitic and Merotic civilisation in North East Africa, the transatlantic slave trade and its abolition, the Windrush generation's history, pre-colonial Black presence in Britain, migration patterns, ethnic and cultural diversity in Britain, the beneficial contributions made by people of all ethnicities to Britain, the role played by the former British empire in both World Wars, Black History Month in the curriculum, Black Lives Matter, and the Civil Rights movement in the USA and abroad should all be covered (Demie 2019; Moncrieffe 2018, 2020).

These topics that engage and raise the aspiration of BAME pupils should be included in the national curriculum from Key Stage One in primary through to Key Stage Four when students take their GCSEs, and across subjects, including history, geography, citizenship, English, and PSHE (personal, social, health, and economic education). However, the government has rejected any review of the English curriculum at present (see Proctor 2020; Leach et al. 2020). The education minister also indicated that in the future, teachers could consider in the history curriculum 'the lives of Mary Seacole and Rosa Park; the achievements of early civilisations such as Benin in west Africa; and the transatlantic slave trade and its abolition' (see Proctor 2020:1). The limited evidence we have indicates that in many schools, the history curriculum is still largely White, male, and Anglocentric. The school curriculum 'reflects the values, perspectives, and experiences of the dominant ethnic group.' It does not add to the growing pride in being BAME students in multicultural Britain. Why should someone be interested in studying history when they don't see themselves represented?

I would argue in the chapter that improving the life chances of young people cannot and will not be achieved if the curriculum is not rigorous and inclusive to reflect modern Britain. There is a need to use an inclusive curriculum that reflects the community the school serves, which has a range of different backgrounds and differs by age, gender, class, ethnicity, and faith. They also bring with them a diverse set of learning styles, educational experiences, cultural capital, complex identities, and differing levels of confidence and self-esteem. An inclusive curriculum understands that this diversity is a key strength that provides learning opportunities for all our students and staff. Other researchers have called for diversity in the school workforce, highlighting the role of Black educators in multi-ethnic schools (Callender 1995; Demie 2019). There is research evidence that shows that in successful schools, the use of an inclusive curriculum is increasingly viewed as a key strategy for student engagement, raising aspiration, and addressing problems such as low attainment, boredom, and alienation of BAME pupils in the classroom (see Demie 2019; Marks 2000; Mortimore 1999).

We also know that one of the weaknesses of educational research in Britain today is that while a plethora of research exists on student achievement, there is very little research evidence on whether inclusive curriculum in schools makes a difference in closing the achievement gap and raising the aspiration of BAME pupils in schools. Research shows that closing the achievement gap between a number of BAME pupils and their peers is the highest challenge faced by policymakers in England. Researchers at the Education Policy Institute (EPI, 2019) argued that little or no headway has been made in closing the gap for Black Caribbean pupils, and it will take a century to close the gap. Other research has also confirmed that Black Caribbeans are consistently the lowest-performing ethnic group regardless of economic disadvantage (see Demie 2019; Demie and Mclean 2017a,b; Clifton and Cook 2012; Cassen and Kingdon 2007).

The reasons for the underachievement are wide-ranging and complex (see Strand 2012; Demie 2003a,b; Demie and Mclean 2017a,b), but researchers have now accepted curriculum barriers and relevance as one of the main factors. The inequalities faced by BAME communities have been deepened by the lack of an inclusive curriculum in the English education system and the failure of the national curriculum to adequately reflect the needs of a diverse, multi-ethnic society (Demie 2019; Gillborn and Mirza 2000; Macpherson 1999; Demie and Mclean 2017a,b; Demie 2005; Mortimore 1999; Swann 1985; Rampton 1981). These concerns persist, and there is still a lack of focus on racial and ethnic diversity in the curriculum. Many people involved in education recognise the need for the decolonisation of the current Eurocentric curriculum, employing a more diverse workforce, inclusion in decision-making bodies across the education sector, and making racial equality part of the curriculum. Many relevant questions and challenges have been posed across the UK on curriculum issues; for example, what is British history being taught in schools? How can decolonising the curriculum transform teaching and learning for the better?

Overall, the evidence from previous research suggests that there is a growing concern that students in the UK are not being taught Black British History as part of the national curriculum, despite numerous findings demonstrating its importance (Demie, 2019; Moncrieffe, 2018). Previous research suggests an inclusive curriculum enhances the school experience for all students, improves student progression and attainment, and addresses achievement gaps. However, there is no Education Endowment Fund (EEF) research on the effectiveness of the use of an inclusive curriculum with pupils in schools. There is a need for developing an inclusive curriculum and incorporating Black History into subjects all year round to provide a sense of belonging and identity to young people, to raise their attainments, and to improve engagement and social cohesion among young people in the UK.

Effective use of inclusive multicultural curriculum: evidence from the case study schools

A complementary methodological approach has been used in the research on the effective use of inclusive curriculum, including reviewing research literature, case studies of schools, and surveys of schools and headteachers involved in diversifying the school curriculum.

The first question we asked during the case study and focus group approach research was, what is the effective inclusive curriculum that is used by schools to support Black and Minority Ethnic (BAME) pupils?' The findings from the case study show schools had effective leadership and used inclusive curriculum to tackle the curriculum barriers. There is evidence that schools face a renewed demand from parents and their children for a more inclusive curriculum where their experience, heritage, and participation in British life are more adequately acknowledged. The response by many teachers to this challenge has been impressive, but it remains a national issue to which the British education system needs to respond. Schools express recognition of the fact that for many Black heritage pupils, the experience of the British school system has not been affirming of Black people. Teachers work hard to make sure this is not passed on, as noted by one of the primary headteachers:

> As we examine the curriculum's ramifications for Black history, we're coming to the realisation that discussing historical events raises the problem of how Black history frequently cannot exist without White history. The inter-relationships are crucial, but the pain of some of those inter-relationships raises broader questions about how history has been presented and mythologised, said one teacher. As part of Black History Month in Year 5, pupils were selected to study the biography of a famous black person and produce their booklets about what they had learned. This forms the basis of a display in the school, and the booklets will go into the school library. We really want to develop pupils' historical skills so that they can understand the background and development of our diverse society.
>
> *(Headteacher, School Y)*

The pupils also spoke with enthusiasm about the work they had done as part of Black History Month. They had studied the lives of a range of people, including Nelson Mandela, Mary Seacole, Mohammed Ali, Jesse Owens, and Bob Marley. This led to a discussion of their own ethnic identities. They were British, and they took it for granted. Their discussion was rooted in an awareness of the importance of family links and associations in shaping their sense of identity. Their definitions were as follows: African Caribbean European; African Caribbean European American: Jamaican English with Canadian and American connections; Mauritian African European; Jamaican English with Maltese connections; and Jamaican English with American connections. Their skills in debating the influences of location, family links, and other factors in developing personal identity were very evident. Their maturity in the discussion was impressive.

There is a powerful sense in the project schools of a multicultural curriculum that is academically robust and well-resourced but also reflects pupils' heritage, culture, and experience. The views of one case study school headteacher summarised the feelings of many:

> The integration of Black History Month-relevant themes into the regular curriculum is indispensable. As a fundamental idea and an important subject of study at our school, "movements of people" is a prominent theme in the National Curriculum, in my opinion. Conflicts and struggles based on economic developments that force upon communities movements and changes are key issues for us in London, the barometer of the world stage. The children knew there were wars in which black people were involved on behalf of the British Empire, and the lesson provided them with the tools to understand and interpret them. Understanding the factors and forces of change and their impact are key to whether pupils are dealing with dinosaurs or volcanoes.
>
> *(Headteacher, School Y)*

In the case study schools, headteachers see their role now as to encourage teachers to use their creative intuition to deepen the quality of pupils' learning by using a 'mesmerizing' curriculum. Many teachers, having been trained in a system where lesson plans and schemes of work were downloaded from the internet, have found it a challenge to develop their own lessons. Schools are engaged in curriculum development, using the richness of their local communities to enrich the foundation subjects and bring greater relevance to the curriculum for Black Caribbean pupils.

These schools offer a rich and varied range of experiences that are not random but arise from a systematic and thought-through approach by headteachers and staff. This is achieved through curriculum activities, visits out of school, visitors to the school, and an extensive and very broad extracurricular programme.

The headteacher reinforced this point by adding:

> This school uses wholeheartedly the culture in the community as a resource for learning by drawing on the languages spoken, e.g., Somali as well as Urdu/Gujarat, Swahili, Arabic, and Polish. They also use local expertise to enhance the learning of their pupils, including Indian dance classes, visits to The Globe theatre and trips away, and study programmes including residential activities to enrich the curriculum. Artists, dance groups, authors, and poets feed into the curriculum creatively and innovatively.
>
> *(Headteacher, School E)*

A secondary school had to rethink the curriculum as the national curriculum is narrowing, especially in English and history. The curriculum now offers extensive opportunities for students, including links with the Young Vic Theatre and educational trips, visits, and workshops with artists in residence. Collaboration is strong.

> We have got to be more creative now to make it relevant to our pupils. Our specialism in performing and visual arts complements and enriches the curriculum, which has been described by Ofsted as "innovative and engaging."

The primary schools also offer a very rich curriculum, drawing on inspiring Black role models whenever possible to encourage pupils to aim high. One of the great strengths of the school is its excellent, enriched curriculum, which very positively supports the aims and ethos of the school. The headteacher highlighted the approach to the school curriculum:

> We looked at our curriculum and assessment. All based on the needs of our children and the community we serve.' Our curriculum values each child as an individual to be able to offer each child possibilities to broaden their experiences and motivations and to learn their history, culture, and languages.
> *(Executive Headteacher, School C)*

Teachers in Years 4 and 6 talked with enthusiasm about how they ensure that the curriculum takes account of the diverse range of pupils and represents them:

> Our key drivers of spirituality, possibilities, excellence, and diversity are threaded through our curriculum. Year 5 has just been doing a project on space, and last year, when we were doing it, we taught about Mae C. Jemison, the first black woman in space. We are very much aware of who our children are, and we also understand what motivates them. It makes our job easier if they are motivated, so we try to weave it in. We cover in the curriculum about Severus, the Black Roman Emperor who was a Moor. We try every way we can to link it to the pupils and London.
> *(Teacher, School C)*

Similarly, educators at School A use the local history to help Black Caribbean students better comprehend their cultural background, as they explain:

> To diversity the curriculum, a lot of work needs to be done on it.
> *(Teacher, School A, sixth grade)*

I try to make things interesting and relevant to them. My enthusiasm is what I bring into the classroom. For example, I showed the children photos of my holiday in Rome, and they commented, "You have a black friend!".

(Year 3 teacher, School A)

We use the Black Cultural Archives for teaching and learning. We take children there to learn their history and see the Black African cultural artifacts. I was amazed that the black Caribbean children did not know their history.' I tried to stand in front of the sign as it could upset young children.

(Year 3 teacher, School A)

Teachers in primary school have continued to develop a rich, diverse, and creative curriculum, as the head of the school described:

One of the first things we did to improve the curriculum was to work hard to develop our subject leaders.' 'We bring the whole school together with a particular theme or topic. We teach math, English, science, and ICT separately but use the themes to support those subjects too. As much as possible, we link the teaching and learning of subjects together through a common theme or topic. When we see our kids, we ask ourselves, "What do they need to learn?"' How can we encourage girls and boys? Our creative curriculum changes each year because we evaluate and see how effective our curriculum is. This way of working allows teachers to become more creative. We also link our homework to the whole school theme, so families become involved.

(Headteacher, School A)

Teachers are enthusiastic about the impact of the curriculum on the children.

There is a lot of flexibility in the curriculum on what I may accomplish in the classroom. I can ask the children what we could do, and they get so much delight out of it since they are participating.

The school's website states that:

The aim of all those at school is to ensure that the curriculum offered to the children is not only fun and enjoyable but also leads to children achieving their full academic potential.

Parents can access 'curriculum guides' each term for each class from EYFS to Year 6, which outline the creative curriculum and homework projects. The school's innovative and exciting partnership with London Music Masters, through The Bridge Project, has contributed to the excellence of the school's curriculum. The project identifies and nurtures young children who might not otherwise have the opportunity to engage in classical music. The project encourages children, their families, and communities to develop a lifelong appreciation for classical music in all its varied forms. Pupils at school have therefore had a range of unique opportunities and experiences, including performing at the Royal Festival Hall. They receive music tuition and participate in various musical workshops and performances throughout the school year.

The rich and diverse curriculum provides many memorable experiences and brings learning to life by creatively linking topic themes between subjects. Boys' writing has greatly improved by developing their skills in contexts they find engaging. Whole school topics cover EYFS to Year 6, which the EYFS team leader views as a very positive feature. She says:

> In many schools, the EYFS is isolated in a little bubble. The kids and I both feel more a part of the school community here. That inspires them. I think it makes a significant difference.
>
> *(Teacher, School A)*

The school's Ofsted report praised its creative curriculum:

> The creative curriculum offers a very broad range of themed activities that are developed extremely well with contributions from pupils. Consequently, the school provides rich and memorable experiences for pupils that prepare them exceptionally well for their next steps in learning. There are many excellent opportunities through the curriculum and in assemblies to promote pupils' spiritual, moral, social, and cultural development. The diversity of the school is celebrated, and pupils are encouraged to consider other faiths and cultures through projects such as Our Heritage. A very wide range of well-attended after-school clubs provide many opportunities for sports, arts, and music activities.
>
> *(Teacher, School A)*

Black History Month is built reflectively into the curriculum in the autumn term and covers influential people and groups in the case study 'School V.' In the nursery cover, Stories from Africa and Reception: Stories from America – the Obamas. Also, we cover Year 1: Ride to Freedom – Rosa Parks – and Year 2: Amazing Adventures of Mary Seacole. Year 3: Blast from the Past WW2 (children's viewpoints), Year 4: Aboriginal Australia: Artists, Year 5: Windrush: Influential People, and Year 6: From Apartheid to Peace: Nelson Mandela.

The school teachers have developed a broad, balanced, and imaginative curriculum, and a curriculum map identifies foundation subjects to be taught through topics presenting a well-structured learning journey for pupils from Year 1 to Year 6. The Humanities Coordinator has taken a leading role in curriculum development and has produced exciting materials for Black History Month that feature local and national 'heroes' or role models, people from the West Indies and Africa who have made a significant contribution to life in Britain.

Teachers talk with enthusiasm about their approach to the curriculum and try to make lessons exciting and relevant to the children.

> We used to use the Creative Learning Journey so people could become imaginative, especially in math, as it starts to make sense to children when you use real-life situations… We did a great math shop last year. Each class came up with things they could make and sell: sandwiches, fruit shops; each class had a stall.
>
> *(Teacher)*

Making connections between subjects is another strength of this curriculum; an example is how drama was incorporated into work on food chains in science. For example, children played the part of bees pollinating flowers.

The schoolchildren in another case study, 'School G,' also use an extensive range of extracurricular activities and visits to places of interest. There is an excellent range of partnerships that have been established; pupils can perform at the Royal Festival Hall and the Young Vic and capitalise on visits to Tate Modern and events at the South Bank.

The school also developed African-influenced art and craft work as part of curriculum initiatives in history, where Benin was chosen as a unit of study. Work of outstanding quality, supported by stimulating and carefully chosen artefacts, was much in evidence in the school. The head teacher highlighted the positive impact of the use of Kingdom of Benin artefacts on teaching and learning and commented that:

> The response of all pupils was enthusiastic, and it has helped to improve the attainment and progress of black pupils in the school.
>
> *(Headteacher, School G)*

Overall, these schools are very aware of the importance that a dynamic, innovative curriculum plays in signalling to the pupils a sense of belonging in the wider community. The case study schools are committed to an innovative curriculum that motivates students of ethnic minority heritage and have developed links with Africa and the rich artistic and sporting communities in London, such as the Royal Ballet, the Royal Festival Hall, the English

National Opera, the London Museums, the British Museums, and the Black Cultural Archives London Artistic Worlds. The schools have created an environment where Black African, Black Caribbean, and Mixed Heritage students feel their history, culture, languages, religion, and individual identities are respected and valued within the curriculum. Every school incorporates Black History Month into its curriculum and celebrates it to the fullest.

It is also important to note here that whatever the curriculum model in the case study schools, every school emphasises the importance of linking it to the national curriculum, having a strong focus on the core curriculum, and high standards in core subjects. Each has a clear rationale for why their school's curriculum is as it is. This is based on a thorough understanding of what kind of school it is and what the students need. These outstanding schools are always looking for ways to improve their curriculum. They consider and plan proposed changes very carefully and only pursue them if there is a clear indication that they will support further gains in pupils' learning, motivation, enjoyment, or achievement. These schools typically offer an impressive range of enrichment opportunities, trips, and visits. This is usually a deliberate strategy, as first, it provides cultural, artistic, and sporting experiences that students are unlikely to encounter at home or in the community, widening horizons and heightening their aspirations and expectations, and giving them access to opportunities that they may take up later in life. Second, it provides opportunities for students to develop greater self-confidence.

Approaches used in diversifying the curriculum in schools: evidence from a school survey

In addition to the case study school evidence, a separate school survey was undertaken to collate the views of headteachers, teachers, and governors about barriers to curriculum and effective inclusive curriculum that is used by schools to support BAME pupils (Demie 2023c). The survey was carried out in the schools that participated in the last five years, one in inner London, LA, in the diversifying the school curriculum project that focussed on improving the achievement of Black and ethnic minority pupils. The survey asks the respondents to rate the level of impact on a seven-point scale covering a range of barriers and interventions. A total of 90 schools participated in the project, and about 50% of the headteachers of the schools involved responded to the survey questionnaire. In addition, there were free text questions in the survey, inviting respondents to describe the most important factors that they feel have contributed to improved results and to give examples of good practice in diversifying the curriculum.

The main findings of the survey suggest that about 96% of the respondents highly agreed that the use of inclusive curriculum has contributed to

Black and ethnic minority achievement in their schools (Demie, 2023a, c). The diversifying the curriculum project focusses on the importance of creating a diverse curriculum to improve educational outcomes for children and young people. It also brings together experienced primary and secondary teachers who share a clear passion for ensuring all children have access to an inclusive curriculum reflecting the Black experience, culture, and history. This involves incorporating stories, facts, and information reflecting Black History, experience, and culture to inspire interest and excitement amongst all pupils about Black History and culture. In doing so, it also encourages Black pupils to have a stronger sense of pride in their heritage. They recruited five primary and five secondary school curriculum developers to inspire content diversity within curriculums across LA (see Demie 2023a, c). The teachers who were involved in the curriculum development project commented on the importance of inclusive curriculum in the school survey as follows:

> The curriculum we develop is geared towards having an impact on the vast communities we serve.
>
> *(Teacher, SP3)*

> There are many possibilities for diversifying the curriculum; we want to broaden the horizons of all of our groups so that we're representative of all voices that we've got in local authority.
>
> *(Teacher, SP3)*

> Diversifying the curriculum allowed us to bring a topic to life for the children. It made them passionate about what they were learning, which in turn made them enthusiastic about learning more and putting to use what they had learned. It gave them a context for their learning and a reason for learning from the past.
>
> *(Teacher, SP3)*

> The tools we have produced are made by teachers for teachers. We have done the hard work for you, creating material that can be embedded into your existing curriculum that meets that requirement and is Ofsted-approved. It is going to be a true curriculum that reflects, inspires, and acknowledges true contributions from the black community.
>
> *(Teacher, SP13)*

> Ensuring that children are increasingly seeing a range of diverse figures (from a range of backgrounds and ethnicities) in subjects to inspire them and allow them to see themselves in the subjects they study.
>
> *(Teacher, SP61)*

As part of curriculum initiatives, several achievements are reported in the survey by headteachers, deputy headteachers, assistant headteachers, school governors, and teachers, including the following positive comments:

> Many schools in the school partnership project are engaged in curriculum development and innovation, using the richness of their local communities to bring greater relevance for students.
> *(Headteacher, SP15)*

> We use a diverse curriculum that meets the needs of black pupils.
> *(Assistant headteacher, SP16)*

> We are using the primary curriculum materials in our school that have been developed by a focus group of teachers. These include KS1 and KS2 material related to the Ancient Kingdom of Benin, Ancient Rome, Ancient Roman Britain, art textiles, history, Romans, geography, math arts, and English. We found the materials developed are useful to engage school leaders to review their school curriculum, inspiring curriculum leads to ensure it is reflective of LA's diverse communities.
> *(Headteacher, SP17)*

> The curriculum used to teach provides their growing pride in being black. The Black experience is used to enrich the curriculum in art, dance, music, geography, history, and technology, e.g., the Kingdom of Benin artefacts, the Kush Kingdom, and the Merotic civilisation. The Kingdom of Benin was well known for its artefacts and the Great Wall, and the Kush Kingdom was an ancient civilisation in Africa and is well known for goldmines, iron, pyramids, and also developed its alphabet.
> *(Headteacher, SP20)*

> The inclusive curriculum was written by teachers to make sure the full contribution of the black community, past and present, is recognised.
> *(Headteacher, SP25)*

> Reworking the curriculum to show more achievement by black people. Greater emphasis on black history and artists, as well as authors.
> *(Governor, SP41)*

> We have worked as a staff team to ensure that we have further diversified the curriculum in all subject areas and that the curriculum is reflective of our school and the much wider community, for example, ensuring Black History is embedded in every term in every year's learning and not just as

part of a Black History month. We feel that this has had a positive impact on pupil engagement.

(Headteacher, SP42)

Explicit inclusion of more diverse texts and figures (historical, scientific, etc.) across the curriculum. CPD for teachers and TAs on a diverse range of images and names within lesson examples.

(Deputy Head, SP43)

We use effectively inclusive curriculum.

(Headteacher, SP47)

Ensuring that a range of identities and cultures are represented in teaching materials for the benefit of all children.

(Governor, SP51)

Excellent planning resources are available to support both teacher subject knowledge and helping to focus lessons on key issues.

(Senior Leadership Team, SP53)

School has reviewed its own curriculum and been supported by grounded sessions.

(Headteacher, SP57)

Conclusions

The substantial body of research into the scale of the curriculum barriers in British schools and the use of inclusive curriculum has offered a valuable background and useful insight for tackling barriers to learning for ethnic minority pupils. Researchers in the field of the curriculum in British schools have now recognised there is a growing concern that students in the UK are not being taught Black British History as part of the national curriculum, despite numerous findings demonstrating its importance (Demie 2019; Moncrieffe, 2018; Moncrieffe, 2018; Macpherson 1999; DfE 2013). All evidence from research suggests that the English school curriculum is Eurocentric from the starting point and focusses on British culture and ignores ethnic minorities in the curriculum (Moncrieffe, 2018,2020). BAME children are not receiving the quality of education they need to thrive in the English education system due to curriculum barriers.

Despite these teachers, school leaders and BAME professionals have continued to champion the need to improve the existing curriculum by adding more BAME experience (see Leach et al. 2020). The evidence from the case study and school survey confirms that the schools have developed an inclusive curriculum that reflects and incorporates the children's heritage. There is strong evidence that ethnic minority contributions and Black experiences are used to enrich the curriculum in history, geography, music, and technology. The case study schools have established connections with rich artistic and sporting communities in London, including the Royal Ballet, the Royal Festival Hall, the English National Opera, London Museums, London Artistic Worlds, the Black Cultural Archives, the British Museum, and the Migration Museum, as well as with Africa. These schools are very committed to an innovative curriculum that inspires students of ethnic minority heritage. The pupils' exposure to these organisations has expanded their perspectives significantly. They have established an atmosphere in which pupils of Black African, Black Caribbean, and mixed descent believe that the curriculum values and respects their individual identities, histories, and cultures. Black History Month is a time when all schools honour the history and contributions of Black people via curriculum-based learning

There is evidence in successful schools that the school curriculum adds to the growing pride in being Black pupils and ethnic minority students in a multicultural society (Demie 2023a,c; 2023b, 2019, 2005; Demie and Mclean 2015). Our findings suggest inclusive curricula are well developed in the case study schools and other schools that have completed our survey. There is evidence that BAME professionals, teachers, and school leaders have continued to champion the need to improve the existing curriculum by adding more BAME experience (see Demie 2023a, c; 2023b; Demie 2019; Demie and Lewis 2010; Demie 2005; and Demie and McLean 2017b). These successful multicultural schools' curricula now include the lives of famous BAME people in Britain, the achievements of early civilisations such as the Benin Kingdom in West Africa, the Cushitic and Merotic civilisations in North East Africa, the transatlantic slave trade and its abolition, the history of the Windrush generation, the pre-colonial Black presence in Britain, migration patterns, ethnic and cultural diversity in Britain, the positive contribution people of all ethnicities have made to Britain, and the role of the countries of the former British empire in both world wars. The national curriculum includes these subjects – history, geography, citizenship, English, and PSHE (personal, social, health, and economic education) – from Key Stage One of primary school through Key Stage Four when students take their GCSEs. These topics are designed to excite and motivate BAME students. We would argue that the case study schools and other schools in the survey have now decolonised the national curriculum. Furthermore, this chapter also raised many relevant questions and challenges for UK curriculum issues, including: What is British history being taught in schools? Many people involved in education now recognise 'the need for the decolonisation of the current Eurocentric curriculum, employing a more diverse workforce in schools, and making diversity and racial equality part of the curriculum' (Demie 2021:2).

Britain is a multi-ethnic and multicultural country, and there is, therefore, a need to develop and use an inclusive curriculum that recognises that students in schools come from a range of different backgrounds. This should differ in ethnicity, gender, language, socioeconomic status, and faith. Our research is about successful schools that have developed and used inclusive curriculum to meet the needs of BAME students in their schools and provide good practices that schools can share to transform their curriculum and improve teaching and learning in primary and secondary schools. The recommendations based on this study and previous research on the school curriculum are that:

The government should ensure that every school develops a curriculum that reflects the rich national cultural diversity.
The schools should develop an inclusive curriculum that engages ethnic minority students. This curriculum should reflect and value cultural diversity and have relevance to their lives.
Students in the UK should be taught Black British History as part of the national curriculum.

References

Callender, C. (1995) A question of 'style': Black teachers and pupils in multi-ethnic schools. *Language and Education* 9(3): 145–159. Doi: 10.1080/09500789509541410

Cassen, R. & Kingdon, G. (2007) *Tackling Low Educational Achievement*. York: Joseph Rowntree Foundation.

Clifton, J. & Cook, W. (2012) *A Long Division: Closing the Attainment Gap in England's Secondary Schools*. London: Institute for Public Policy Research (IPPR).

Demie, F. (2003a) Using value-added data for school self-evaluation: A case study of practice in inner city schools. *School Leadership and Management*, 23 (4): 445–467.

Demie, F. (2003b) Raising the achievement of Black Caribbean pupils in british schools: Unacknowledged problems and challenges for policy makers. *London Review of Education*, 1 (3): 229–248.

Demie, F. (2005) Achievement of Black Caribbean pupils: Good practice in Lambeth schools. *British Educational Research Journal* 31(4): 481–508.

Demie, F. (2019) *Educational Inequality: Closing the gap*. London: UCL IOE press.

Demie, F. (2021) *Transforming the Secondary Curriculum*. British Educational Research Association. https://www.bera.ac.uk/blog/transforming-the-secondary-curriculum

Demie, F. (2023a) *Raising the Achievement of Black Caribbean pupils: Barriers and Good Practice in Schools*. London: Lambeth Research and Statistics Unit.

Demie, F. (2023b) *Tackling Educational Inequality: Lessons from London Schools*. Equity in Education & Society. https://doi.org/10.1177/27526461231161775

Demie, F. (2023c) *A School Survey of Barriers to Learning, Success Factors, And Effective Inclusive Curriculum That Contributed to Improving Black And*

Demie, F. & Lewis, K. (2010) *White Working Class Achievement: An Ethnographic Study of Barriers to Learning in Schools*. https://doi.org/10.1080/03055698.2010.506341

Demie, F. & Mclean, C. (2015) *Narrowing the Achievement Gap: Good Practice in Schools*. London: Lambeth Research and Statistics Unit.

Demie, F. & Mclean, C. (2017a) *Black Caribbean Underachievement in Schools in England*. Lambeth LA: Lambeth Research and Statistics Unit.

Demie, F. & Mclean, C. (2017b) *The Achievement of Black Caribbean Pupils: Good Practice*. London: Lambeth Research and Statistics Unit.

DfE. (2013) *History Programmes of Study: Key Stages 1 and 2. National Curriculum in England*. London: Department for Education.

EPI. (2019) *Education in England: Annual Report 2019*. London: Education Policy Institute, July. https://epi.org.uk/publications-and-research/annual-report-2019/

Gillborn, D. & Mirza, H.S. (2000) *Educational Inequality: Mapping Race and Class*. London: Office for Standards in Education.

Harris, R. (2020) *Decolonising the History Curriculum*. BERA Research Intelligence, Spring.

Harris, R. & Reynolds, R.(2018) Exploring teachers' curriculum decision making: insights from history education *Oxford Review of Education* 44(2):1–17. Doi: 10.1080/03054985.2017.1352498

Leach, A., Voce, A. & Kirk, A. (2020) Black British History: The Row Over the Curriculum in England. *Guardian*. https://www.theguardian.com/education/2020/jul/13/black-british-history-school-curriculum-england

Macpherson, W. (1999) *The Stephen Lawrence Inquiry*. London: The Stationery Office.

Marks, H. (2000) Student engagement in instructional activity: Patterns in the elementary, middle, and high school years. *American Educational Research Journal* 37(1): 156.

Moncrieffe, M.L. (2018) *Arresting-Epistemic-Violence-Decolonising-The-National-Curriculum-For-History*. BERA blog. https://www.bera.ac.uk/blog/arresting-epistemic-violence-decolonising-the-national-curriculum-for-history

Moncrieffe, M.L. (2020) Decolonizing the curriculum: Transnational perspectives. In Race, R. & Harris, R. (eds.) *Research Intelligence*, 142. London: British Educational Research, Spring. Association. https://www.bera.ac.uk/publication/spring-2020

Moncrieffe, M.L. (2022) *Decolonising Curriculum Knowledge: A Scholarly Journey From The Local, To National And International Perspectives*. https://www.bera.ac.uk/blog/decolonising-curriculum-knowledge-a-scholarly-journey-from-the-local-to-national-and-international-perspectives

Mortimore, P. (1999) *The Road to Improvement: Reflections on School Effectiveness*. Lisse: Sweets and Zeitlinger.

Proctor, K. (2020) Tone-deaf' ministers reject BAME review of English curriculum. *Guardian*, July. https://www.theguardian.com/education/2020/jul/30/exclusive-tone-deaf-ministers-reject-bame-review-of-english-curriculum

Rampton, A. (1981) *West Indian Children in Our Schools*. London: HMSO.

Stamou, E., Popv, A. & Sovtemel, E. (2020) *Decolonisation of the Curriculum from the Side Lines? Responsivity Transfer and Neo-Colonialism*. BERA blog. https://www.bera.ac.uk/blog/decolonisation-of-the-curriculum-from-the-sidelines-responsibility-transfer-and-neo-nationalism

Strand, S. (2012) The White British-Black Caribbean achievement gap: tests, tiers, and teacher expectations. *British Educational Research Journal* 38(1): 75–101.

Swann, L. (1985) *Education for All: Final Report of the Committee of Inquiry into the Education of Children from Ethnic Minority Groups*. London: HMSO.

9
TACKLING SCHOOL EXCLUSIONS OF ETHNIC MINORITY PUPILS

Introduction

There has been considerable concern about the growing number of exclusions in schools in England among teachers, school leaders, parents, communities, and education policymakers. In particular, several studies have drawn attention to the rise in school exclusions and suspensions (see DfE 2019; Demie, 2019a,b; Parsons 2009,2010; Timpson, 2019; EPI, 2019; IPPR 2017; Demie and Mclean 2017; Wright et al. 2008). This has brought exclusion issues to the forefront of the public and education policy debate in England.

The review of previous research also suggests that Black and Special Educational Needs (SEN) pupils represent the most excluded groups of pupils in British schools (Demie, 2022a, b; Timpson, 2019; EPI, 2019; House of Common Library, 2018; Ofsted, 2018; DfE, 2019; Power and Taylor, 2018; IPPR, 2017; EHRC, 2015; Parsons, 2010, 2009, 2008). In addition to Black Caribbean students, Gypsy/Roma and Traveller pupils and Mixed White and Black Caribbean pupils' are over-represented in the exclusion statistics in England. There were several factors highlighted in the literature for a negative impact on school exclusions and reasons for the over-representation of Black Caribbean, Mixed White, and Black Caribbean, Gypsy/Roma pupils, and Travellers of Irish Heritage pupils in schools in exclusion.

The review of the literature shows the reasons for the over-representation of Black and ethnic minorities in exclusions are related to factors such as low teacher expectation, institutional racism, pupil behaviour, rigid school policies, and sociocultural factors outside the school's control (Strand and Fletcher, 2014; McClusky et al. 2016). The literature review also highlighted racism as one explanation for the enduring nature of the disproportionate

DOI: 10.4324/9781003499633-12

exclusion rate of Black Caribbean pupils (IPPR 2017, Demie 2022a,b), when factors such as socioeconomic background or additional needs were not taken into account. Racism was considered to influence schools' views on acceptable behaviour and expectations of different sets of pupils. The review of the literature confirms that Black students are more than twice as likely as White students to be suspended or expelled, and in urban districts, the disparity has been found to range from 3 to 22 times as likely (Raffaele Mendez & Knoff, 2003) in the USA.

Empirical data from England further supports the extent of the issue with school expulsions.

For example, the Department for Education (DfE,2022) data show that 6,495 pupils were permanently excluded from state-funded primary, secondary, and special schools in England in 2021/2022 compared to 4,630 in 2012/13. This was an increase in the exclusion number by 1865 pupils, or 40%, during the period. The evidence of the fixed term exclusion also suggests about 578,280 pupils were excluded compared to 265,520 in the same period, an increase of 312760 pupils, or 118% (DfE 2019). The DfE (2021/2022) data also shows schools exclude pupils they are responsible for educating in schools to alternative provision settings. There were 30,129 fixed-period exclusions in pupil referral units in 2021/22, up from 15,536 in 2013/2014 (see DfE 2023).

- The empirical evidence in England shows a worrying picture of disproportionality in school exclusions by ethnic background. Of particular concern is that Black Caribbean and Mixed White and Black Caribbean pupils had the highest exclusion rates over the period (see Figure 9.1 and Table 9.1) with Black Caribbean students being more than twice as likely as the whole student body to be excluded for a certain amount of time. Two relatively small groups had the highest permanent exclusion rates, Gypsy/Roma pupils and Travellers of Irish Heritage at 0.36% and 0.29%, respectively, an incidence about three times higher than that of the overall school population.
- Other recent DfE statistics on exclusions also show that Black Caribbean are over-represented in both permanent and fixed-term exclusions. Table 9.1 shows that:
- 19.3% of Travellers, 13.6% of White and Black Caribbean, and 11.7% of Black Caribbean pupils had a fixed-period of exclusion. They were followed by 6% of Gypsy/Roma heritage The boys' exclusion rate was three times higher than that of the girls, with 0.02% of girls and 0.05% of boys being permanently expelled. This rate was even higher for White and Black Caribbean and Black Caribbean pupils, suggesting that the high exclusion rate was partly due to boys of that ethnic group.

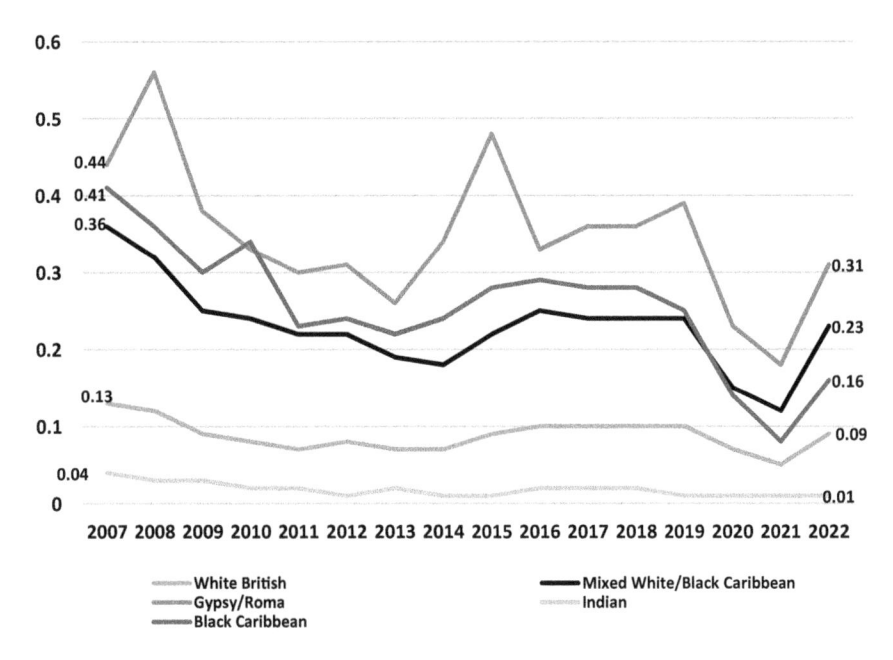

FIGURE 9.1 Trend in permanent exclusions in England by main ethnic groups.

Source: Permanent exclusions in England: 2007 to 2022, DfE SFR26/2022.

- About 7.05% of those not eligible and 17.1% of those eligible had fixed-term exclusions. It demonstrates unequivocally that students who were known to be eligible for free school meals were also more likely to be permanently excluded over their whole school career or to be excluded for a certain amount of time.
- The data also shows pupils eligible for free school meals were about four times as likely to receive a permanent exclusion as other pupils in 2021/2022.

Tackling school exclusions

The schools use a range of approaches and practices related to preventing exclusion. In recent years, the need for detailed case studies of schools that have successfully tackled school exclusions has become apparent as a means of increasing our understanding of how schools can tackle school exclusions. For these reasons, several British studies looked at examples of schools that provide an environment in which pupils flourish without taking the drastic action of suspension and exclusion (Demie and Mclean, 2019; RSA, 2021; DfE, 2019). The research's lessons validate that effective case study schools have defied national trends by removing students very infrequently, if at all.

TABLE 9.1 Exclusions by pupil characteristics in schools in England, percentage of population 2021/2022

Pupils characteristics	Ethnic background	Permanent Exclusions	Suspensions
	Number	6,495	578,280
	Gypsy Roma	0.31	25.6
Ethnic background	Traveller of Irish heritage	0.31	19.3
	White and Black Caribbean	0.23	13.6
	Black Caribbean	0.16	11.7
	Irish	0.11	8.1
	White and Black African	0.1	7.9
	Any other Black background	0.09	7.3
	White British	0.09	7
	White and Asian	0.06	6
	Any other Mixed background	0.06	5.1
	Pakistani	0.05	5
	Black African	0.05	4.2
	Any Other Ethnic Group	0.05	4.2
	Any other White background	0.04	4
	Any other Asian background	0.03	2.3
	Bangladeshi	0.02	2.3
	Indian	0.01	1.1
	Chinese	0.01	0.7
Gender	Girls	0.02	2.09
	Boys	0.05	3.78
Free school meals status	FSM – eligible	0.1	7.05
	FSM – not eligible	0.02	1.71
SEN	EHCP	0.07	7.78
	SEN support	0.12	8.16
	No SEN	0.02	1.94
All Pupils	All	0.08	6.91

Source: (DfE 2022).

There is a need for evidence of what works in tackling school exclusions and suspensions. Although we have extensive evidence of the rise in school exclusions, there is little research evidence on what works to tackle school exclusions. Given the paucity of robust evidence about the impact of reducing school exclusions in the context of the UK, we have used the findings of the DfE literature review (2019a) and RSA's own Pinball Kids research project (2021), Demie and Mclean's (2019) research into what works for tackling school exclusions, and Moore et al. (2019) EEF research into improving behaviour in the context of England.

There are many reasons why schools are bucking national trends and successfully managing school exclusions. For example, the research by Demie and Mclean (2020:67–82) and Demie (2022a:128–130) on tackling school exclusions in England identified the following factors that proved successful in tackling school exclusions and suspensions:

- '*A strong leadership team that is committed to diversity and race equality*: in these schools, leaders demonstrated an acute awareness of the challenging circumstances many pupils experience, and they have endeavoured to create safe and secure environments, where pupils are regarded as assets and are shown respect. Pupils have at least one named member of staff that they can go to when they are experiencing difficulties that might get out of hand and lead to more serious consequences. There is tight planning, and communication systems have been established to ensure that there is consistency in approach, thus minimising confusion or misunderstanding.
- *Well-developed, effective teachers CPD*: Teachers' professional learning is a feature of these schools' investments, with a significant proportion of the budget in one school spent on CPD. Post-graduate qualifications are pursued by teachers, and they take a research-based approach to developing practice. Another effective approach is to train staff to recognise symptoms of childhood trauma, for example, as a result of challenging home environments, knife crime, gangs, etc., within their students' neighbourhoods.
- *Use of innovative inclusive curriculum*: They recognise the need to develop a curriculum that reflects the reality of pupils' lives. Successful schools use innovative and engaging learning opportunities that convince pupils that learning can be fun and memorable. Above all, it has relevance to the lives of pupils. Enriched by opportunities to be creative, gain confidence, and develop their self-esteem, pupils enjoy visits to museums, galleries, theatres, and visits from well-known artists and performing companies.
- *Use of effective inclusion strategies and practice*: Effective schools are fully inclusive schools, and the staff is wholly committed to providing equal opportunities for all pupils. They are also committed to overcoming barriers to learning and meeting any special educational needs to ensure that all students make good progress. They recognise that negative behaviour is often a consequence of social, emotional, and mental health issues or trauma, which pupils find difficult to communicate. Considerable investment is made in pastoral support, with highly skilled non-teaching support staff, with their ability to personalise learning, to address the issue of exclusion. Many problems of extreme behaviour arise because of students' difficulty in accessing the curriculum which, in turn, can be linked to inadequate literacy and lack of success. Successful schools respond with a focus on relationships, providing early interventions, restorative justice, and learning support.

Inclusion is at the heart of everything the schools do, ensuring that pupils feel they are included academically and socially, and early intervention is key to the school's approach to preventing school exclusion.
- *Use a diverse multi-ethnic workforce*: There is great diversity in the workforce in the case study schools in terms of the range of roles, skills, and ethnicity. They have recruited good quality teaching and non-teaching staff that reflect the languages, cultures, ethnic backgrounds, and faiths of the pupils in the school. Successful schools also pride themselves on recruiting from the local community, and this has sent a strong message to the community that they are valued, helped the schools become a central point of the wider community, and built trust. Teaching assistants are great and play a key role in communicating with parents and supporting pupils.
- *Providing excellent care and guidance for pupils*: successful schools provide exceptional care and guidance for pupils, and they make every effort to meet the individual and often complex needs of children when they enter school, including ADHD and child mental health needs.
- *Use effective targeted Intervention and support*: carefully targeted support has a significant impact in preventing the exclusion of pupils. Schools' intervention and targeted support strategies are effective because they are driven by pupils' academic, emotional, and social needs. Successful schools do have an excellent range of interventions to break down barriers for children with SEND and support them to be able to access the curriculum within their classroom.
- *Effective behaviour policy that is based on inclusion in mind*: It ensures that the behaviour policy does not discriminate against pupils on the grounds of race, gender, SEND, or sexual orientation.'

(see Demie 2022b:128–130)

Similar beneficial approaches to those mentioned above to address school expulsions are also suggested by Graham et al.'s (2019) literature review of other research conducted in the setting of England, which highlighted promising methods including establishing a positive school ethos and culture to assist and direct personnel in comprehending, recognising, and handling behaviour in constructive ways; assist families and kids by utilising the recommended high-quality outside resources and Offer 'targeted' support to certain students, such as one-on-one tutoring or counselling.

Based on their research on good practices in schools, Demie and Mclean (2019) contended that good practice was nearly universal and included a strong ethos and core values, a culture of high expectations, a culture of clarity and routines, and a focus on fostering excellent, supportive relationships where kids are valued, their talents are developed, and they can thrive. In addition, there were evident ties to the community and a dedication to equitable opportunity.

There are other effective good practices to tackle school exclusions that we have identified from the review of literature. These include:

- Effective, inclusive, and nurturing practice
- Effective use of local authority (LAs) and multi-agency teams
- Trauma-informed practice
- Restorative approaches
- Effective behavioural management

Effective use of inclusive and nurturing

The Department for Education's (DfE, 2019) study review suggests that the implementation of caring and inclusive policies can effectively address school exclusions and assist children. This strategy tries to eliminate needless exclusions while implicitly assisting all students in thriving in mainstream classrooms and developing the social and emotional skills essential for lifetime flourishing. According to the DfE literature assessment, the available data does offer some helpful insight into the variety of strategies and tactics linked to preventing exclusions in various circumstances by promoting inclusive and supportive schools. The following crucial aspects of inclusive practice were identified in the DfE literature review:

- 'A positive school ethos and culture that guides and supports staff in understanding, identifying, and managing behaviour in positive ways
- Support for families and children, using high-quality external provision where needed
- Targeted support to some pupils through effective use of one-to-one tuition or counselling.'

(DfE, 2019:8)

The RSA's 'Pinball Kids' research project by Partridge et al. (2020) also shows the challenges with school exclusions and how vulnerable children are disproportionately represented in special educational needs. The research identified the following five conditions necessary for change to tackle school exclusions and suspensions:

- 'Every child has a strong relationship with a trusted adult in school.
- All children's parents or carers are engaged as partners in their education.
- Every child attends school with an inclusive ethos.
- Every child is assessed for learning and other needs throughout their school career, and there is the capacity to provide appropriate support.'

(Partridge et al. 2020:5)

Stronger ties between students and instructors or other school personnel, as well as the efficient application of focussed interventions and support through one-on-one assistance, small groups, and pastoral care, are crucial to averting harmful school exclusions, according to this research.

The RSA's own Pinball Kids (2020) report recommends that every pupil should have at least one supportive and positive relationship with a member of the school staff. This is especially critical for students who are considered to be at-risk, since they may have experienced trauma or instability in their adult relationships at home, or they may equate unpleasant interactions involving discipline with relationships with school staff.

Recent RSA (2021) studies as part of developing an inclusive and nurturing schools toolkit also provide good practice in tackling school exclusions in England. An inclusive and nurturing education was described by the RSA as one that supports students to thrive in mainstream schools, develops the social and emotional capabilities necessary for lifelong flourishing, and reduces needless exclusions (RSA, 2021). The toolkit highlights features of inclusive and nurturing practice. It shows some evidence of a positive impact on inclusion and learner outcomes for all pupils. The case studies were developed from interviews with school leaders and practitioners from eight case study schools, multi-academy trusts, and local authorities. Key recommendations of the RSA research findings and toolkit for all pupils include the use of trauma-informed practice, consistent, and restorative approaches to addressing challenging behaviour, and a strong focus on relational practice. Their findings also highlighted how early identification, counselling, and therapeutic support, engaging with families, multi-agency and community sector response and academic engagement and support, use of staff-teacher networks, and inclusive practice tackled school exclusions in the school and local authorities (RSA, 2021).

Restorative approach

A review of the literature on restorative approaches to addressing challenging behaviour seeks to address conflicts and tension by repairing challenging relationships/or behaviours. It suggests that schools that use restorative approaches can create a more inclusive atmosphere and address challenging behaviour in a non-punitive way (see Moore et al., 2019).

A report on Restorative Approaches in Primary Schools (2008) reduced fixed-term exclusions by just over half (51%). It also shows how the restorative approach helped to improve the child's behaviour within the school and provided positive messages for both the staff and pupils.

Restorative approaches to school discipline are used throughout the USA to tackle the racial inequality gap and reduce school exclusions (Gregory et al. 2006). Numerous studies that show restorative practice has the ability to improve education have benefited from this strategy. According to the study, targeted support and encouragement of student voice are useful for children's developmental needs. Teachers and parents have also found it to be helpful. The findings of the study showed that teachers with high restorative practice teachers had more positive relationships with their diverse students. Students see this as more respectful and friendly. As a result, they issued fewer suspensions. The findings also show that well-used restorative approaches to discipline have helped close the racial gap in the discipline. The study found that 'higher restorative practice implementation was associated with lower use of disruption/defiance disciplinary referrals with Latino and African American students compared with lower restorative practice implementers.' (Gregory et al. 2006).

Overall, Gregory et al.'s (2006) study confirms that higher Minnesota, California, Colorado, and Florida. It is also used internationally, including in England, Australia, Scotland, Canada, and Hong Kong (González, 2011, 2014). The restorative practice was associated with lower suspensions for Latino and African American students.

Other models that primarily focus on restoring relationships have been used in the USA in states such as Minnesota, California, Colorado, and Florida It is also used internationally in countries such as England, Australia, Scotland, Canada, and Hong Kong (González, 2011; McCluskey et al., 2019, 2016) and has been instrumental in reducing suspension.

Effective use of LAs and multiagency team

Parsons's (2010) study also examined how committed local authorities, along with their communities, can successfully reduce or eliminate permanent exclusions. This study was part of the Strategic Alternatives to Exclusion from a school project and focussed on three low-excluding LAs and five high-excluding LAs. The principal aim of the study was to investigate whether LAs should stop requiring permanent or fixed-period exclusions. The findings of the study show that all schools had reduced their rates of school exclusions with support, coordination, and brokered by the LA or through local partnerships. Based on this empirical evidence (Parsons 2010) suggests 'Zero exclusion schools are possible' and local authorities have a powerful influence on tackling school (Parsons 2010:395). He gave reasons for a reduction in school exclusions to the work of the LA and its strategic developments, including:

- 'Shared commitment across schools and LA members and officers working with explicit principles and procedures.
- Broadening the school by making more diverse and multi-level provision in schools.

- Building bridges so that managed moves can be organised, and school clusters can share the responsibilities.
- Alternative provision involves finding or making a place for every child.
- Joining up the dots to make multi-agency work effective.
- Ethos, attitudes, and sharing a vision, working at hearts and minds to gain support for including all children and responding to all needs.'

(Parsons, 2010: 402)

The key recommendation of the RSA's Pinball report by Partridge (2020) also supports Parson's findings and argues the need to invest in multi-agency team education, social work, youth work, mental health, and police professionals working together to provide and support children at risk of exclusions beyond the school gate across the LAs. They argued, based on the research findings, that multi-agency teams make a huge difference in supporting children and tackling school exclusions.

Trauma-informed practice

Additional research indicates that social and emotional learning that will promote a child's development can be taught using a trauma-informed method. Effective social and emotional learning interventions, such as teaching social and emotional learning skills through whole school ethos and activities, among others, can support positive relationships, mental health, and learning gains of +4 months per year, according to the EEF's review Improving Social and Emotional Learning in Primary Schools (EEF, 2019).

This EEF evidence also highlighted that teacher-pupil relationships are key to good pupil behaviour. Pupil effort and academic achievement may be impacted by these associations.

Effective behaviour management

Another approach used by successful schools in Australia, Canada, England, New Zealand, and the USA is developing good practices for behaviour management to control student conduct in schools. Research by Armstrong (2018) highlighted the need for accommodating the behavioural needs of the student. However, it has been argued that using evidence-based initiatives designed to tackle behaviour issues in the USA and the UK through the use of effective behaviour support has made a positive change in reducing school exclusions. One of the key recommendations from these behaviour management initiatives in tackling behaviour problems is to use targeted support for teachers experiencing occupational burnout. He also argued the need to encourage schools to include and keep students who might otherwise face suspension or exclusion on behavioural grounds using an incentive policy (Armstrong, 2018).

Garner (2011:14) also argued that schools that are successful in reducing school exclusions of pupils with challenging behaviour are characterised by effective leadership that has ensured several measures to prevent exclusions, including:

The use and promotion of well-integrated in-class support to teachers; clear, well-understood behaviour expectations; consistent but fair use of rewards and light-touch sanctions; strongly established, well-staffed learning support units and mentors; strongly embedded multi-agency support; and a strong commitment to inclusion.

There is a lack of research into successful schools in the USA for tackling school exclusions. Much of the research focusses on the causes and consequences of exclusions, including the over-representation of African Americans and Latinos in school exclusions compared to White pupils (see Raffaele Mendez & Knoff, 2003; Skiba, Michael, Nardo, & Peterson, 2002; Eitle and Eitle, 2004; Raffaele Mendez & Knoff, 2003; Skiba et al., 2011). However, Valdebenito et al. (2019) researched to examine the impact of interventions to reduce exclusions from school. The review covered 37 studies, with 33 studies from the USA and four elsewhere. The study shows that:

Four intervention types – enhancement of academic skills, counselling, mentoring/monitoring, and skills training for teachers – had significant desirable effects on exclusion.

(Valdebenito et al. 2019:1)

There are also lessons from other studies in the USA and elsewhere. The main findings from the USA suggest that school-based intervention; enhancement of academic skills, counselling, mentoring/monitoring, and skills training for teachers; restorative practice, and good behavioural management can be effective in reducing school exclusions (Armstrong 2018; González, 2011; Garner 2011; McCluskey 2008).

There is evidence that successful schools in Australia, Canada, England, New Zealand, and the USA are developing good practices for behaviour management, including targeted support for teachers experiencing occupational burnout and

Promotion of well-integrated in-class support to teachers; clear, well-understood behaviour expectations; consistent but fair use of rewards and light-touch sanctions; strongly established, well-staffed learning support units and mentors; strongly embedded multi-agency support; and a strong commitment to inclusion.

(Garner, 2011:8)

What is also clear from the review is that restorative approaches to school discipline are increasingly used to reduce student suspension and to close the racial discipline gap in the USA and elsewhere. The findings from the USA and elsewhere also show that teachers with high restorative practices had more positive relationships with their diverse students. These include Latino and African American students compared with lower restorative practice users.

Conclusions

This chapter seeks to understand success factors in tackling exclusion. This research confirms there is a disproportionate rate of exclusion of some ethnic groups, including Gypsy/Roma pupils, Travellers of Irish Heritage pupils, Black Caribbean, Mixed White, and Black Caribbean, in schools. Our findings indicate ethnic disparities were caused by multiple factors, including institutional racism, teachers' low expectations, poverty, a lack of diversity in the school workforce, and race issues (Demie, 2023).

However, the findings in this chapter show it is possible to tackle school exclusions. Evidence from the study shows that successful schools rarely, if ever, exclude pupils (Partridge et al. 2020; Demie and Mclean 2019; DfE 2019; Moore et al. 2019; Timpson 2019). These schools are effective in supporting pupils at risk of exclusion, and they have the following key features:

- An effective leadership team committed to equality and diversity
- Diverse workforce
- Excellent care and guidance of pupils
- Targeted intervention and support
- Effective behavioural management policy and practice
- Effective, inclusive, and nurturing practice
- Restorative approaches to school discipline
- Strong multi-agency support
- Effective alternative provisions and learning support units

The review of research literature suggested that the good practice discussed above has been used in England, the USA, Canada, Australia, Hong Kong, and internationally to tackle school exclusions and suspensions (see for details DfE 2019; RSA's 2021; Demie and Mclean, 2019; Partridge et al. 2020; Valdebenito et al. 2019; Graham et al. 2019; Garner 2011; Parsons 2010; González, 2011; McCluskey 2008; Gregory, et al. 2016). These could be considered by schools, practitioners, and policymakers to reduce and plan to manage the alternative pathways of learners at risk of school exclusions.

There is evidence from the literature reviewed also that successful schools are using good practices related to school exclusions, ranging from the commitment to individual teachers through effective use of school discipline policy that is not rigid and a whole-school approach to vulnerable children and their behaviours (Demie 2022a; DfE 2019; RSA, 2021). These successful schools put a premium on the education of the child and not on the financial cost of its education, which is used as a reason to exclude vulnerable Black and ethnic minority and SEN children. They all have high expectations for everyone. They want to do their best for every child. In these successful schools, children come first by ensuring the behaviour policy is based on inclusion and does not discriminate against pupils on the grounds of race.

References

Armstrong, D. (2018) Addressing the wicked problem of behaviour in schools. *International Journal of Inclusive Education* 22(9): 997–1013, DOI: 10.1080/13603116.2017.141373

Demie, F. (2019a) The experience of Black Caribbean pupils in school exclusion in England. *Educational Review.* https://doi.org/10.1080/00131911.2019.1590316

Demie, F. (2019b) *Exclusions of pupils from schools in England: Extent, causes and consequences: Research Project Brief.*, London: Lambeth School Research and Statistics Unit. https://www.lambeth.gov.uk.rsu/sites/www.lambeth.gov.uk.rsu/files/school_exclusions_in_england_research_brief.pdf

Demie, F. (2022a) *Understanding the Causes and Consequences of School Exclusions: Teachers, Parents and Schools' Perspectives.* London: Routledge.

Demie, F. (2022b) 'Tackling teachers' low expectations of Black Caribbean students in English schools. *Equity in Education and Society Journal* 1(1): 32–49. https://doi.org/10.1177/27526461211068511

Demie, F. (2023) *Raising the Achievement of Black Caribbean pupils: Barriers and Good Practice in Schools.* London: Lambeth Research and Statistics Unit. https://www.lambeth.gov.uk/sites/default/files/2023-05/Raising_Achievement_of_Black_Caribbean_Pupils_-_Barriers_and_Good_Practice.pdf

Demie, F. & Mclean, C. (2017) *Black Caribbean Underachievement in Schools in England.* Lambeth LA. London: School Research and Statistics Unit.

Demie, F. & Mclean, C. (2019) *Tackling Educational Disadvantage: What works in schools.* London: Lambeth Research and Statistics Unit.

Demie, F. & Mclean, M. (2020) *Tackling School Exclusions: Good Practice.* London: School Research and Statistics Unit, October.

DfE. (2019) *Permanent and Fixed-period exclusions in England 2017–2018.* London: Department for Education, 25 July. https://www.gov.uk/government/statistics/permanent-and-fixed-period-exclusions-in-england-2017-to-2018

DfE. (2021) *Permanent and Fixed-period exclusions in England 2019–2020.* London: Department for Education.

DfE. (2022) *Permanent and Fixed-period exclusions in England 2020–2021.* London: Department for Education.

DfE. (2023) *Permanent and Fixed-period exclusions in England 2021–2022.* London: Department for Education.

EEF. (2019) *Teaching and Learning Tool Kit.* London: Education Endowment Foundation. https://educationendowmentfoundation.org.uk/evidencesummaries/teaching-learning-toolkit/

EHRC. (2015) *Is Britain Fairer? The State of Equality and Human Rights*. London: Equality and Human Rights Commission. https://www.gov.uk/government/publications/is-britain-fairer-the-state-of-equality-and-human-rights-2015

Eitle, T.M.N. & Eitle, D.J. (2004) 'Inequality, segregation, and the overrepresentation of African Americans in school suspensions'. *Sociological Perspectives*, 47, 269–287.

EPI. (2019) *Unexplained pupil exits from schools: a growing problem?* London: Education Policy Unit, April. https://epi.org.uk/wp-content/uploads/2019/04/EPI_Unexplained-pupil-exits_2019.pdf

Garner, P. (2011) *Promoting the conditions for positive behaviour, to help every child succeed Review of the landscape*. National College for School Leadership (NCSL).

González, T. (2011) Restoring justice: Community organizing to transform school discipline policies. *U.C. Davis Journal of Juvenile Law & Policy* 15(1): 9–10.

González, T. (2014) Addressing racial disparities in school discipline: Restorative alternatives to exclusionary practices in schools. In Losen, D. (ed.), *Closing The School Discipline Gap*. New York, NY: Teachers College Press.

Graham, B., White, C., Edwards, A., Potter, S., & Street, C. (2019) *School Exclusion: A Literature Review On The Continued Disproportionate Exclusion Of Certain Children*. Department for Education, May. https://assets.publishing.service.gov.uk/government/uploads/system/uploads/attachment_data/file/800028/Timpson_review_of_school_exclusion_literature_review.pdf

Gregory, A., Clawson, K., Davis, A. & Gerewitz, J. (2016) 'The promise of restorative practices to transform teacher-student relationships and achieve equity in school discipline'. *Journal of Educational and Psychological Consultation*, 26 (4): 325–353.

Gregory, A., Nygreen, K. & Moran, D. (2006) The discipline gap and the normalization of failure. In Noguera, P.A. & Wing, J.Y. (eds.), *Unfinished business: Closing the racial achievement gap in our schools*, 121–150. San Francisco, CA: Jossey-Bass.

House of Common Library. (2018) *Off-rolling in English schools*. London: House of Common Library brief, Number 08444, 10 December. https://researchbriefings.parliament.uk/ResearchBriefing/Summary/CBP-8444

IPPR. (2017) *Making the Difference: Breaking the link between school exclusion and social exclusion*. London: Institute for Public Policy Research. https://www.ippr.org/files/2017-10/making-the-difference-report-october-2017.pdf

McCluskey, G. (2008) 'Exclusion from school: what can 'include' pupils tell us?' *British Educational Research Journal*, 34 (4): 447–466.

McCluskey, G., Cole, T., Daniels, H., Thompson, I. & Tawel, A. (2019) Exclusion from school in Scotland and across the UK: Contrasts and questions. *British Educational Research Journal* 45(6): 1140–1159.

McClusky, G., Riddell, S., Weedon, E. & Fordyce, M. (2016) Exclusion from school and recognition of difference. *Discourse: Studies in the Cultural Politics of Education* 37(4): 529–539. https://doi.org/10.1080/01596306.2015.1073

Moore, D., Benham-Clarke, S., Kenchington, R., Boyle, C., Ford, T., Hayes, R. & Rogers, M. (2019) *Improving Behaviour in Schools: Evidence Review*. London: Education Endowment Foundation. https://educationendowmentfoundation.org.uk/public/files/Improving_Behaviour_in_Schools_Evidence_Review.pdf

Ofsted. (2018) *Off-rolling: using data to see a fuller picture*, Blog Posted by: Jason Bradbury, June. https://educationinspection.blog.gov.uk/2018/06/26/off-rolling-using-data-to-see-a-fuller-picture/

Parsons, C. (2008) Race relations legislation, ethnicity and disproportionality in school exclusions in England. *Cambridge Journal of Education* 39(3): 401–419. Cambridge.

Parsons, C. (2009) Explaining sustained inequalities *in* ethnic minority school exclusions *in* England—passive racism *in a* neoliberal grip. *Oxford Review* of *Education* 35(2): 249–265.

Parsons, C. (2010) 'Achieving zero permanent exclusions from school, social justice and economy'. *FORUM 52* (3): 395–404. www.wwwords.co.uk/FORUM

Partridge, L., Strong, F., & Lobley, E. (2020) *Pinnball Kids: Preventing school exclusions*. RSA. https://www.thersa.org/globalassets/reports/2020/the-rsa-pinball-kids-preventing-school-exclusions.pdf

Power, S. & Taylor, C. (2018) Not in the classroom, but still on the register: Hidden forms of school exclusion. *International Journal of Inclusive Education*. https://doi.org/10.1080/13603116.2018.1492644

Raffaele Mendez, L.M. & Knoff, H.M. (2003) Who gets suspended from school and why: A demographic analysis of schools and disciplinary infractions in a large school district. *Education and Treatment of Children* 26: 30–51.

RSA. (2021) Inclusive and nurturing schools toolkit. https://www.thersa.org/reports/inclusive-nurturing-schools-toolkit

Skiba, R.J., Horner, R.H., Chung, C.-G., Rausch, M.K., May, S.L. & Tobin, T. (2011) Race is not neutral: A national investigation of African American and Latino disproportionality in school discipline. *School Psychology Review* 40(1): 85–107.

Skiba, R.J., Michael, R.S., Nardo, A.C. & Peterson, R. (2002) The colour of discipline: Sources of racial and gender disproportionality in school punishment. *Urban Review* 34(4): 317–342.

Strand, S., & Fletcher, J. (2014) *A Quantitative Analysis Of Exclusions From English Secondary Schools*. Oxford: University of Oxford, Department of Education.

Timpson, E. (2019) *Timpson Review of School Exclusion*. London: Department for Education. https://assets.publishing.service.gov.uk/government/uploads/system/uploads/attachment_data/file/807862/Timpson_review.pdf

Valdebenito, S., Eisner, M., Farrington, P., Ttofi, M. & Sutherland, A. (2019) School-based interventions for reducing disciplinary school exclusion: a systematic review. *Campbell Systematic Reviews* 14(1): 1–216. https://www.researchgate.net/publication/322397442_School-based_interventions_for_reducing_disciplinary_school_exclusion_a_systematic_review

Wright, C., Weekes, D. & McGlaighlin, A. (2008) *Race, Class, and Gender in Exclusion from School*. Routledge.

PART IV

The International Experience in Raising the Achievement of Black and Ethnic Minority Students

10
THE INTERNATIONAL EXPERIENCE IN RAISING THE ACHIEVEMENT OF BLACK AND ETHNIC MINORITY STUDENTS

Introduction

The racial achievement gaps have long been discussed and researched in education. One of the major debates in education in the USA has been how to raise achievement and close the achievement gap between White students and Black and Hispanic students (Gottfried et al. 2023; Shirrell et al. 2023; Rudasill et al. 2023; Gershenson et al. 2023; Dirmeyer, 2021; Lindsay et al. 2021; OECD 2020; Hung et al. 2020; Dietrichson et al. 2017; Ansell, 2011; Olneck 2005; Coleman 1966). This chapter explores the international experience of closing the achievement gap for Black American, Hispanic, Indigenous American, Asian American, and other ethnic minority students in the USA and other English-speaking countries. Drawing on a systematic literature review and standardised score results about the achievement gap in the USA and the variety of explanations for the existence of the gap, it will argue where England sits to the USA in closing the achievement gap to draw implications for tackling Black and ethnic minority students' achievement. This is followed by school strategies to tackle educational inequalities and the attainment gap. The last section draws conclusions and lessons from the USA to drive improvement and close the achievement gap of Black and ethnic minority students.

The racial achievement gap in the USA

The achievement gap in the USA is alarming, and there has been a long-standing debate about the gap between Black, White, and Hispanic students in educational achievement. Researchers argued that Black Americans,

DOI: 10.4324/9781003499633-14

Hispanics, and racial groups are more likely to earn lower grades and score lower on standardised tests and less likely to enter and complete college than Whites, while Asian Americans achieved higher than Whites (Gottfried et al., 2023; Hughes and Cymon, 2023; Gershenson et al., 2023; Bradley, 2022; Pollard, 2022; Minus-Vincent, 2022; Lindsay et al., 2021; Assari et al., 2021; Hung et al., 2020; OECD 2020; Dietrichson et al., 2017; McKown, 2013; Ansell, 2011). Researchers in our review used to measure the racial achievement gaps in standardised test scores, high school dropout rates, high school completion rates, college acceptance, and retention rates. For example, according to Phillips et al. (1998), who examined the Black-White test score gap after Children Enter School, children of Latino, Native American, and African American descent begin kindergarten and first grade with lower levels of oral language, reading, and mathematics than do White and Asian American children. This accounts for about half of the test score gap between Black and White students.

Reardon and Galindo (2009) and Clotfelter et al. (2009) study suggest that on average, Hispanic and Black students begin kindergarten with math scores three-quarters of a standard deviation lower than those of White students. The reading scores were a half standard deviation lower than those of White students. These studies also found that Black-White gaps in both math and reading scores are around half a standard deviation.

Hedges and Nowell's (1998) analysis of the Scholastic Assessment Test (SAT), which is used as an admission test in the USA, also shows the largest gap between White and African American students, with scores of about 82 to 1.18 standard deviations lower than White students in composite test scores. White and Hispanic students are closely behind Black Americans, with Asian American students achieving higher than that of White students and other ethnic minorities.

Vanneman et al.'s 2009 study using the National Assessment of Educational Progress (NAEP) reports the national Black-White gap and the Hispanic-White gap in math and reading assessments; the data show a Black-White gap in mathematics, a 26-point difference at the 4th-grade level and a 31-point difference at the 8th-grade level. The reading evidence suggests a 27-point difference at the 4th grade and a 26-point difference at the 8th-grade level.

Hemphill's (2011) study of the Hispanic-White gap also suggests a 21-point difference in mathematics at the 4th-grade level and a 26-point difference at the 8th-grade level. There is a 25-point difference at the 4th-grade level in reading and a 24-point difference in reading at the 8th-grade level.

Dirmeyer (2021) and Hung et al. (2020) also confirm that Black and Hispanic students significantly underperform on standardised tests compared to their White peers, and they are more likely to receive lower grades, drop out of high school, and score lower on standardised tests; they are less likely to complete college education than White students. Recent NAEP data evidence also shows a big gap between Black Americans, Hispanics, and White Europeans (see Table 10.1).

The NAEP reading and mathematics assessment for grades 4, 8, and 12 trend data between 2022 and 2019 also shows an interesting pattern by racial and ethnic groups in the USA (see Table 10.1).

TABLE 10.1 The National Assessment of Educational Progress (NAEP) trend in reading and mathematics average scores for Black, Hispanic, and White students in the USA

	Reading								
	Grade 4			Grade 8			Grade 12		
Year	White	Black	Hispanic	White	Black	Hispanic	Black	White	Hispanic
2022	246	217	205	268	244	251	N/A	N/A	N/A
2019	249	224	209	272	244	252	263	295	274
2017	248	223	209	275	249	255	266	295	276
2015	248	224	208	274	248	253	268	297	276
2013	250	224	207	276	250	256	269	296	274
2011	249	224	206	274	249	252	267	293	272
2009	248	222	205	273	246	249	267	292	273
2007	248	222	205	272	245	247	269	297	275
2005	246	220	203	271	243	246	271	297	276
2003	243	216	200	272	244	245	265	293	270
2000	234	203	201	272	245	247	273	297	279
1996	232	198	190	270	244	243			

	Mathematics Average score								
	Grade 4			Grade 8			Grade 12		
	Black Grade 4	Hispanic	White	Black American	Hispanic	White	Black	Hispanic	White
2022	217	224	246	253	261	285	**N/A**	**N/A**	**N/A**
2019	224*	231*	249*	260*	268*	292*	128	138	159
2017	223*	229*	248*	260*	269*	293*	130	139	160
2015	224*	230*	248*	260*	270*	292*	132*	141*	162*
2013	224*	231*	250*	263*	272*	294*	131	138	161
2011	224*	229*	249*	262*	270*	293*	127	133*	157*
2009	222*	227*	248*	261*	266*	293*			
2007	222*	227*	248*	260*	265*	291*			
2005	220*	226	246	255	262	289*			
2003	216	222*	243*	252	259*	288*			
2000	203*	208*	234*	244*	253*	284			
1996	198*	207*	232*	240*	251*	281*			

Source: https://www.nationsreportcard.gov/mathematics/nation/groups/?grade=4

In reading at grade 4, there was a 29% achievement gap in 2022 compared to 34% in 1996. However, the data shows that White 4th-grade students outperformed Black and Hispanic students. Similarly, at grade 8, the average score in reading for White 8th-grade students declined in 2022 compared to 1996. At grade 12 there was a 32-point White-Black score gap in 2019. While average reading scores for White and Black 12th-grade students were not significantly different in 2019 compared to 2015, the scores for both groups were lower than in 1996. Overall, the reading evidence from the data shows that the White and Black achievement gap was 25% in 2022 at grade 4 compared to 25% at grade 8 and 32% at grade 12 in 2022. However, the Hispanic gap in the same period is less than that of Blacks. At grade 4, the gap was 22% compared to 25% at grade 8 and 21% at grade 12.

In mathematics, in 2022, among racial/ethnic groups, the average mathematics score for White 4th-grade students was 32 points higher than their Black peers (compared to 33 points in 2019). The data also shows in mathematics for 8th graders there are no significant changes for the White-Black and White-Hispanic score gaps in 2022 compared to 2019. Similarly, the average mathematics score in grade 12 for White students was 31 points higher than the average score for their Black peers in 2019. The data also shows that 22 points higher than the average mathematics score for 12th-grade Hispanic students.

Factors associated with the achievement gap in the USA

Researchers have offered a variety of explanations for the existence of the racial achievement gap in the USA. Previous research identified several factors as important risk factors associated with the achievement gap and as having a significant impact on the academic achievement of Black and ethnic minority students in the USA. These include factors such as race, socioeconomic status (SES), parental influence, family background, parental factors, quality of the school, high-quality teaching, school funding, and the geography of the school neighbourhood. Institutional and structural factors (attending low- and highly segregated schools), school exclusions, cultural differences (African American cultural factors, Latino American cultural factors, Asian American cultural factors), and bias in standardised tests. Each of these factors is a potential risk factor and contributed to the widening of the achievement gap in the USA, as can be seen from the discussions that follow.

One of the important factors contributing to the achievement gap in the USA is race background. Research identified that the gap is influenced by the race and ethnicity of the students, and racial background played a key role. Ford et al. (2008), based on SAT and NACEP data, argued that the underachievers with the lowest academic achievement are African Americans. The educational gap between African American students and their White counterparts is an education problem (Leach and Williams, 2007), and the racial achievement gap suggests that students from African families are twice as likely to have repeated a grade, 73% more likely to be suspended from school, and 23% attend special classes (Kaushal and Nepomnyaschy, 2009).

Leach and Williams (2007) studies also show African Americans are placed in fewer academically challenging courses in high school based on racial background. Griffin's (2002) research also shows that African American and Hispanic communities are comparatively less interested in education, and there was evidence that supported the idea that African American and Hispanic students place less importance on academic performance. This finding is important as it identifies the value of keeping African American and Hispanic students engaged in the learning process through means other than good grades. African American and Hispanic students do not stay in school solely because of their grades. It is important that students feel connected through an understanding of their significance in the academic setting (Steele, 1997).

There is now a consensus in the USA that racial background matters in education. There is a deep-rooted gap between people of colour and Whites in terms of beliefs and culture, and the ethnic and racial backgrounds of students play an integral role in their expectations for education (Ogbu, 1992a,b,1993). This intractable nature of differences in academic achievement due to racial background is a major concern and has contributed to the achievement gap identified in the SAT and NACEP statistics shown above.

Another important factor highlighted in the literature was SES. Researchers have examined SES as a determinant of the achievement gap. There is now evidence that shows a strong link between SES and the achievement gap in the USA (Assari et al., 2021; Easterbrook and Hadden, 2021; Hung et al., 2020). The NAEP (2009) shows that 36% of all African American children and 33% of all Hispanic children are poor, and poverty factors play a key role in achievement.

Recent data by Bradley (2022) also shows that 32% of Black children were living in poverty, 31% of Native American children, 25% of Hispanic children, and 25% of Pacific Islander children. Assari et al. (2021) and Bradley (2022) also argued that poverty has been consistently associated with the achievement gap. There is a huge over-representation of African Americans in poverty statistics in the USA compared to any other ethnic group, and as a result, poverty has important detrimental effects on schooling, including poor performance (Dirmeyer, 2021; Perry, 2009; Assari et al., 2021, 2020; Talbert-Johnson, 2004; West, 2007; Harwell and LeBeau, 2010). Living in poverty usually means families are less able to afford good healthcare, secure nutritious food, or provide enriching cultural or educational experiences for their children; these are all essential preconditions for success in schools for ethnic minority students (Assari et al., 2021; Talbert-Johnson,

2004; West, 2007). More importantly, there is now strong research evidence that poor families are less likely to invest in educational enrichment items (e.g., educational toys, books, and participation in educational activities), which are useful for the learning and development of children (Kaushal and Nepomnyaschy, 2009).

All previous research has shown persistent racial inequalities due to the low quality of education at urban schools and poverty (Assari et al., 2020, 2021; Talbert-Johnson, 2004; Sandy and Duncan, 2010; Rutkowski et al., 2018; Harwell and LeBeau, 2010; Dirmeyer, 2021).

Parental influence and family background factors were also identified as reasons for the achievement gap between African Americans, Hispanics, and other ethnic groups in the USA. Several research studies and reviews show that parental involvement in children's education is influential in children's success at school, and family involvement affects student achievement (see Lambert et al., 2022; Barton et al., 2004; Cooper et al., 2010; Hill and Tyson, 2009; Patall et al., 2008; Jeynes, 2003, 2005, 2007, 2012; Fan and Chen, 2001). Teachers and school leaders see low parental involvement as a barrier to student success. We would argue that the school cannot accomplish its purpose without at least the implicit support of the family and parents. Barton et al research (2004) shows that low parental education expectations and a lack of homework monitoring or study aids are all linked to lower school performance. Leach and Williams (2007) argue that family support and setting early educational goals are two of the strongest predictors of student development and academic success, but there is low parental and family involvement from African and Hispanic families compared to their White peers, and this is one factor contributing to the achievement gap (Leach and Williams, 2007).

Researchers also identified cultural differences as the reasons for the achievement gap in education. For example, Ogbu (1992a), in his research 'Understanding Cultural Diversity and Learning,' argued that cultural factors contribute to the racial achievement gap. He highlighted that students from minority cultures face language barriers, differences in cultural norms in interactions and learning styles, and varying levels of acceptance of White American culture. In particular, it has been found that ethnic minority students' cultures generally do not align with the mainstream culture in American society, and they have a harder time in school. In addition, views of the value of education differ among Whites. Research suggests that African American and Hispanic children often receive mixed messages about the importance of education and, as a result, perform below their academic potential (Noguera, 2003).

The Hispanic student is particularly affected by Latino-American cultural factors, which see their parents as having immigrated to the USA and a high school diploma as being a sufficient amount of schooling and do not know the importance of continuing to college (Suárez-Orozco and Marcelo

Suárez-Orozco 1995). Additionally, some students prioritise their obligations to assist their families over their educational aspirations. Surveys have shown that while Latino American families would like their children to have a formal education, they also place a high value on getting jobs and marrying, which conflicts with the goal of educational achievement. Latino American students also face barriers such as financial stability and insufficient support for higher education within their families (Hemphill et al., 2011; Suárez-Orozco and Marcelo Suárez-Orozco, 1995). Latino Americans over the age of 25 have the lowest percentage of obtaining a bachelor's degree or higher among all other racial groups, with only 11% (U.S. Census Bureau, 2003).

Research suggests Hispanic children are more likely to be raised in poverty, with 33% of Hispanic families living below the economic poverty level, compared to African American (39%), Asian (14%), and White (13%) counterparts. Furthermore, language is a problem with Spanish families as they are not English speakers (Hemphill et al. 2011). As a result, some Hispanic students have difficulty getting help and assistance with their homework at home (Suárez-Orozco and Marcelo Suárez-Orozco, 1995). This affects the achievement gap compared to Whites in America.

Similarly, in the case of African Americans, the community culture may play a role in the achievement gap. Jencks and Phillip's (1998) research into achievement test: closing the Black-White test score gap argues that African American parents may not encourage early education in toddlers. As a result of cultural differences, African American students tend to begin school with a lower vocabulary than their White classmates. The children enter school with decreased word knowledge, which can affect their language skills, influence their experience with books, and create different perceptions and expectations in the classroom context. Poverty also often acts as a factor, and many children who are poor and come from homes that lack stability, continuity of care, adequate nutrition, and medical care create a level of environmental stress that can affect the young child's development compared to White. Studies show there is a problem for many African American students due to the large number of single-parent households. Students from single-parent households frequently struggle to find time for their parents to offer assistance (Carola Suárez-Orozco and Marcelo Suárez-Orozco, 1995).

Research also shows that African American students are likely to receive different messages about the importance of education from their peer group and their parents, and they are more likely to place less emphasis on education. Some researchers point out that African American and Hispanic students may feel little motivation to do well in school. They do not believe education will pay off in the form of a better job or upward social mobility (Jencks and Phillips, 1998).

Asian American cultural factors also played a key role in their education in the USA (Kao, 1995; Hsin and Xie, 2014). There is strong evidence that suggests Asian American students are more likely to view education as a means to social mobility and career advancement compared to ethnic groups such as African Americans and Hispanics (Lee, 1994; Shirrell et al., 2023; Shortell and Romine, 2020; Gottfried et al., 2023). They also see education as a means to overcome discrimination as well as language barriers in the USA. This notion comes from cultural expectations and parental expectations of their children, which are rooted in the cultural belief that education and hard work are the keys to educational and eventually occupational attainment. This factor has helped narrow the achievement gap with their White American peers. As a concluding remark, there is now a consensus that African American, Hispanic, and Asian American cultural differences contribute to the achievement gap compared to Whites in the USA.

Institutional factors and neighbourhood segregation are also highlighted as the reasons for the achievement gap (see Rushing, 2017; Orfield et al., 2012; Card and Rothstein, 2007; Charles, 2003; Crain and Mahard, 1978). In the USA, according to the districting patterns within the school system, ethnic minority students are more likely to originate from low-income households, attend low-achieving, highly segregated schools, and get inadequate funding. Schools in lower-income districts tend to employ less qualified teachers and have fewer educational resources. Rothstein's (2004; Card and Rothstein's 2007) study provides insight into neighbourhood segregation and its contribution to the gap, as well as further evidence that the achievement gap between Black and White students is higher in more segregated cities in the USA. All this research suggests that the gap is wider when looking at the scores within a highly segregated city. These researchers also consistently found a strong correlation between neighbourhood segregation and lower scores. They also found both school and neighbourhood segregation to have negative effects on Black achievement, thus adding to the national achievement gap between Black and White students.

VanderHart's (2006) study also shows that ethnic minority groups are also affected by school tracking systems within schools that have proven to be detrimental to students. The tracking system assigns students to ability groups or tailors lesson plans for different groups of learners in the school. In this practice, schools tend to emphasise SES and cultural capital when placing students in groups, and ethnic minority students are over-represented in lower educational tracks. Hispanic and African American students are often wrongly placed into lower tracks as administrators or teachers have low expectations of them compared to White groups or Asian Americans. Such expectations of race are a form of institutional racism and should never be allowed. Once students are in these lower tracks, researchers argue that they tend to have a less challenging curriculum, less qualified teachers, and few opportunities to move into higher-ability groups or tracks. This has also contributed to the achievement of Hispanic and African American students (VanderHart, 2006).

The lack of diversity and the effect of own-race teachers on student achievement are also raised by research for reasons of underachievement and the gap. The disproportionality of the number of ethnic minority teachers is particularly a concern in the USA, as a growing body of research suggests that the under-representation of ethnic minority teachers in schools is a contributing factor to the racial test score gap in the USA, and ethnic minority students could benefit from assignments to teachers of their race and ethnicity (Ingersoll and May, 2011; Kirby, Berends, and Naftel, 1999; Villegas, Strom, and Lucas, 2012; Clotfelter, Ladd, and Vigdor, 2007; Dee, 2004; Ehrenberg, Goldhaber, and Brewer, 1995; Meier, Wrinkle, and Polinard, 1999).

Dee (2004) analysed test score data for Black and White students participating in Tennessee's large-scale randomised experiment designed to measure the relationship between class size and student achievement. He found evidence that assignment to an own-race/ethnicity teacher increases the math and reading achievement of both Black and White students by between 6 and 6 percentile points.

Yarnell and Bohrnstedt's (2018) analysis of students and teachers from the NAEP Grade 4 Reading Assessment also showed that having a Black teacher is associated with higher levels of achievement for Black students. Gottfried et al. (2023) NCES Early Childhood Longitudinal Study also shows that students with a racial match to their teachers had slightly higher math and reading scores, even after controlling for other factors. Easton-Brooks et al. (2009) study using data from the Early Childhood Longitudinal Study about African American students taught by either African American or European American teachers in the public school system shows African American students with at least one African American teacher scored higher on reading at the end of kindergarten compared to students with no exposure to an African American teacher.

Minus-Vincent's (2022) study in New Jersey schools reported that Black students taught by Black teachers achieved better scores than peers not taught by teachers of the same ethnicity. Kamau's (2011) study in a multi-ethnic public high school also confirmed that students whose race and ethnicity matched their teachers' race and ethnicity achieved higher mean scores in English and math. Banerjee (2019) also reported that Black students who are taught by Black teachers have higher expectations for their performance than White teachers do in English (effect size 0.24) and math (0.33).

Several other studies also suggested that ethnic minority students, especially Black students in the USA, have higher attainment at school when taught by teachers of the same ethnicity (Clotfelter et al. 2010, Daniels 2022). Pollard's (2022) research also highlighted that there is no link between student-teacher ethnic match and improved attainment. Studies in the USA have also identified some teachers' biases in assessing the academic performance of ethnic minority students. Teachers' perceptions are sensitive to the lowest-performing Black students in early classrooms but less responsive to the highest-performing students (Rangel and Shi 2020; Blazar 2021). Research indicates that White teachers may be more inclined to assess the writing of Black students as below expected levels compared to that of White students, compared to teachers of colour who are themselves people of colour and appear not to exhibit this same bias in their evaluations (Quinn 2020). These patterns of teachers' bias in assessments persist, and the teaching of weak teachers and White teachers may be argued to have a link to achievement and low attainment.

Other factors that are identified in the literature are student-teacher relationships. Many studies argue that same ethnicity teachers are more culturally responsive to their teachers (Castro and Calzada 2021; Rudasill et al. 2023; Brooms 2017), and ethnic minorities and students with teachers of the same ethnicity tend to have better relationships. Such good relationships with their teachers tend to lead to higher attainment and fewer discipline referrals (Crosnoe et al., 2004; Pollard, 2022). These studies also found Black students tend to see Black male teachers as having better relationships with them, making an important contribution to their development and attainment (Brooms 2017). This is further confirmed by the Gershenson et al. (2016) study, which found that non-Black teachers had lower educational expectations for Black students compared to Black teachers. With diversity in school staffing, Chan et al. (2023) state that there is less racial and ethnic bias in relationships.

Several USA studies also found that many White European teachers perceived Black students as being lower-achieving and worse-behaved than White students (Minor 2014). There is considerable variation between teachers in their expectations for specific students (Papageorge et al. 2020). US Black, Hispanic, and Native American students are more likely to be judged as having a disability than White and especially Asian American students. Black students are also more likely to be excluded or drop out of school and less likely to be assigned to gifted and talented programmes than White or Latino students (Redding 2019). In general, the evidence shows that ethnic disproportion between students and teachers in schools affects student treatment and outcomes, as well as the achievement gap in the USA.

Brown's (2018) study, which focussed on student perceptions of teacher effectiveness and the student-teacher relationship, found that the presence of a same-race teacher was associated with more positive student perceptions of the teacher's classroom environment, expectations, and rigour. The impact on the perception of the perception of the student-teacher relationship was more pronounced among White students compared to Black students. Other studies in the USA have found that many teachers perceived Black students as being lower-achieving and worse-behaved than White students (Minor 2014). There is considerable variation between teachers in their expectations for specific students, and expectations can be linked to students enrolling in and completing post-compulsory education (Papageorge et al. 2020). Different perceptions of some ethnic groups are even linked to judgements about whether students have a learning challenge or disability (Cooc 2017). US Black, Hispanic, and Native American students are more likely to be judged as having a disability than White and especially Asian American students. Black students are also less likely to be assigned to gifted and talented programmes than White or Latino students (Redding 2019). They are more likely to be excluded or drop out from school.

Another racial factor is also related to school exclusions. Black students' higher rate of out-of-school suspensions may impact overall academic achievement, contributing to a gap in overall performance when compared to White students (Dirmeyer, 2021). Particularly, African Americans and Hispanics are disproportionately suspended from schools when compared to their White classmates. Research confirms that African American students in particular are suspended on average two to three times more frequently than White students (Brooks, Schiraldi, and Ziendenberg, 1999) research also found that African American students reported a more negative perception of racial climate and had lower grades and more disciplinary issues. White teachers reported the behaviour of African American students as more disruptive Stearns and Glennie (2007) states that the achievement gap is occurring due to cultural and attitudinal differences between students. Ogbu writes similarly about an 'oppositional culture' of African American youth who go against mainstream expectations and disengage from school because they fear being accused of 'acting white.'

Analysis of the national data by Leung-Gagné et al. 2022 also confirms that racial and ethnic disparities in the use of out-of-school suspensions within the USA have persisted over the years. The suspension data shows Black students were excluded from school at the highest rate, with more than 1 in 8 Black students (12%) receiving one or more out-of-school suspensions in 2017–2018. The suspension rates of Hispanic, Pacific Islander, and White students were quite similar across the years in elementary schools, but Native American students were excluded at rates higher than the national average (see Leung-Gagné et al. 2022 and Figure 10.1).

A review of the literature on school exclusion and suspension also suggests that Black students are more often disciplined than other students because of a lack of cultural differences. Ethnic minority students with similar ethnic minority teachers are less likely to be seen as disruptive (Dee, 2005), excluded (Lindsay and Hart 2017), suspended from schools, or dropped out. Blake et al. (2016) study of Texas public schools over five

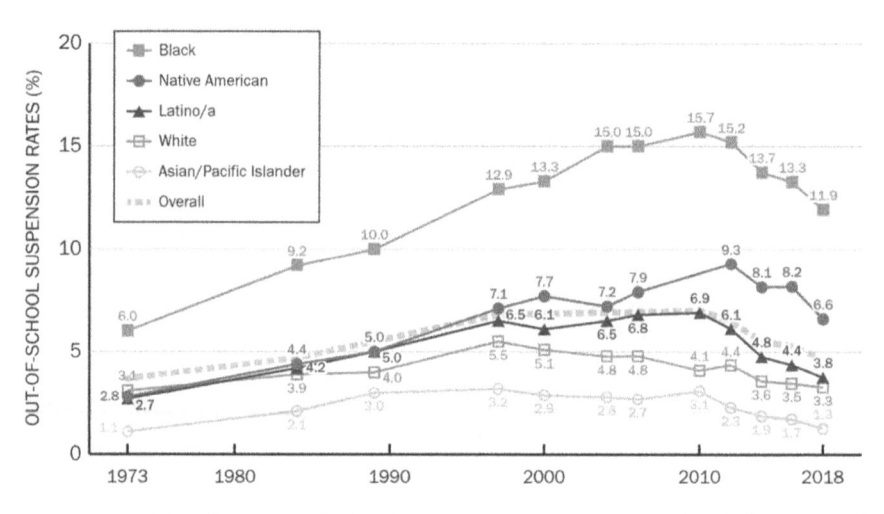

192 Black and Ethnic Minority Achievement in Schools

FIGURE 10.1 Trends in out-of-school suspension rates in K-12 schools by race and ethnicity, 1973–2018.

Source: Leung-Gagné et al. (2022:5) Pushed Out: Trends and Disparities in Out-of-School Suspension.

years shows that because of the similarity of the faculty and students, there was less likelihood of punishment of Black and Hispanic students.

Shirrell et al. (2023) studies using The New York City Department of Education (NYCDOE) data spanning 10 academic years show greater proportions of ethnically matched teachers decrease the likelihood of suspension for Black and Latinx students. It also suggests that diversifying the teacher workforce could significantly decrease exclusionary discipline in urban districts.

Lindsay and Hart (2017) and Lindsay et al. (2021) studied in North Carolina and Texas and found that the use of same-race teachers reduced rates of exclusionary discipline for Black students. Hughes et al. used data from Florida middle and high schools and also suggested that greater racial and ethnic diversity among district teaching faculties was associated with a reduction in Black and Latino suspension disparities compared to White students. This is further supported by Gershenson et al.'s (2023) study, which confirms that having a Black same-grade colleague reduces the suspension rates of White teachers' Black students, suggesting a strong argument for diversity in the teaching workforce.

The overall conclusion from the review is that the achievement gap is a major issue in the USA, and the data shows lower performance in test scores and grades, high dropout rates, high exclusion rates, low graduation rates, and low enrolment in post-secondary education for Black Americans and Hispanics. The main reasons for the gap are related to racism, SES, teachers' low expectations, school exclusions and suspensions, cultural differences, and lack of diversity in the teaching workforce.

Effective strategies to tackle educational inequalities and the racial achievement gap

There have been few systematic reviews of strategies to tackle educational inequalities and close the achievement gap in USA schools. For instance, Cabral-Gouveia et al. (2023) pointed out that a significant portion of inequality stems from membership in historically marginalised SES groups. Being Black, Hispanic, or gipsy, or having any other racialised condition, strongly influences academic attainment, school dropout rates, and career choices in the USA. Sirin's (2005) and White's (1982) studies also confirmed a moderate effect size between SES and achievement and a strong effect between school area and achievement. Berkowitz et al. (2017) produced a critical literature review by examining whether a positive school and class climate can successfully interfere with the association between low SES and poor academic achievement. His findings show an overall positive contribution to academic achievement for students of disadvantaged backgrounds and in free schools (Berkowitz et al., 2017). Another comprehensive systematic review and meta-analysis by Dietrichson et al. (2017), which focussed on effective academic interventions for primary school students with low SES, also suggests several possibilities for closing the gap using parent training programmes, health interventions, role model interventions, and early childhood intervention programmes to increase the academic achievement of children with low SES. Using a treatment-control design, Dietrichson et al. (2017) gathered interventions implemented by schools, researchers, and local stakeholders and concluded that there is a positive impact for low-SES students with interventions such as tutoring, feedback and progress monitoring, and cooperative learning.

However, there was little review of the useful strategies to close the racial achievement gap, which is critical in the US context. This is despite strong evidence that the gap between the academic achievement of students from ethnic minority groups and that of the White majority is at the forefront of educators and policymakers in the USA. Research in the area does not point to any dramatic 'breakthrough' interventions but to a series of apparently straightforward changes that schools could make to close the gap. However, research evidence indicates that addressing some of the factors mentioned earlier can boost the academic achievement of economically disadvantaged and ethnic minority children (Dietrichson et al., 2017; Corallo and McDonald, 2002). The strongest research evidence is for high-quality pre-schools and school-related factors. This may be partly because more research has been done on factors within the school's purview in the USA.

In examining effective strategies to close the achievement gap, we will now consider strategies to close the school readiness gap as well as the school achievement gap.

Closing the school readiness gap in the early years

Several researchers pointed out the need for high-quality early childhood. Many African American, Hispanic, and other ethnic minority children start school so far behind, and the gap between the students by the time they reach kindergarten is already wide. There is also strong evidence that good early childhood programmes can produce substantial immediate gains for disadvantaged children (see Peisner-Feinberg, 1999; Snow et al., 1998).

In the early years, there is a need to extend high-quality, academically focussed childhood education to all the children at risk of failure, including African American, Hispanic, Asian American, White, and all other children. The most promising strategy from research is to increase access to high-quality, centre-based early childhood education programmes for 3- and 4-year-olds and support for parents that begin earlier than kindergarten with programmes that engage parents.

Studies by Monk (2001), Neuman (2003), Sherman (2002), and Thompson and O'Quinn (2001) indicate the Future Children programmes emphasise developing cognitive skills, which tends not to be an emphasis of Head Start programmes and can have a long-lasting impact on the school success of low-income and minority children. There is research evidence that such high-quality programmes have low child-staff ratios, well-educated staff, and strong supervision and likely narrow the school readiness gap considerably (Monk, 2001; Neuman, 2003; Sherman, 2002; Thompson and O'Quinn, 2001).

These research evidence also recommends preschool programmes serving disadvantaged children with a high-quality, stimulating curriculum delivered by well-qualified teachers and training in early childhood education in small classes with high teacher-student ratios. Parent training to better equip parents to foster their children's development and reinforce what the teacher is doing through such things as reading to the child daily and dealing effectively with behaviour problems is also suggested, as it has a significant impact. Home visits to all families in the programme to enable staff to identify health problems in children, assist parents in getting ongoing health care for their children, and screen for parents' mental health problems or other issues have also demonstrated a positive impact in the context of the USA.

The evidence from several studies does show that an overall high-quality early childhood programme that tackles the early readiness gap by focussing on academic preparation for school can reduce the gap sharply and also deliver long-term benefits to children, families, and society that last into the school process.

Closing the achievement gap in school

The achievement gap persists for many reasons in US schools, and it divides American Indian, Asian, African American, Latino, and White students in the USA from grade-school test scores through high school graduation and higher education in the USA. A review of published research identified factors related to the school, home, and community associated with the achievement gap by race and income (see Barton & Coley 2010; Mueller, 2006a, 2006b). This research evidence indicates that students from higher-income and White counterparts tend to have comparatively rigorous curricula, high-quality teachers, good teacher preparation time, teacher experience, attendance, low teacher absenteeism, low teacher turnover, small class sizes (fewer than 25 students per class), safe schools (little or no fear of being attacked, no gang presence), parent participation and attendance at school events, teachers' high ratings of parent involvement, student stability and rarely changing schools, adequate nutrition, and reading to young children daily for 3- to 5-year-olds. In contrast, students from lower-income families and racial/ethnic minorities (Black and Hispanic students, in particular) tend to have fewer of these success factors than normal White Americans.Borman et al.'s (2003) review and research also highlighted how comprehensive school reform programmes bring together many of the core elements just described into one package. These programmes seek to integrate instruction, testing, classroom management, teachers' professional development, parent involvement, and school management to achieve school-wide academic improvement. The best of these models has boosted student academic achievement and reduced achievement gaps. Models with the strongest evidence for their effectiveness include Success for All, Direct Instruction, the School Development Programme, and No Child Left Behind (Borman et al. 2003).

Addressing some of the factors listed above that affect the achievement gap can close the achievement gap for disadvantaged and minority children. Previous research and evaluation studies have also identified key characteristics of schools closing the gap and some core elements of schools that effectively improve the academic achievement of low-income and minority children (Hughes and Cymon, 2023; Borg et al., 2012; Berkowitz et al., 2017; Dietrichson et al., 2017; Mueller, 2006a,2006b; Kober, 2001; Haycock, 2001, Haycock & Jerald, 2002; Corallo and McDonald, 2002; Muijis et al., 2004; Reynolds, 2002; Navarro and Natalicio, 1999). Some of the key evidence that research points to are:

Providing effective leadership

Strong school leadership is very important to closing the achievement gap and raising achievement in schools. The principal of the school has a key role to play in setting vision and direction and creating a positive school culture to drive school improvement. Leithwood & Seashore Lewis (2012:2); Leithwood (2007:2) identified successful leadership as:

- 'Defining the vision, values, and direction
- improving conditions for teaching and learning
- redesigning the organisation: aligning roles and responsibilities
- enhancing teaching and learning
- redesigning and enriching the curriculum
- enhancing teacher quality, including succession planning
- building relationships inside the school community
- building relationships outside the school community
- placing an emphasis on common values.' Leithwood & Seashore Lewis (2012:2); Leithwood (2007:2)

There is a consensus from research that in successful schools, school leaders focus attention on student achievement as the work of the school and set the expectation that all students will achieve high levels (Muijs et al., 2004; Reynolds, 2002). For example, Corallo and McDonald (2002) argued that no specific style of leadership is most effective in creating and sustaining the kinds of school features just described. This may be because leadership style needs to be adjusted to fit the circumstances. In the long run, a more distributed or democratic form of leadership, involving teachers, probably works best. Teaching quality is the main priority of the leadership, not administration, management, or other problems (Corallo and McDonald, 2002; Muijs et al., 2004).

High quality in teaching and learning

The first key strategy to close the gap is to improve teaching and learning and ensure that African American children are taught by able, well-prepared, and experienced teachers. There is considerable research evidence that the quality of the teachers who teach ethnic minority groups and, indeed, White Americans, is among the most important determinants of how much the student will learn (Thompson and O'Quinn, 2001). We would argue that teacher quality is the most important school-level factor affecting student achievement. Ensuring that students in high-poverty and high-minority schools have excellent, well-qualified, well-prepared, and experienced teachers can make a big difference (Haycock, Jerald, and Huang, 2001; Sherman, 2002;

Monk, 2001; Thompson and O'Quinn, 2001; Reynolds, 2002; Singham, 2003). The 1966 Coleman report, 'Equality of Educational Opportunity,' in the USA found that teacher characteristics explain more variance in student achievement than any other school factor (Coleman et al., 1966). Hanushek also found that students learning with the most effective teachers outperformed their peers who were learning with the least effective teachers by as much as one grade level. We would argue that, first and foremost, the school must have a strong focus on teaching and learning. That is, the instructional programme needs to be at the heart of what the school is about, driving daily efforts to make a difference in teacher education. This may mean protecting instructional time against intrusions and minimising other distractions during the school day (Corallo and McDonald, 2002; Muijs et al., 2004).

In addition, ethnic minority children are assigned less qualified, less experienced teachers than White children. Researchers argued that students from low-income families and ethnic minorities may benefit the most from learning with very effective teachers (Sanders and Rivers, 1996). The USA research gave attention to the need to ensure that African American, Hispanic, and other ethnic minority children are taught by able, well-prepared, experienced teachers who are White Europeans. Studies suggest that assigning well-abled teachers could eliminate the gap between White and ethnic minorities (Looney, 2011; Thompson and Quinn, 2001; Sanders and Rivers, 1996).

Using a rigorous, inclusive curriculum

All students need a challenging and inclusive curriculum if the achievement gap is to be reduced (Burris et al., 2008). This is particularly key for African Americans, Hispanics, and other ethnic groups. Large racial disparities currently mark participation rates in more rigorous or advanced courses or Advanced Placement coursework in high school. To even out this disparity, students of all races need to be offered a challenging, inclusive curriculum that meets the needs of the community the school serves. Students' efforts and performance are greatly impacted by their teachers' expectations (Haycock, Jerald, and Huang, 2001; Kober, 2001; Thompson and O'Quinn, 2001; Lucas and Garmoran, 2002; Singham, 2003).

Researchers also argued for the need to align the curriculum, the way it is implemented in the classroom, the standards of performance that students are expected to reach, and the assessment of student progress towards those standards. This helps to channel efforts towards the same goals and makes those goals clear to teachers, students, and parents (Corallo and McDonald, 2002; Muijs et al., 2004; Snipes and Casserly, 2004).

Small class size

Smaller class sizes are associated with higher student engagement, fewer discipline problems, and greater teacher satisfaction and enthusiasm (Anderson, 2000). Anderson (2000) identified a number of these factors and argued that children benefit from small class sizes (17–20 students), especially in kindergarten through third grade. To benefit, children need to be in smaller classes for at least two years during the early elementary grades. Research results show that minority students and students from low-income families benefit the most from smaller classes. It also helps students receive more individualised attention from the teacher.

All other previous research and systematic reviews into class size also suggest small class sizes have advantages and are useful for closing the achievement gap and improving teaching and learning in the classroom. As class sizes became smaller, there were more times when pupils were the focus of a teacher's attention, and pupils were engaged with teachers (Hattie, 2005a,b; Biddle and Berliner, 2002; Ehrenberg, Brewer, Gamoran, and Willms, 2001; Anderson, 2000; Blatchford and Mortimore, 1994; Blatchford, Goldstein, and Mortimore, 1998; Galton, 1998).

Effective use of assessment data and test results to improve

High-quality assessment, tracking, and target setting for individuals and groups are the features of all the successful schools in the USA. The systematic collection and analysis of data enable schools to identify needs and employ resources. Research in the USA also shows that student assessment is tied to the curriculum being taught, and the use of student performance data in decision-making characterises effective schools. Test results help identify gaps in learning and can be used to guide or adjust instruction. To use test results effectively, teachers require assistance and training (Corallo and McDonald, 2002; Muijs et al., 2004; Snipes and Casserly, 2004). Many successful schools in the USA also found systematic and detailed ethnic monitoring to be an effective method for raising the achievement levels of African Americans, Hispanics, and other ethnic groups. In successful schools, ethnic monitoring was not viewed negatively as a way of stereotyping children but as a means of identifying learning problems. The schools kept careful records about each student by ethnic and socioeconomic background. Through ethnic monitoring, it is possible for schools to monitor the performance of different groups and to consider possible explanations and strategies for action to close the achievement gap and tackle educational inequalities. The data allows schools to look at achievement at standardised scores and test results for each subject by any combination of ethnic origin, gender, level of socioeconomic disadvantage, EAL, SEN, years in school, and suspension and absence rates (Snipes and Casserly, 2004; Corallo and McDonald, 2002).

Teacher's continuous professional development (CPD) programme

Teacher professional development is a critical part of a strong curriculum and instructional programme. Professional development must be focussed on implementing the curriculum effectively in the classroom. Elements of an effective teacher training programme include both theory and practical application to the classroom, demonstration, coaching, and feedback as the teacher implements the curriculum (Corallo and McDonald, 2002; Muijs et al., 2004; Snipes and Casserly, 2004).

Other intervention strategies

Other promising intervention strategies also have proven evidence in closing the achievement gap and tackling inequality in the USA and are recommended based on research evidence (see Corallo and McDonald, 2002; Muijs et al., 2004; Monk, 2001; Peterson, 2013; Smalley and Reyes-Blanes, 2001). These recommended strategies and practices in the context of the USA are outlined below:

- *Using targeted interventions and support*: Individual tutoring for students in need and one-on-one tutoring that supplements the regular curriculum can be an effective approach to improving student achievement. It is most effective when it is provided early to students in danger of falling behind. Certified teachers are the most effective tutors (Monk, 2001; Thompson and O'Quinn, 2001). In some cases, tutoring may occur as part of after-school or summer programmes.
- *Involving parent and community engagement:* Parent and broader community involvement in schools can substantially increase student achievement. However, it is important to recognise that parent engagement in high-poverty schools tends to be challenging (Smalley and Reyes-Blanes, 2001).

The achievement gap in other English-speaking countries

Our review of the literature shows limited research has attempted to compare the educational opportunities and outcomes of Indigenous populations in other English-speaking countries such as New Zealand and Australia (e.g., Song et al., 2014; Thompson et al., 2010; Ford & Moore 2013; Rubie-Davies 2006). However, the limited available research and review of literature so far show similar evidence in the USA and England, which is discussed above, and there are widespread school achievement gaps between ethnic minorities and non-Indigenous White ethnic groups. In many other English-speaking countries, students from some ethnic minority groups have consistently lower educational outcomes than their peers from ethnic majority groups.

For example, Turkish students (Song, 2011) and Roma students have consistently lower educational outcomes than their peers from dominant ethnic groups. These substantial differences in educational outcomes between groups of individuals are cause for concern. For example, the Song et al. (2014) study examines long-standing gaps in educational achievement between Indigenous and non-Indigenous students in Australia and New Zealand. In both countries, there are longstanding and substantial disparities in achievement between ethnic groups, and the ethnic minority groups that have the lowest academic performance are Indigenous and Māori students, respectively.

> The New Zealand PISA scores of Māori and Pacifika students are much lower than the average for Päkehä/European students. Students identify as Päkehä/European (71% of all students) achieved an average reading score of 541 score points in reading literacy on PISA 2009 compared to Māori (19%). and Pacifika (10%) who scored 478 score points and 448 score points, respectively.
>
> *(Song et al. 2014:4)*

The PISA findings analysed by Thompson et al. (2010) also showed that Indigenous pupils' reading literacy scores were, on average, 82 points lower than those of their non-Indigenous peers. This gap equates to more than one PISA proficiency level and more than two years of schooling, and for Australian Indigenous students, the picture may be even bleaker. Australian Indigenous students also perform significantly lower (57 score points) than the OECD average. On average, however, substantial difficulties remain for Indigenous Australians, who, in comparison to their non-Indigenous peers, are less likely to attend preschool, have less access to secondary school in the communities where they live, have 2–3 times the rate of absenteeism of other students, leave school much younger than non-Indigenous students, and have a low completion rate with less than half finishing secondary school (Thompson et al. 2010).

Ford's & Moore's 2013 achievement gaps study in Australia using NAPLAN data also reveals education inequality in Australia between Indigenous and non-Indigenous Australians. The findings suggest a significant gap in reading, writing, and numeracy between Indigenous students and their non-Indigenous counterparts. The national gap for reading was 19.7 percentage points, for writing 16.7 percentage points, and for numeracy 21.2 percentage points. In terms of actual percentages, this means that 94% of non-Indigenous students achieved the NMS or above, compared with 75% of Indigenous students by year.

Rubie-Davies (2006) study in New Zealand also investigated teacher expectations in reading and math of four ethnic groups in New Zealand, controlling for achievement and confirming the lower expectations of teachers for the Indigenous Māori and Pasifika ethnic groups. This was responsible for the achievement gap between Māori and Pasifika students, who often underachieve, and their more advantaged White and Asian peers. The research also confirms that teachers in New Zealand had high expectations for New Zealand White and Asian students but not for Indigenous Māori achievement.

It is difficult to come across data on the achievement gap in Canada, as it has not been common practice like in the USA and England, where researchers have used identity-based data to identify achievement gaps between groups of students based on race, gender, SES, and social identities. Much of Canada's data is focussed on qualification attainment, immigrant status, languages spoken at home, and fluency in English, and not on race or ethnicity to study the racial achievement gap. However, Shah (2019) highlighted that researchers in Canada have also demonstrated that in Toronto public schools, the gap for Black, Latino, Middle Eastern, and Indigenous students is as high as 30% on standardised student scores (Shah, 2019). The evidence available so far suggests there is a significant gap based on standardised scores in Canada between ethnic minority groups and White people, as in the USA, England, and New Zealand.

In summary, Australia, New Zealand, and Canada have been high-performing countries in international assessments of educational achievement, including PISA. In these countries, however, significant challenges remain around equity of access and outcomes for Indigenous students. There is a large portion of the reading achievement gap between Indigenous and non-Indigenous students that is associated with substantial inequities in student resources. On average, parents of Indigenous students have lower levels of education, lower occupational status, and fewer books and computers at home compared to their non-Indigenous peers.

Summary and conclusions

This chapter examined the racial and SES gap, the reasons for the gap, and some of the school strategies to tackle inequalities and close the achievement gap in the USA. The research draws evidence from systematic reviews of literature and standardised score results that are widely used in the USA. The main findings and conclusion from the above review of literature on the racial achievement gap and the factors responsible for the gap in the USA confirm that, on average, African American, Hispanic, and ethnic minority children in American public schools are disproportionately disadvantaged. The evidence from the review also confirms lower performance in test scores and grades, high dropout rates, high exclusion rates, low graduation rates, and low enrolment in post-secondary education (NAEP, 2023; Gaddis and Lauen, 2014; Jencks and Phillips, 1998; Noguera, 2001, 2003; Kao and Thompson, 2003).

Several factors were responsible for the achievement gap. These include racial background, socioeconomic factors, parental and family background, the quality of schools, funding issues, the geography of the school neighbourhood, which is segregated, cultural differences between White and African American, Hispanic, Asian American, and other ethnic minority groups, and bias of standardised scores and tests towards African American, Hispanic, and Asian American compared to Whites. What is also a concern is that African American students experience lower teacher expectations and lower ability tracks (Hanushek and Rivkin, 2009; Burris et al., 2008; McKown and Weinstein, 2008; Flores, 2007), over-representation in special education placement (Codrington and Halford, 2012; Ahram et al., 2011; Zion and Blanchett, 2011), and receive exclusionary school discipline practices more than other racial groups (Finn and Servoss, 2015; Losen et al., 2014; Carter et al., 2014). In addition, Hispanic and Black African American pupils mainly attend schools with high teacher mobility, high levels of poverty, and high ethnic minority children. The highest percentage of teachers teaching subjects in these schools are not qualified to teach (Harper, 2015; Orfield et al., 2012), and they experience school segregation (Rushing, 2017; Condron et al., 2013; Card and Rothstein, 2007; Diamond, 2006; Noguera, 2001). The evidence from the literature reviewed above suggests that all these factors have contributed to the racial achievement gap of Black, Hispanic, and other ethnic minority groups in the USA, reflecting on the national SAT and NACEP assessment scores.

Addressing the disparity in the national test score and educational inequality between White and Black, Hispanic, and Asian Americans remains one of the greatest educational challenges in the USA. We would argue that education is a basic right. Yet in the USA, for Black, Hispanic, Asian, Indigenous American, and ethnic minority students, that right is yet a reality. There is a long way to go before closing the achievement gap and tackling racial and socioeconomic gaps and challenges. The evidence from the review strongly suggests that underachievement is likely tied to schooling and policy environments that do not meet their needs, not students themselves.

Despite these challenges, there is a lot of research into the achievement gap to address educational inequality in the USA. The literature review shows there are promising strategies to close the gap (see Cabral-Gouveia et al., 2023; Borg et al., 2012; Berkowitz et al., 2017; Dietrichson et al., 2017; Mueller, 2006a, 2006b; Kober, 2001; Haycock, 2001; Haycock and Jerald, 2002; Corallo and McDonald, 2002; Muijs et al., 2004; Reynolds, 2002; Anderson, 2000; Navarro and Natalicio, 1999). These include focussing on reading, writing, math, and science skills; high-quality teaching; reducing class size; effective use of data and assessment to monitor achievement by ethnic groups and social background factors; using a teaching workforce that reflects the school population and the community school serves; providing effective teaching, providing strong leadership, and effective use of an inclusive curriculum; providing CPD; encouraging staff collaboration; effective targeted support, including one-to-one tutoring, small group support, parental and community engagement, and targeted support for mental health and nutrition.

One key strategy for closing achievement gaps is to ensure that African American, Hispanic, and other ethnic minority populations have access to high-quality teaching. This makes a huge difference in the children's education. There is also compelling research evidence that shows programmes to attract high-quality teachers to high-poverty, high-minority schools can help to close the gap in teaching quality. The research evidence from the review shows one of the main problems in the USA is that teachers are often less willing to teach in disadvantaged schools because of lower salaries, fewer resources, and more challenging environments. In addition to getting these teachers where they are needed most, it is important to provide them with high-quality professional development (CPD) so that they can continue to support the achievement of their students.

All the above points are worth considering to close the achievement gaps for African Americans, Hispanics, Indigenous Americans, Asian Americans, and all other ethnic minority groups. We know from the research that all students of different ethnic and racial groups can and do succeed in the USA.

References

Ahram, R., Fergus, E. & Noguera, P. (2011) Addressing racial/ethnic disproportionality in special education: case studies of suburban school districts. *Teachers College Record* 113: 2233–2266.

Anderson, L.W. (2000) Why should reduced class size lead to increased student achievement? In M.C. Wang and J.D. Finn (eds.) *How Small Classes Help Teachers Do Their Best*. Philadelphia: Temple University Center for Research in Human Development.

Ansell, S. (2011, July 7) *Achievement Gap*. Education Week. https://www.edweek.org/leadership/acheivement-gap/2004/09

Assari, S., Mardani, A., Maleki, M., Boyce, S. & Bazargan, M. (2021) Black-White Achievement Gap: Role of Race, School Urbanity, and Parental Education. *Pediatric Health Med Ther*. 12: 1–11.

Assari, S., Caldwell, C.H. & Zimmerman, M.A. (2020) Diminished returns of parental educational attainment on school achievement of non-Hispanic black high school students. *Under Review* 1: 1254.

Banerjee, N. (2019) Student–teacher ethno-racial matching and reading ability group placement in early grades. *Education and Urban Society*, 51(3): 395–422.

Barton, A.C., Drake, C., Perez, J.G., St. Louis, K. & George, M. (2004) Ecologies of parental engagement in urban education. *Educational Researcher* 33(4): 3–12. doi:10.3102/0013189X033004003. S2CID 144012401

Barton, P. & Coley, R. (2010) *The Black-White Achievement Gap When Progress Stopped*. Policy Information Report.

Berkowitz, R., Moore, H., Astore, R. & Benbensishty, R. (2017) A research synthesis of the associations between socioeconomic background inequality school climate and academic achievement. *Review of Educational Research* 87(2): 425–469. doi: 10.3102/0034654316669821

Biddle, B.J. & Berliner, D.C. (2002) *What research says about small classes and their effects. Part of series In Pursuit of Better Schools: What research says* www.WestEd.org/policyperspectives or http://edpolicyreports.org

Blake, J., Smith, D., Marchbanks, M., Seibert, A., Wood, S. & Kim, E. (2016) Does student-teacher racial/ethnic match impact Black students' discipline risk? In R. Skiba, K. Mediratta and K. Rausch (eds.), *Inequality in School Discipline: Research and Practice to Reduce Disparities*, 79–98. New York, NY: Palgrave MacMillan.

Blatchford, P., Goldstein, H. & Mortimore, P. (1998) Research on class size effects: a critique of methods and a way forward. *International Journal of Educational Research* 29(8). DOI:10.1016/S0883-0355(98)00058-5

Blatchford, P. & Mortimore, P. (1994) The issue of class size in schools: what can we learn from research? *Oxford Review of Education* 20(4): 411–428.

Blazar, D. (2021) *Teachers of Color, Culturally Responsive Teaching, and Student Outcomes: Experimental Evidence from the Random Assignment of Teachers to Classes*. WorkingPaper No. 21-501. Annenberg Institute for School Reform at Brown University.

Borg, J.R., Borg, M.O. & Stranahan, M.A. (2012) Closing the achievement gap between high-poverty schools and low-poverty schools. *Research in Business and Economics Journal* 5: 1. https://www.aabri.com/manuscripts/111012.pdf

Borman, G., Hewes, G., Overman, L. & Brown, S. (2003) Comprehensive school reform and achievement: a meta-analysis. *Review of Educational Research* 73: 2, 125–230. https://doi.org/10.3102/00346543073002125

Bradley, K. (2022) *The Socioeconomic Achievement Gap in the US Public Schools*. Ballard Brief. December 2022. www.ballardbrief.byu.edu. https://ballardbrief.byu.edu/issue-briefs/the-socioeconomic-achievement-gap-in-the-us-public-schools

Brooks, K., Schiraldi, V. & Ziendenberg, J. (1999) *Schoolhouse type: Two years later*. www.cjcj.org

Brooms, D. (2017) Black other fathering in the educational experiences of Black males in a single-sex urban high school. *Teachers College Record* 119(11): 1–46.

Brown, B. (2018) *The effect of teacher race on student perceptions in low-income schools*. University of Arkansas.

Burris, C.C., Wiley, E., Welner, K.G. & Murphy, J. (2008) Accountability, rigor, and detracking: achievement effects of embracing a challenging curriculum as a universal good for all students. *Teachers College Record* 110: 571–607.

Cabral-Gouveia, C., Menezes, I. & Nevesm, T. (2023) Educational strategies to reduce the achievement gap: a systematic review. *Frontiers Education* 8: 1155741. doi: 10.3389/feduc.2023.1155741. https://www.frontiersin.org/articles/10.3389/feduc.2023.1155741/full

Card, D. & Rothstein, J. (2007) Racial segregation and the Black-White test score gap. *Journal of Public Economics* 91: 2158–2184.

Carter, P., Fine, M. & Russell, S. (2014) *Discipline disparities series: overview*. Bloomington, IN: Center for Evaluation and Education Policy.

Castro, A. & Calzada, E. (2021) Teaching Latinx students: do teacher ethnicity and bilingualism matter? *Contemporary Educational Psychology* 66: 101994.

Chan, M., Sharkey, J., Nylund-Gibson, K. & Dowdy, E. (2023) Associations of school diversity with students' race-based victimization and school connectedness: a combined influence of student and teacher racial/ethnic diversity and socioeconomic diversity. *Journal of Youth and Adolescence* 52(1): 44–60.

Charles, C.Z. (2003) The dynamics of racial residential segregation. *Annual Review of Sociology* 29: 167–207. doi:10.1146/annurev.soc.29.010202.100002. S2CID 145272311.

Clotfelter, C.T., Ladd, H.F. & Vigdor, J.L. (2007) *How and why do teacher credentials matter for student achievement?* (NBER Working Paper No. 12828). http://www.nber.org/papers/w12828

Clotfelter, C.T., Ladd, H.F. & Vigdor, J.L. (2009) The academic achievement gap in grades 3 to 8. *Review of Economics and Statistics* 91(2): 398–419. doi:10.1162/rest.91.2.398. S2CID 57564132

Clotfelter, C., Ladd, H. & Vigdor, J. (2010) Teacher credentials and student achievement in high school: a cross-subject analysis with student fixed effects. *Journal of Human Resources* 45(3): 655–681.

Codrington, J. & Halford, F. (2012) *Special education and the mis-education of African American children: A call to action.* Washington, DC: The Association of Black Psychologists. https://abpsi.org/pdf/specialedpositionpaper021312.pdf

Coleman, J.S. (1966) *Equality of Educational Opportunity.* Washington, DC: U.S. Department of Health, Education and Welfare.

Coleman, J.S., Campbell, E.Q., Hobson, C.J., McPartland, J., Mood, A.M., Weinfeld, F.D., et al. (1966) *Equality of Educational Opportunity.* Washington: U.S. Department of Health, Education, and Welfare, Office of Education.

Condron, D.J., Tope, D., Steidl, C.R. & Freeman, K.J. (2013) Racial segregation and the Black/White achievement gap, 1992 to 2009. *Sociological Quarterly* 54: 130–157.

Cooc, N. (2017) Examining racial disparities in teacher perceptions of student disabilities. *Teachers College Record* 119(7): 1–32.

Cooper, C.E., Crosnoe, S. & Pituch (2010) Poverty race and parental involvement during the transition to elementary school. *Journal of Family Issues* 31(7): 859–883. doi:10.1177/0192513X09351515. S2CID 145197192

Corallo, C. & McDonald, D. (2002) *What works with low-performing schools: a review of research.* Charleston, West Virginia: AEL, Inc.

Crain, R. & Mahard, R. (1978) Desegregation and black achievement: a review of the research. *Law and Contemporary Problems* 42: 17–56.

Crosnoe, R., Johnson, M. & Elder, G. (2004) Intergenerational bonding in school: the behavioral and contextual correlates of student-teacher relationships. *Sociology of Education* 77(1): 60–81.

Daniels, K. (2022) *Teacher Workforce Diversity: Why It Matters for Student Outcomes.* Hunt Institute.

Dee, T. (2004) Teachers, race, and student achievement in a randomized experiment. *Review of Economics and Statistics* 86(1): 195–210.

Dee, T. (2005) A teacher like me: does race, ethnicity, or gender matter? *American Economic Review* 95: 158–165.

Diamond, J.B. (2006) Still separate and unequal: Examining race, opportunity, and school achievement in "integrated" suburbs. *The Journal of Negro Education* 75: 495–505.

Dietrichson, J., Bøg, M., Filges, T. & Klint Jørgensen, A.M. (2017) Academic interventions for elementary and middle school students with low socioeconomic status: a systematic review and meta-analysis. *Review of Educational Research* 87, 243–282. doi: 10.3102/0034654316687036

Dirmeyer, H. (2021) *Black and White Student Achievement Gaps in Tennessee*, Electronic Theses and Dissertations. Paper 3862. https://dc.etsu.edu/etd/3862

Easterbrook, M.J. & Hadden, I.R. (2021) Tackling educational inequalities with social psychology: identities, contexts, and interventions. *Social Issues Policy Review* 15: 180–236. doi: 10.1111/sipr.12070

Easton-Brooks, D., Lewis, C. & Zhang, Y. (2009) Ethnic-matching: the influence of African American teachers on the reading scores of African American students. *National Journal of Urban Education and Practice* 3(1): 230–243.

Ehrenberg, R., Goldhaber, D. & Brewer, D. (1995) 'Do teachers' race, gender, and ethnicity matter? Evidence from the National Educational Longitudinal Study of 1988. *Industrial and Labor Relations Review* 48: 547–561.

Ehrenberg, R.G., Brewer, D.J., Gamoran, A. & Willms, J.D. (2001) Class size and student achievement. *Psychological Science in the Public Interest* 2(1).

Fan, X., & Chen, M. (2001) Parental involvement and students' academic achievement: a meta-analysis. *Educational Psychology Review* 13: 1–22. doi: 10.1023/A:1009048817385

Finn, J.D. & Servoss, T.J. (2015) Misbehavior, suspensions, and security measures in high school: Racial/ethnic and gender differences. *Journal of Applied Research on Children: Informing Policy for Children at Risk* 5(2): Article 11.

Flores, A. (2007) Examining disparities in mathematics education: achievement gap or opportunity gap? *The High School Journal* 91: 29–42.

Ford, D.Y., Grantham, T.C., & Whiting, G.W. (2008) Another Look at the Achievement Gap: Learning From the Experiences of Gifted Black Students. *Urban Education*, 43(2): 216–239. https://doi.org/10.1177/0042085907312344

Ford, D.Y., & Moore, J.L. (2013) Understanding and reversing underachievement, low achievement, and achievement gaps among high-ability African American males in urban school contexts. *Urban Review* 45: 399–415.

Gaddis, S.M. & Lauen, D.L. (2014) School accountability and the black-white test score gap. *Social Science Research* 44: 15–31.

Galton, M. (1998) Class size: a critical comment on the research. *International Journal of Educational Research* 29: 809–818.

Gershenson, S., Holt, S. & Papageorge, N. (2016) Who believes in me? The effect of student–teacher demographic match on teacher expectations. *Economics of Education Review* 52: 209–224.

Gershenson, S., Lindsay, C., Papageorge, N.W., Campbell, R. & Rendon, J. (2023) *Spillover Effects of Black Teachers on White Teachers' Racial Competency: Mixed Methods Evidence from North*. https://papers.ssrn.com/sol3/papers.cfm?abstract_zid=4631011

Gottfried, M., Little, M. & Ansari, A. (2023) Student-teacher ethnoracial matching in the earliest grades: benefits for executive function skills? *Early Education and Development* 1–17. https://doi.org/10.26300/42eb-rw67

Griffin, B. (2002) Academic disidentification, race, and high school dropouts. *The High School Journal* 85(4): 71–81 DOI:10.1353/hsj.2002.0008

Hanushek, E.A. & Rivkin, S.G. (2009) Harming the best: how schools affect the black-white achievement gap. *Journal of Policy Analysis and Management* 28(3): 366–393.

Harper, S.R. (2015) Success in these schools? Visual counternarratives of young men of color and urban high schools they attend. *Urban Education* 50: 139–169.

Harwell, B. (2010) Student eligibility for a free lunch as an SES measure in education research. *Educational Research* 39(2): 120–131. doi:10.3102/0013189X10362578

Hattie, J. (2005a) The paradox of reducing class size and improving learning outcomes. *International Journal of Educational Research* 43: 387–425.

Hattie, J. (2005b) *What is the Nature of Evidence That Makes A Difference to Learning? Conference Papers.* Melbourne: ACER. http://www.acer.edu.au/workshops/documents/Proceedings_000.pdf

Haycock, K. (2001) Closing the achievement gap. *Educational Leadership* 58(6): 6–11.

Haycock, K. & Jerald, C. (2002) Closing the achievement gap. *Principal* 82(2): 20–23.

Haycock, K., Jerald, C. & Huang, S. (2001) Closing the gap: done in a decade. *Thinking K-16* 5(2): 3–22.

Hedges, L.V. & Nowell, A. (1998) Black-white test score convergence since 1965. In C. Jencks & M. Phillips (Eds.), *The Black-White Test Score Gap*, 149–181. Washington, DC: The Brookings Institution.

Hemphill, F., Vanneman, A. & Rahman, T. (2011) *How Hispanic and White Students in Public Schools Perform in Mathematics and Reading on the National Assessment of Educational Progress.* NCES.

Hill, N.E. & Tyson, D.F. (2009) Parental involvement in middle school: A meta-analytic assessment of the strategies that promote achievement. *Developmental Psychology* 45(3): 740–763. https://doi.org/10.1037/a0015362

Hsin, A. & Xie, Y. (2014) *Explaining Asian Americans' Academic Advantage Over Whites.* https://doi.org/10.1073/pnas.140640211

Hughes, D. & Cymon, I. (2023) *The Impact of Effective Teaching in Closing the Achievement Gap for Minority Students Entering Post-Secondary Education: A Case Study.* Doctoral Dissertations and Projects. 5098. https://digitalcommons.liberty.edu/doctoral/5098

Hung, M., Smith, W.A., Voss, M.W., Franklin, J.D., Gu, Y. & Bounsanga, J. (2020) Exploring student achievement Gaps in School Districts Across the United States. *Education and Urban Society* 52(2): 175–193.

Ingersoll, R.M. & May, H. (2011) *Recruitment, Retention and the Minority Teacher Shortage (Report No. 69).* Philadelphia, PA: The Consortium for Policy Research in Education.

Jeynes, W.H. (2003) A meta-analysis: the effects of parental involvement on minority children's academic achievement. *Education & Urban Society* 35(2): 202–218. doi:10.1177/0013124502239392. S2CID 145407192

Jeynes, W.H. (2005) A meta-analysis of the relation of parental involvement to urban elementary school student academic achievement. *Urban Education* 40(3): 237–269. https://doi.org/10.1177/0042085905274540

Jeynes, W.H. (2007) The relationship between parental involvement and urban secondary school student academic achievement: a meta-analysis. *Urban Education* 42(1): 82–110. https://doi.org/10.1177/0042085906293818

Jeynes, W. (2012) A meta-analysis of the efficacy of different types of parental involvement programmes for urban students. *Urban Education* 47(4): 706–742. https://doi.org/10.1177/0042085912445643

Kamau, N. (2011) *Race, Culture, and Academic Achievement: An Historical Overview and an Exploratory Analysis in a Multi-Ethnic, Urban High School*. Temple University.

Kao, G. (1995) Asian Americans as model minorities? A look at their academic performance. *Am. J. Educ.* 103: 121–159.

Kao, G. & Thompson, J. (2003) Racial and ethnic stratification in educational achievement and attainment. *Annual Review of Sociology* 29: 417–442. doi:10.1146/annurev.soc.29.010202.100019

Kaushal, N. & Nepomnyaschy, L. (2009) Wealth, race/ethnicity, and children's educational outcomes. *Children and Youth Services Review* 31(9): 963–971. https://www.sciencedirect.com/science/article/pii/S019074090900108X

Kirby, S.N., Berends, M. & Naftel, S. (1999) Supply and demand of minority teachers in Texas: problems and prospects. *Educational Evaluation and Policy Analysis* 27(1): 47–66.

Kober, N. (2001) *It Takes More Than Testing Closing the Achievement Gap. A Report of the Center on Education Policy*. Distributed by ERIC Clearinghouse. OCLC 1062989819.

Lambert, M.C., Duppong Hurley, K., January, S.-A. & Huscroft D'Angelo, J. (2022) The role of parental involvement in narrowing the academic achievement gap for high school students with elevated emotional and behavioral risks. *Journal of Emotional and Behavioral Disorders* 30(1): 54–66. https://doi.org/10.1177/10634266211020256

Leach, M.T. & Williams, S.A. (2007) The impact of the academic achievement gap on the African American family: a social inequality perspective. *Journal of Human Behaviour in the Social Environment* 15(2–3): 39–59. https://doi.org/10.1300/J137v15n02_04

Lee, J. (1994) Behind the model-minority stereotype: voices of high- and low-achieving Asian American students. *Anthropology & Education Quarterly* 25(4): 413–429. doi: 10.1525/aeq.1994.25.4.04x0530j. ISSN 1548-1492. S2CID 146627243.

Leithwood, K. & Seashore Lewis, K. (2012) *Linking Leadership to Student Learning*. New York, NY: Wallace Foundation.

Leithwood, K. (2007) What we know about educational leadership. In J. Burger, C. Webber and P. Kleinck (eds.), *Intelligent Leadership: Constructs for Thinking Educational Leaders*, 41–66. Dordrecht: Springer.

Leung-Gagné, M., McCombs, J., Scott, C. & Losen, D. (2022) *Pushed Out: Trends and Disparities in Out-of school Suspension*. Learning Policy Institute. https://files.eric.ed.gov/fulltext/ED626581.pdf

Lindsay, C.A. & Hart, C.M.D. (2017) Exposure to same-race teachers and student disciplinary outcomes for Black students in North Carolina. *Educational Evaluation and Policy Analysis* 39(3): 485–510. https://doi.org/10.3102/0162373717693109

Lindsay, C., Monarrez, T. & Luetmer, G. (2021) *The Effects of Teacher Diversity on Hispanic Student Achievement in Texas*. Policy Brief. Texas Education Research Center.

Looney, J. (2011) Developing high-quality teachers: teacher evaluation for improvement on becoming a teacher: a lifelong process. *European Journal of Education* 46(4): 440–455.

Losen, D., Hewitt, D. & Toldson, I. (2014) *Eliminating Excessive and Unfair Exclusionary Discipline in Schools: Policy Recommendations for Reducing Disparities*.

Discipline Disparities: A Research-To-Practice Collaborative. Bloomington, IN: The Equity Project at Indiana University Center for Evaluation and Education Policy.

Lucas, S.R. & Garmoran (2002) Tracking and the achievement gap, in Bridging the achievement gap. In: J.E. Chubb and T. Loveless (eds.). Washington, D.C.: Brookings Institution.

Mckown, C. (2013) Social equity theory and racial-ethnic achievement gaps. *Child Development* 84: 1120–1136. doi: 10.1111/cdev.12033

McKown, C. & Weinstein, R.S. (2008) Teacher expectations, classroom context, and the achievement gap. *Journal of School Psychology* 46(3): 235–261.

Meier, K.J., Wrinkle, R. & Polinard, J.L. (1999) Representative bureaucracy and distributional equity: addressing the hard question. *Journal of Politics* 61: 1025–1039.

Minor, E. (2014) Racial differences in teacher perception of student ability. *Teachers College Record* 116(10): 1–22.

Minus-Vincent, D. (2022) *The Impact of Teacher and Student Racial and Ethnic Matching on Student Outcomes: A Quantitative Study* (Doctoral dissertation, Seton Hall University).

Monk, T. (2001) *The Black-White Achievement Gap: What Does the Research Show?* Learn North Carolina, November. http://www.learnnc.org/index.nsf.

Mueller, D. (2006a) *Smaller Class Size is Associated with Higher Engagement of Students, Fewer Discipline ... Students Receiving More Individualized Attention From The Teacher.* https://www.wilder.org/sites/default/files/imports/SchoolSuccess PointPaper_3-06.pdf

Mueller, D. (2006b) *Tackling the Achievement Gap Head on A Background and Discussion Paper on the Wilder Foundation's School Success Focus Area.* https://www.wilder.org/sites/default/files/imports/SchoolSuccessPointPaper_ 3-06.pdf

Muijis, D., Harris, A., Chapman, C., Stoll, L. and Russ, J. (2004) Improving schools in socioeconomically disadvantage areas - a review of research evidence. *School Effectiveness and School Improvement* 15 (2): 149–175.

National Assessment of Educational Progress (NAEP). (2023) *Trends in Academic Progress.* The Nation's Report Card.

Navarro, M.S. & Natalicio, D.S. (1999) Closing the achievement gap in El Paso: a collaboration for K-16 renewal. *Phi Delta Kappan* 80: 597–601.

Neuman, S.B. (2003) From rhetoric to reality: the case for high-quality compensatory pre-kindergarten programs. *Phi Delta Kappan* 85(4). https://doi.org/10.1177/ 003172170308500408

Noguera, P.A. (2001) Racial politics and the elusive quest for excellence and equity in education. *Education and Urban Society* 34: 18–41.

Noguera, P.A. (2003) The trouble with Black boys: the role and influence of environmental and cultural factors on the academic performance of African American males. *Urban Education* 38(4): 431–459.

OECD. (2020) *Education at a Glance 2021: OECD Indicators.* Paris: OECD. https://www.oecd-ilibrary.org/sites/db0e552c-en/index.html?itemId=/content/ component/db0e552c-en

Ogbu, J.U. (1992a) Understanding Cultural Diversity and Learning. *Educational Researcher* 21(8): 5–14. doi:10.3102/0013189x021008005. S2CID 20086710

Ogbu, J.U. (1992b) Understanding cultural diversity and learning. *Educational Researcher* 21 (8): 5–14. doi:10.3102/0013189x021008005. S2CID 20086710

Ogbu, J.U. (1993) Differences in Cultural Frame of Reference. *International Journal of Behavioral Development* 16: 483–506.

Olneck, N. (2005) Economic consequences of the achievement gap for African Americans. *Marquette Law Review* 89: 95–104.

Orfield, G., Kucsera, J. & Siegel-Hawley, G. (2012) *E pluribus... separation: deepening double segregation for more students*. https://civilrightsproject.ucla.edu/research/k--12-education/integration-and-diversity/mlk-national/e-pluribus...separation-deepening-double-segregation-for-more-students

Papageorge, N., Gershenson, S. and Kang, K. (2020) Teacher expectations matter. *Review of Economics and Statistics* 102(2): 234–251.

Patall, E.A., Cooper, H. & Robinson, J.C. (2008) Parent involvement in homework: a research synthesis. *Review of Educational Research* 78(4): 1039–1101. https://doi.org/10.3102/0034654308325185

Peisner-Feinberg, H. (1999) *The Children of the Cost, Quality, and Outcomes Study Go to School: Public Report*. Chapel Hill, C.

Perry, L. (2009) Characteristics of equitable systems of education: a cross-national analysis. *European Education* 41(1): 79–100. doi: 10.2753/EUE1056-49344 10104. ISSN 1056-4934. S2CID 144485252

Peterson, K. (ed.) (2013) *Expanding Minds and Opportunities: Leveraging the Power of Afterschool and Summer Learning for Student Success*. Washington, D.C.: Collaborative Communications Group.

Phillips, M., Crouse, J. and Ralph, J. (1998) Does the Black-White test score gap widen after children enter school? In: Jencks and Phillips (eds.), *The Black-White Test Score Gap*. Brookings.

Pollard, C. (2022) *Teaching, Learning, and Race: Toward the Identification of Mechanisms Underlying Own-and Other-Race Teacher Effects* (Doctoral dissertation). Harvard: Harvard University Graduate School of Arts and Sciences. https://dash.harvard.edu/handle/1/37372027?show=full

Quinn, D. (2020) How to reduce racial bias in grading. *Education Next* 21(1).

Rangel, M. & Shi, Y. (2020) *First impressions: the case of teacher racial bias*. IZA Discussion Paper No. 13347.

Reardon, S.F. & Galindo, C. (2009) The Hispanic-White achievement gap in math and reading in the elementary grades. *American Educational Research Journal* 46(3): 853–891. doi:10.3102/0002831209333184. S2CID 46738093

Redding, C. (2019) A teacher like me: a review of the effect of student–teacher racial/ethnic matching on teacher perceptions of students and student academic and behavioral outcomes. *Review of Educational Research* 89(4): 499–535.

Reynolds, G.M. (2002) Identifying and eliminating the achievement gaps: A research-based approach. In *Viewpoints Vol. 9, Bridging The Great Divide: Broading Perspectives On Closing Achievement Gaps*. Naperville, IL: North Center Regional Educational Laboratory.

Rothstein, R. (2004) *Class and Schools: Using Social, Economic, and Educational Reform to Close the Black-White Achievement Gap*. New York, NY: Columbia.

Rubie-Davies. (2006) Teacher expectations and student self-perceptions: exploring relations. *Psychology in the Schools* 43(5): 527–651.

Rudasill, K., McGinnis, C., Cheng, S., Cormier, D. & Koziol, N. (2023) White privilege and teacher perceptions of teacher-child relationship quality. *Journal of School Psychology* 98: 224–239.

Rushing, W. (2017) School segregation and its discontents: chaos and community in post–civil rights Memphis. *Urban Education* 52(1): 3–31.

Rutkowski, D., Rutkowski, L., Wild, J. & Burroughs, N. (2018) Poverty and educational achievement in the US: A less-biased estimate using PISA 2012 data. *Journal of Children Poverty* 24(1): 47–67. doi:10.1080/10796126.2017.1401898

Sanders, W. & Rivers, J. (1996) *Residual Effects of Teachers*. https://www.beteronderwijsnederland.nl/files/cumulative%20and%20residual%20effects%20of%20teachers.pdf

Sandy, J. & Duncan, K. (2010) Examining the achievement test score gap between urban and suburban students. *Education Economics* 18(3): 297–315. doi:10.1080/09645290903465713

Shah, V. (2019) Racialised student achievement gap are red alert. https://theconversation.com/racialized-student-achievement-gaps-are-a-red-alert-108822

Sherman, L. (2002) To realize the dream. *Northwest Education Magazine* 8: 1. Fall, Northwest Regional Educational Laboratory.

Shirrell, M., Bristol, T. & Britton, T. (2023) The effects of student–teacher ethno-racial matching on exclusionary discipline for Asian American, Black, and Latinx students: Evidence from New York city. *Educational Evaluation and Policy Analysis*. https://doi.org/10.3102/01623737231175461

Shortell, D. & Romine, T. (2020) *Justice Department accuses Yale of discriminating against Asian American and White applicants*. CNN.

Singham, M. (2003) The achievement gap: myths and reality. *Phi Delta Kappan* 84(8). April. https://doi.org/10.1177/003172170308400808

Sirin, S.R. (2005) Socioeconomic status and academic achievement: a meta-analytic review of research. *Review of Educational Research* 75: 417–453. doi: 10.3102/00346543075003417

Smalley, S.Y. & Reyes-Blanes, M.E. (2001) Reaching out to African American parents in an urban community: a community-university partnership. *Urban Education* 36(4): 518–533. https://doi.org/10.1177/0042085901364005

Snipes, J. & Casserly, M. (2004) Urban school systems and education reform. *Journal of Education for Students Placed at Risk* 9: 2, 127–141.

Snow, C., Susan Burns, M. & Peg Griffin. (eds.) (1998) *Preventing Reading Difficulties in Young Children*. Washington, D.C.: National Academy Press.

Song, S. (2011) Second-generation Turkish youth in Europe: Explaining the academic disadvantage in Austria, Germany, and Switzerland. *Economics of Education Review* 30: 938–949.

Song, S., Perry, L., McConney, A. (2014) Explaining the achievement gap between Indigenous and non-Indigenous students: An analysis of PISA 2009 results for Australia and New Zealand. *Educational Research and Evaluation* 20(3) DOI:10.1080/13803611.2014.892432

Stearns, E. & Glennie, E. (2007). When and Why Dropouts Leave High School, *Youth & Society*, 38(1). https://doi.org/10.1177/0044118X05282764

Steele, C. (1997) A threat in the air: how stereotypes shape intellectual identity and performance. *American Psychologist*, 52: 613–629. https://pubmed.ncbi.nlm.nih.gov/9174398/

Suárez-Orozco, C., & Suárez-Orozco, M.M. (1995) *Transformations: Immigration, Family Life, And Achievement Motivation Among Latino Adolescents*. Stanford University Press.

Talbert-Johnson, C. (2004) Structural inequities and the achievement gap in urban schools. *Education and Urban Society* 37(1): 22–36. doi:10.1177/0013124504268454

Thompson, S., De Bortoli, L., Nicholas, M., Hillman, K. & Buckley, S. (2010). *PISA in brief, highlights from the full Australian report: Challenges for Australian Education: Results from PISA 2009*. Melbourne, Australia: Australian Council for Educational Research.

Thompson, C. & Quinn, D. (2001) *Eliminating the Black-White Achievement Gap: A Summary of Research*. https://archive.org/details/ERIC_ED457250

VanderHart, P.G. (2006) Why do some schools groups by ability? *American Journal of Economics and Sociology* 65: 435–462.

Vanneman, A., Hamilton, L., Baldwin Anderson, J. & Rahman, T. (2009) *Achievement Gaps: How Black and White Students in Public Schools Perform in Mathematics and Reading on the National Assessment of Educational Progress, (NCES 2009-455)*. Washington, DC: Institute of Education Sciences, U.S. Department of Education. https://nces.ed.gov/nationsreportcard/pdf/studies/200945 5.pdf

Villegas, A.M., Strom, K. & Lucas, T. (2012) Closing the racial/ethnic gap between students of color and their teachers: an elusive goal. *Equity and Excellence in Education* 45(2): 283–301.

West, A. (2007) Poverty and educational achievement: why do children from low-income families tend to do less well at school? *Benefits* 215: 283–297.

White, K.R. (1982) The relation between socioeconomic status and academic achievement. *Psychological Bulletin* 91 (3): 461–481. https://doi.org/10.1037/0033-2909.91.3.461

Yarnell, L.M. & Bohrnstedt, G.W. (2018) Student-teacher racial match and its association with black student achievement: an exploration using multilevel structural equation modeling. *American Educational Research Journal* 55(2): 287–324. https://doi.org/10.3102/0002831217734804

Zion, S.D. & Blanchett, W. (2011) [Re]conceptualizing inclusion: can critical race theory and interest convergence be utilized to achieve inclusion and equity for African American students? *Teachers College Record* 113: 2186–2205.

PART V

What are the Lessons for Those Concerned with Black and Ethnic Minority Achievement?

11
SUMMARY, CONCLUSIONS, AND LESSONS TO RAISE ACHIEVEMENT AND TACKLE INEQUALITY

Introduction

This chapter brings together the key findings from the research evidence used in writing the book and the lessons to be drawn from successful schools. The book is a story of a search for lessons about what works in education and how to improve schools. The book arose from our research into the barriers to learning and what works in raising the achievement of Black and ethnic minority students in the last 20 years and looks to answer, in detail, our main research questions: what are the barriers to learning in schools, and what are strategies and good practices in driving school improvement and addressing educational inequality?

Drawing on original evidence of KS2 and GCSE attainment data, case studies, school survey evidence, focus groups, and interviews with headteachers, teachers, school staff, policymakers, parents, pupils, and governors, the author tries to chart the road to improvement and tackle inequality in education by examining the factors behind the success story of the transformation of schools. It also draws on international comparative literature on Black and minority ethnic groups' achievement in the various studies he has been involved with and his 20 years of experience working with local authorities, the London Challenge, government departments, national strategies, schools, and governors as a researcher, school adviser, and Continuing Professional Development (CPD) trainer.

The evidence used in this book also addressed the main questions that motivated me to write the book on strategies and good practices to close the achievement gap in successful case study schools. The key messages from the book are summarised below. The first section of the chapter provides a summary and conclusion of the experience in England and at the international level in tackling inequality. Implications for policy, practice, and future research will follow this.

Summary and conclusions

The barriers to learning: challenges

A growing body of research suggests many barriers to learning and factors that contribute to the underachievement of Black and ethnic minority pupils in schools (DfES, 2006; Demie, 2005, 2019, 2023a,b, 2022a, b). The findings of the survey of headteachers and teachers identified barriers to learning, including factors such as teachers' low expectations, institutional racism, lack of diversity in the school workforce, lack of parental engagement, lack of parental aspiration, low literacy levels, poverty, a social class issue, curriculum barriers, lower tier entry in school ability group, school exclusions, lack of parental involvement, curriculum barriers, racism, and lack of funding. These research findings are also supported by previous research on barriers to learning and reasons for the underachievement of ethnic minority and disadvantaged pupils in English schools (see Gillborn and Youdell, 2000; Crozier, 2005; Maylor et al., 2009; DCSF, 2008; DfE 2015; Cabinet Office, 2017; EHRC, 2016; MacPherson, 1999; DfES, 2006; Demie 2005, 2003a,b; 2022a, b; Demie and Mclean, 2017a,b; Ofsted, 2009b; Strand, 2015). Other researchers also noted the lack of adequate support of schools from parents, economic deprivation, poor housing, and home circumstances (Rampton 1981; Swann 1985); the failure of the national curriculum to reflect adequately the need for a diverse and multi-ethnic society (Macpherson, 1999; Demie 2023a,b).

The evidence from the data and the survey confirms tackling educational inequality and closing the gap is one of the biggest challenges faced by policymakers, teachers, and school leaders in England. Some Black and ethnic minority group pupils are consistently the lowest-performing group, and the gap widens, particularly at the end of secondary school. The data suggests there is still a long way to go in closing the achievement gap.

Success factors in closing the achievement gap: good practice

However, despite challenges in closing the achievement gap, the situation is not always doom and gloom. In several successful schools, Black and ethnic minority students buck the national trend. There are many reasons why Black and ethnic minorities are doing well in these successful schools (Demie and Mclean 2017b; Demie 2019, 2005; Ofsted 2002a,b; McKenley et al. 2003; Tikly et al. 2006). Chapters 3–8 detail the success factors behind outstanding achievement. The chapters carry discussions and case study interviews with headteachers, teachers, school staff, parents, governors, and children from a range of perspectives, including the quality of school leadership and management, the school curriculum, the quality of teaching and learning, pupil performance, targeted intervention strategy and support, English as an Additional Language (EAL) pupils assessment and support, school exclusions, pupils' views about the school. race, and ethnicity in the curriculum, and school parental engagement and diversity in the school workforce. This is further supported by school surveys and literature reviews over 20 years. Key features Identified as success factors for raising achievement and tackling educational inequality include are:

- Strong leadership on equality and diversity
- Effective teaching and learning
- High expectations
- Diversifying the curriculum
- Diversity in the school workforce
- Tackling school exclusions
- Parental engagement
- Use of data to identify underachieving groups and track performance
- Effective support for ethnic minorities and EAL pupils
- Targeted intervention and support for pupils
- Celebration of cultural diversity

These findings are similar to previous surveys by Demie (in 1998 and 2023c) and other several studies (Demie and Mclean 2017a,b; Demie 2005, DfES 2003; Blair and Bourne 1998). Each of the above school strategies and good practices is explored in detail in the book to reveal exactly what the schools do to ensure they provide the very highest quality of education for all their students.

It is important to note that the most important factors that link all successful schools are the excellence of their leadership in driving school improvement and tackling inequality, high-quality teaching, effective use of inclusive curriculum, effective targeted intervention strategies to support underachieving groups, and effective use of data to track individual pupils' performance. The successful schools draw a wide range of data to track the progress of individual pupils and ethnic groups. The book argues that policymakers and school practitioners need more evidence on 'what works to tackle educational inequality. What works for Black and ethnic minorities in disadvantaged areas will work for all groups. No one can claim special privileges. Work works must work for everyone.' However, there is no 'pick and mix' option. It is recommended that schools develop all these characteristics through the effective use of data to monitor achievement to pinpoint and tackle the underperformance of individual pupils.

Targeted intervention strategies in addressing inequality

The book also explored in detail the schools' targeted intervention strategies to raise achievement and close the gaps. Drawing on evidence collected through case study interviews, focus groups, and surveys of headteachers, teachers, and school staff, and a review of literature on the London Challenge and the Education Endowment Fund (EEF) evidence, the book identified a range of effective targeted interventions used by schools to close the achievement gap. These include:

- Early intervention,
- Additional small-group teaching,
- One-to-one tuition,
- Peer tutoring,
- Parental involvement,
- Booster class,
- Mastery learning,
- Pastoral care,
- Improving behaviour and attendance,
- Homework,
- Phonics,
- EAL support, and
- Enrichment programmes.

The book discusses a wealth of targeted interventions that work well in school. The findings of the case study and school survey used in the book are also in line with recent EEF (2019) research and the London Challenge evidence. These intervention strategies are very popular in the case study schools and are used effectively to raise achievement and close the gap between disadvantaged pupils and their peers.

Similarly, Snyder et al. (2019) review of the international evidence also suggested that targeted interventions are effective in raising achievement and closing the gap' in schools. Other research on what works also suggests similar to the findings of the case study and the school survey used to write the book and confirm many schools use targeted interventions to close the achievement gap between disadvantaged pupils and their peers (Demie 2019, 2023a; 2023b; Demie and Mclean 2016a,b; Mongon and Chapman 2008; Ofsted 2009a,b; EEF 2023).

Lessons to raise achievement and tackle inequality in schools

The experience in English schools

A body of previous research evidence shows that inequality in educational outcomes has grown, and there are long-standing achievement gaps in England associated with socioeconomic status and ethnic background

(Hutchinson et al., 2019; Demie, 2019; 2005; Mortimore and Whitty, 1997; Ofsted, 2014). Although overall educational attainment for Black and ethnic minorities increased steadily, the achievement gap is not closing between White British and their peers. Despite the rhetoric of equality in schools in England, the school experiences of Black and ethnic minority students continue to be unequal. This is further supported by the national data that suggests clear evidence that racial and socioeconomic inequities are the most significant contributors to the achievement gap. The data confirm that Chinese and Indian pupils tend to significantly outperform the White British majority, while Black Caribbean, Pakistani, Black African, and Bangladeshi (not fluent in English), Traveller, and Gypsy children tend to underperform. Moreover, worryingly, the gap in Black Caribbean achievement increases rather than narrows as a child progresses through compulsory education. The empirical evidence also confirms that ethnic minority disadvantaged pupils' underachievement in education is real and persistent and that some are consistently the lowest-performing group in the country.

However, in recent years, detailed case studies of successful schools that raise the achievement of pupils against the odds have improved our understanding of how schools can enhance pupils' academic achievement and tackle educational inequality. A substantial body of research into school effectiveness and improvement now shows that schools make a difference, albeit with certain limits, and about 8–15% of the attainment difference between schools is accounted for by what they do in school. The rest is attributed to factors beyond the school gate, such as school intake characteristics and the family's racial and socioeconomic status, and the geography of the school neighbourhood where pupils live (Sammons 2007; Tikly et al. 2006; Strand 2012, 2014, 2015; Demie and Mclean 2015, 2016a,b, 2017a,b, Ofsted 2002a,b, 2009a,b; Ofsted 2013; Demie 2005, 2022b; Strand 2015; Edmonds 1982; Demie and Lewis 2010a,b,c).

Many of the previous research studies looked at examples of schools that provide an environment in which pupils flourish in areas of challenging circumstances. These identified the key characteristics of successful schools in raising achievement, including strong leadership, high expectations, effective teaching and learning, an ethos of respect for diversity, and good parental involvement (see for details Demie 2019; Demie and Lewis 2010a,b,c; Demie and Mclean 2015, 2016a,b, 2017a,b; DfES 2003).

Ofsted's (2009a, b) case study research in schools also highlighted the prime contribution of leadership and management, together with some other features responsible for the success of each of the case study schools. The schools succeed in their study for the following reasons:

- 'A strong and caring ethos and high expectations
- A positive "can do" culture where praise and encouragement prevail and self-esteem is high,
- Outstanding teaching by consistently high-quality staff,

- A focus on improving standards of attainment,
- A clear stand on racism and a strong commitment to equal opportunities
- Enriching the curriculum
- Partnership with parents and the community
- High-quality planning, assessment, and targeted intervention to enable all children to achieve the best they can.'

(Ofsted 2009a, b; Ofsted 2002a,b)

Another Ofsted research study into what works in outstanding schools also identified similar effective strategies in raising achievement and closing the gaps in schools. They included: 'rigorous monitoring of data, effective use of feedback, planning, support, and interventions, ensuring access to high-quality teaching, having a strong and visionary Headteacher and working with parents to increase engagement and raise aspirations.' (Ofsted 2013:31)

The findings and conclusions in this book, which is summarised above from English schools, also confirm similar evidence related to barriers and success factors in addressing educational inequality in England.

The international experience

The international literature review in the book on closing the achievement gap also examined the racial and socioeconomic status gap. Research into successful schools in the USA and at the international level by Edmonds (1982) and Williams et al. (2005) has also provided similar insights into common practices in high-performing schools serving high-poverty student populations. This study uses high-performing schools to identify the common characteristics that could be the source of their success. The most recent body of research on school effectiveness has found that successful schools in the USA have strong leadership, high-quality teaching and learning, effective use of data for monitoring student progress, parental involvement, and a positive school climate.

Muijis et al. (2004) review of the international literature also demonstrates that effective leaders exercise an indirect and powerful influence on the effectiveness of the school and the achievement of students in most countries. They argued that headteachers of effective and improving schools focus on teaching and learning issues. In addition, they are also good at proving constantly that disadvantage need not be a barrier to achievement, that speaking English as an additional language can support academic success, and that schools really can be learning communities (see Demie and Strand, 2006). These findings of research into successful schools have increased our understanding of how schools can enhance pupils' academic achievement and close the achievement gap.

The USA literature review also shows the reasons for the racial and socioeconomic achievement gap and some of the school strategies to tackle inequalities and close the achievement gap (Easterbrook and Hadden, 2021; Shirrell et al., 2023; Dirmeyer, 2021; OECD, 2020; Coleman 1966). The research also draws evidence for systematic reviews of literature and standardised score results that are widely used in the USA. The main findings and conclusion from the systematic review of literature on the racial achievement gap and the factors responsible for the gap in the USA confirm that, on average, African American, Hispanic, Indigenous American, American Asian, and other ethnic minority children in American public schools are disproportionately disadvantaged. The evidence from the review in the USA also confirms an increase in the achievement gap, lower performance in test scores and grades, high dropout rates, high exclusion rates, low school completion rates, and low attendance in post-secondary education. Several factors were responsible for the achievement gap in the USA. These include racial background, socioeconomic factors, parental and family background, the quality of schools, teachers quality where teachers are not qualified to teach, funding issues, and the geography of the school neighbourhood. The USA evidence also identified as a barrier to cultural differences between White and African American, Hispanic, Asian American, and other ethnic minority groups, bias of standardised scores and tests towards African Americans, Hispanics, and Asian Americans compared to Whites. Many researchers also reported in the USA the lower teacher expectations and lower ability tracks, the over-representation of ethnic minorities in special education placement and high exclusionary school discipline practices more than other racial groups, attending schools with high teacher mobility, high levels of poverty, and high ethnic minority children, and school segregation as the main reasons for the achievement gap. The evidence from the literature reviewed in the book suggests that all these factors have contributed to the racial achievement gap of Black, Hispanic, and other ethnic minority groups in the USA, reflected in the national SAT and NACEP assessment scores.

Despite these challenges, there is so much research into the achievement gap to address the educational inequality in the USA. The literature review shows several strategies to close the gap including focussing on reading, writing, maths, and science skills; high-quality teaching; reducing class size, effective use of data and assessment to monitor achievement by ethnic groups and social background factors, employing a teaching workforce that reflects the school population and the community school serves; providing effective teaching, providing strong leadership, and effective use of inclusive curriculum, providing CPD, encouraging staff collaboration, effective targeted support including one-to-one tutoring, small group support, parental and community engagement, and targeted support for mental health and nutrition.

Many of the approaches and strategies used in the USA to close the achievement gap are similar to those used in the UK.

The limited available research and review of literature in other English-speaking countries such as New Zealand, Australia, Canada, and Europe, also show similar evidence in the USA and England. The evidence in the book suggests that students from some ethnic minority groups, such as indigenous students in Australia and New Zealand, Turkish and Roma students in Europe, and Black and ethnic minority students in Canada, have consistently achieved lower educational outcomes than their peers from ethnic majority groups. These substantial differences in educational outcomes between groups of individuals are a cause for concern.

The lessons to be drawn from successful schools

This book tells the remarkable story of barriers to learning and how schools have successfully addressed educational inequalities and closed the achievement gap in England. The evidence from our research confirms the wide range of effective strategies and good practices to raise educational attainment, including:

1. Providing strong school leadership and excellent teaching to raise the achievement of all schoolchildren.
2. Giving extra support to disadvantaged pupils, minority ethnic pupils, and pupils who are learning the English language. This approach enables children to reach a high level of educational attainment, which closes the gap between the groups that underachieve nationally and their peers.
3. Using an inclusive curriculum that engages the students and also values cultural diversity. These schools have rich and imaginative curricula, both within and beyond the classroom.
4. Rigorous tracking and monitoring of each student's progress and achievement through the effective use of data and good-practice research. Effective data can generate both optimism and urgency about where improvement is most needed to tackle underachievement and inequalities in provision.
5. Providing outstanding pastoral care that is inclusive and offers unstinting support to their families.
6. Using effective, targeted intervention strategies and support in class in a small group, or one-to-one support tailored to individual needs.
7. Effective parent partnership with class, teachers, senior leaders, SENDCos, TAS, and learning mentors who generally come from the local community and can break down barriers and establish confidence and trust of parents.

8. Providing effective multicultural education that provides students with knowledge about the histories, culture, and contributions of diverse groups in contemporary and future British society. The experience of the case study schools has shown that multicultural education matters, and the school celebrates cultural diversity and encourages racial and ethnic harmony and cross-cultural understanding as part of community cohesion.
9. Developing inclusive schools that incorporate the idea that all students who have different cultural characteristics should have equal opportunities to learn in school.
10. Providing funding for additional targeted interventions and initiatives to support schools. One could also argue that the key factors for improvement in the case study schools were related to funding and government initiatives to transform urban schools. The successful schools no doubt have been well funded to challenge poverty and support teaching and learning in challenging schools.

The good practice stories of how these successful schools have succeeded in closing the achievement gap are of local and national significance. Our study confirms, beyond doubt, that the excellent education provided in the schools is the reason for improvement and closing the achievement gap. The two-decade-long research has proved what works and identified the factors that make a difference. This good practice needs to be shared between schools.

References

Blair, M. & Bourne, J. (1998) *Making the Difference: Teaching and Learning Strategies In Successful Multi-Ethnic Schools*. London: Department for Education and Employment Publication Research Report RR59.

Cabinet Office. (2017) *Race Disparity Audit Summary Findings from the Ethnicity Facts and Figures website*. London: Cabinet Office. At https://assets.publishing.service.gov.UK/government/uploads/system/uploads/attachmentdata/file/6860

Coleman, J.S. (1966) *Equality of Educational Opportunity*. Washington, DC: U.S. Department of Health, Education and Welfare.

Crozier, G. (2005) There is a war against our children: Black educational underachievement revisited. *British Journal of Sociology of Education* 26(5): 585–598.

DCSF. (2008) *The Extra Mile: How Schools Succeed in Raising Aspiration In Deprived Communities*. London: Department for Children, Schools and Families. https://bit.ly/3CSBw31

Demie, F. (2003a) Using value-added data for school self-evaluation: a case study of practice in inner city schools. *School Leadership and Management* 23(4): 445–467.

Demie, F. (2003b) Raising the achievement of Black Caribbean pupils in British schools: unacknowledged problems and challenges for policy makers. *London Review of Education* 1(3): 229–248.

Demie, F. (2005) 'Achievement of Black Caribbean pupils: Good practice in Lambeth schools'. *British Educational Research Journal*, 31 (4): 481–508.

Demie, F. (2019) *Educational Inequality: Closing the gap*. London: UCL IOE Press, July. https://www.ucl-ioe-press.com/books/social-justice-equality-and-human-rights/educational-inequality/

Demie, F. (2022a) *Understanding the Causes and Consequences of School Exclusions: Teachers, Parents and Schools' Perspectives*. London: Routledge.

Demie, F. (2022b) 'Tackling teachers' low expectations of Black Caribbean students in English schools. *Equity in Education and Society Journal* 1(1): 32–49. https://doi.org/10.1177/27526461211068511

Demie, F. (2023a) *Raising the Achievement of Black Caribbean pupils: Barriers and Good Practice in Schools*. London: Lambeth Research and Statistics Unit.

Demie, F. (2023b) 'Tackling educational inequality: Lessons from London schools'. *Equity in Education & Society*. https://doi.org/10.1177/27526461231161775

Demie, F. (2023c) *A School Survey of Barriers to Learning, Success Factors, And Effective Inclusive Curriculum That Contributed to Improving Black and Minority Ethnic (BAME) Pupils Attainment in Schools*. London: Lambeth Research and Statistics Unit.

Demie, F. & Lewis, K. (2010a) *Outstanding Secondary Schools: Good Practice*. London: Lambeth Research and Statistics Unit.

Demie, F. & Lewis, K. (2010b) 'Raising the Achievement of Portuguese pupils in British Schools: a case study of Good Practice'. *Educational Studies*, 36 (1): 95–109.

Demie, F. & Lewis, K. (2010c) *White Working Class Achievement: An Ethnographic Study of Barriers to Learning in Schools*. https://doi.org/10.1080/03055698.2010.506341

Demie, F. & Mclean, C. (2015) *Narrowing the Achievement Gap: Good Practice in Schools*. London: Lambeth Research and Statistics Unit.

Demie, F. & Mclean, C. (2016a) 'Tackling disadvantage: what works in narrowing the achievement gap in schools'. *Review of Education*, 3 (2): 138–174. https://doi.org/10.1002/rev3.30

Demie, F. & Mclean, C. (2016b) *What Works in School Improvement: Examples of Good Practice*. Lambeth LA: Lambeth Research and Statistics Unit.

Demie, F. & Mclean, C. (2017a) *Black Caribbean Underachievement in Schools in England*. Lambeth LA: Lambeth Research and Statistics Unit.

Demie, F. & Mclean, C. (2017b) *The Achievement of Black Caribbean Pupils: Good Practice*. London: Lambeth Research and Statistics Unit.

Demie, F., & Strand, S. (2006) English Language Acquisition and Educational Attainment at the End of Secondary School. *Educational Studies*, 32 (2): 215–231.

DfE. (2015) *Supporting the Attainment of Disadvantaged Pupils: Articulating Success and Good Practice Research Report*. London: Department for Education. https://bit.ly/3bLxCNq

DfES. (2003) *Aiming High: Raising the Achievement of Minority Ethnic Pupils*. London: DfES Consultation.

DfES. (2006) *Exclusion of Black Pupils Priority Review: Getting it, getting it right*. London: Department for Education and Skills.

Dirmeyer, H. (2021) *Black and White Student Achievement Gaps in Tennessee*. Electronic Theses and Dissertations. Paper 3862. https://dc.etsu.edu/etd/3862

Easterbrook, M.J. & Hadden, I.R. (2021) 'Tackling educational inequalities with social psychology: identities, contexts, and interventions'. *Social Issues Policy Review* 15: 180–236. doi: 10.1111/sipr.12070

Edmonds, R. (1982) 'Programmes of school improvement: An overview'. *Educational Leadership* 40 (3): 8–11.

EEF. (2019) *Teaching and Learning Tool Kit*. London: Education Endowment Foundation. https://educationendowmentfoundation.org.uk/evidencesummaries/teaching-learning-toolkit/

EEF. (2023) *Teaching and Learning Tool Kit*. London: Education Endowment Foundation. https://educationendowmentfoundation.org.uk/education-evidence/teaching-learning-toolkit

EHRC. (2016) *Healing a Divided Britain: The Need for a Comprehensive Race Equality Strategy*. London: Equality and Human Rights Commission. https://www.equalityhumanrights.com/sites/default/files/healing_a_divided_britain_-_the_need_for_a_comprehensive_race_equality_strategy_final.pdf

Gillborn, D. & Youdell, D. (2000) *Rationing Education: Policy, Practice, Reform and Equity*. Buckingham: Open University Press

Hutchinson, J., Bonetti, S., Crenna-Jennings, W. & Akhal, A. (2019) *Education in England: Annual Report 2019*. Education Policy Institute. https://bit.ly/3ETGflu

Macpherson, W. (1999) *The Stephen Lawrence Inquiry*. London: The Stationery Office.

Maylor, U., Smart, S., Kuyok, K.A. & Ross, A. (2009) *Black Children's Achievement Programme Evaluation*. London: Department for Children and Schools.

McKenley, J., Power, C., Ishani, L. & Demie, F. (2003) *Raising the Achievement of Black Caribbean Pupils in British Schools: Good Practice in Lambeth Schools*. Research and Statistics Unit, Lambeth Education.

Mongon, D. & Chapman, C. (2008) *Successful leadership for promoting the achievement of White Working Class pupils*. National College for School Leadership (NCSL).

Mortimore, P. & Whitty, G. (1997) *Can School Improvement Overcome the Effects of Disadvantage?* London: Institute of Education, University of London.

Muijis, D.; Harris, A.; Chapman, C.; Stoll, L.; and Russ, J. (2004) Improving Schools in Socioeconomically Disadvantage Areas- A review of research evidence, School Effectiveness and *School Improvement*, 15 (2), 149–175.

OECD. (2020) *Education at a Glance 2021: OECD Indicators*. Paris: OECD. https://www.oecd-ilibrary.org/sites/db0e552c-en/index.html?itemId=/content/component/db0e552c-en

Ofsted. (2002a) *Achievement of Black Caribbean Pupils: Good Practice in Secondary Schools*. London: Office for Standards in Education, HMI 448.

Ofsted. (2002b) *Achievement of Black Caribbean Pupils: Good Practice in Primary Schools*. London: Office for Standards in Education, HMI 448. https://dera.ioe.ac.uk/id/eprint/10139/1/Achievement_of_black_caribbean_pupils_-_three_successful_primary_schools.pdf

Ofsted. (2009a) *Twelve Outstanding Secondary Schools: Excelling Against the Odds*. London: Office for Standards in Education, HMI: 080240. https://dera.ioe.ac.uk/id/eprint/11232/2/Twelve.pdf

Ofsted. (2009b) *Twenty Outstanding Primary Schools: Excelling Against the Odds*. http://dera.ioe.ac.uk/11216/1/Twenty%20outstanding%20primary%20schools.pdf

Ofsted. (2013) *Unseen children: access and achievement 20 years on*. Ofsted. http://www.ofsted.gov.uk/resources/unseen-children-access-and-achievement-20-years

Ofsted. (2014) *Written evidence to House of Commons Education Select Committee, In Education Committee (2014). Underachievement in Education by White Working Class Children*. London: House of Commons 142, The Stationery Office Limited.

Rampton, A. (1981) *West Indian Children in Our Schools*. Cmnd 8273. London: HMSO.

Sammons, P. (2007) *School Effectiveness and Equity: Making Connections - A Review School Effectiveness and Improvement Research-Its Implications for Practitioners and Policymakers*. Reding: CFBT Education Trust.

Shirrell, M., Bristol, T. & Britton, T. (2023) 'The Effects of Student–Teacher Ethnoracial Matching on Exclusionary Discipline for Asian American, Black, and Latinx Students: Evidence From New York City'. *Educational Evaluation and Policy Analysis*. https://doi.org/01623737231175461

Snyder, K., Fong, C., Paintwer, K., Pittard, C. Barr, S. and Patall, E. (2019) *Interventions for academically underachieving students: A systematic review and meta-analysis*. https://www.sciencedirect.com/science/article/abs/pii/S1747938X18306316?via%3Dihub

Strand, S. (2012) The White British-Black Caribbean achievement gap: tests, tiers, and teacher expectations. *British Educational Research Journal* 38(1): 75–101.

Strand, S. (2014) School effects and ethnic, gender and socio-economic groups in educational achievement at age 11. *Oxford Review of Education* 40(2): 223–245

Strand, S. (2015) *Ethnicity, Deprivation, and Educational Achievement at Age 16 in England: Trends Over Time*. University of Oxford.

Swann, L. (1985) *Education for All: Final Report of the Committee of Inquiry into the Education of Children from Ethnic Minority Groups*. Cmnd 9453. London: HMSO.

Tikly, L., Haynes, J., Caballero, C., Hill, J. & Gillborn, D. (2006) *Evaluation of Aiming High: African Caribbean Achievement Project*. Bristol. https://research-information.bris.ac.uk/ws/portalfiles/portal/128456398/RR801.pdf

Williams, T., Kirst, M., Haertel, E., et al. (2005) *Similar students, different results: Why do some schools do better? A large scale survey of California elementary schools serving low-income students*. Mountain View, CA: EdSource.

12
IMPLICATIONS FOR POLICY AND PRACTICE

Introduction

Raising achievement and tackling educational inequality of Black and ethnic minority children is one of the biggest challenges faced by policymakers, teachers, and school leaders in England (Hutchinson et al., 2019; Demie, 2019a; Mortimore and Whitty, 1997; Strand 2012, 2014, 2015a, b). The international research literature reviewed above also suggests that the achievement gap and educational inequality are challenging in the USA and other English-speaking countries (see Edmonds 1982; Muijis et al. 2004; Easterbrook and Hadden, 2021; Hung et al. 2020; Rudasill et al. 2023; Gershenson et al. 2023; Dirmeyer, 2021; Lindsay et al. 2021; OECD 2020; Dietrichson et al., 2017). There is also evidence from the review literature that shows good practice is used to tackle inequality in successful schools (Demie 2019a,b, c, 2023a, b; 2022a, b; Demie and Mclean, 2017a,b, Ofsted 2002, 2009a, b; Baars et al. 2014; Cabral-Gouveia et al. 2023). The successful case study schools and school survey findings in this book also provide effective strategies and good practices evidence to drive school improvement and tackle educational inequality. These success stories have also implications for policy and practice, schools, central government, local authorities, multi-academy trusts (MATs), school governors, and the research community.

Implications for schools

Key messages for schools and school improvement practitioners have emerged from the experience in England and internationally. The finding suggests that disadvantage need not always be a barrier to achievement, and schools can challenge the potentially adverse impact of poverty. The case study schools evidence shows that schools can and do make a difference in the life chances of young people. They demonstrate outstanding practice in all areas to support disadvantaged pupils. Many approaches are not new or different, but they require leadership teams and staff across the school to ensure that every member of staff is aware of which children are disadvantaged and that they take clear and accountable action to accelerate those students' progress. The approach and strategies used by the case study schools can be used elsewhere and widely disseminated. The key ingredients are, as we have seen, strong leadership on equality and diversity, high-quality teaching, the effective use of data to monitor performance and deliver an inclusive curriculum, and targeted support interventions. These can be replicated in schools nationally and internationally.

Another important message for schools and policymakers is that there is no pick-and-mix option. An effective school will seek to develop all the approaches, underpinning them with practical data that monitors the achievement of the target groups to pinpoint and tackle underperformance. To help raise the achievement of disadvantaged, ethnic minority, and EAL pupils, these schools:

1. Develop leadership capacity. As a matter of good practice, the school should audit the current workforce and pursue diversification at all levels, including senior management and teachers, to ensure that it reflects the school population.
2. Use data to identify underachieving groups and to improve teachers' and management's understanding of how and why some students underachieve and what teachers can do about it. It is important to recognise ethnic monitoring is key in enabling schools to keep track of what is happening to pupils.
3. Audit the curriculum to ensure that it reflects the diversity of the school community and the needs of all pupils, including representation of the different cultural, ethnic, linguistic, and religious groups in the area.
4. Celebrate cultural diversity through the effective use of International Day, Black History Month, and, above all, an inclusive curriculum that meets the needs of a multicultural society.
5. Ensure to provide continuous professional development (CPD) for teachers. Teachers need additional training that makes them aware of Black and ethnic minority cultural differences, the issue of diversity, racism, and curriculum barriers relating to the education of Black and ethnic minority students. Teachers also need training and guidance in conflict and behavioural management. The impetus for change in schools must start with the headteacher.

6. To be effective in addressing the needs of Black and ethnic minority pupils, schools have to ensure the right culture and ethos are created. This requires vision and leadership by the headteachers and governors in establishing values to which the school is committed. The school needs to set and maintain high standards of behaviour and high expectations of its pupils and staff.

Implications for headteachers and teachers

The most important factor in raising achievement and tackling inequality in education is the headteachers' and teachers' commitment to diversity and equality in schools. Headteachers and teachers' high expectations of Black and ethnic minority students played a key role in the high achievement. Some headteachers and teachers nationally were unaware that their expectations were lower for some pupils than others, particularly ethnic minority students. This is unacceptable. Where they differ for groups of pupils – girls rather than boys, Black rather than White – they are perpetuating differences in achievement that are deeply unjust. The implications for headteachers must be the need to focus on classroom practice and to challenge the existence of such differentiations. A positive view of children, whatever their background, will allow teachers to take into account the difference between ethnic minorities and their peers without allowing them to lower expectations. The successful schools in this study had high expectations of all children, whatever their background, and this has made a huge difference in teaching and learning in the classroom. We need to recognise that England is a multicultural country, and teachers must be well-trained to take on the challenge in the classroom. The impetus of organising training for teachers and for change in schools must start with the headteacher.

Implications for central government

Our research shows that when the government stipulates changes, change at the school level begins to happen. It, therefore, is important that the government recognise that tackling the underachievement of certain ethnic groups is an important part of raising standards for all in schools. To tackle underachievement, the central government and schools need to develop targeted initiatives to identify and address the needs of pupils of ethnic minorities. In the past, the Ethnic Minority Achievement Grant (EMAG) was introduced by the government as a means of supporting the attainment of pupils from ethnic minority groups and ending the shocking underachievement of ethnic minority pupils compared with their White British peers. The government's EMAG funding given to schools was designed to provide greater resources for schools with a high proportion of ethnic minority students. It appears that the government has become ineffective in using evidence to tackle inequality and race issues and has recently ended the funding. Our data shows clearly that the achievement gap has widened nationally. Our evidence confirms that the performance of some ethnic minority groups consistently lags behind that of their peers. And it shows what can be done to address educational inequality. We need to take action to tackle the problem at the national level. The recommendations for central government that emerge from the present study are:

1. Educational inequalities should be tackled at national and local levels. The DfE needs to recognise the fact that schools and local authorities, MAT, need to target funding to support pupils from underachieving minority ethnic groups and pupils learning English as an additional language. The DfE needs to reintroduce targeted funding to schools in which ethnic minority pupils are underachieving to provide the foundation for an education system that values social justice.
2. Building on the lessons learned from the present research and the lessons learned from the London Challenge, the DfE needs to establish a national project for raising the achievement of ethnic minority children to be applied where ethnic minority students are being failed by their schools.
3. The national data indicates that teachers in England tend to be from White British monocultural backgrounds. Fewer than one in seven come from an ethnic minority group. The government needs to encourage schools to employ a workforce that reflects the community and the area they serve. All schools in England need to be aware of diversity and multicultural education.

Implications for local education authorities and multi-academy trusts

Our research findings have implications for local authorities. We argue that school improvement and area-based school systems cannot be driven successfully by the central government for many reasons. Central government lacks local knowledge and the capacity to provide oversight to meet local needs and to monitor performance to identify problems early (Mortimore, 1999; Demie and McLean, 2015). This is best carried out by local authorities and MATs.

Although recent legislation has diminished the power of LAs, they remain accountable to their communities and are uniquely placed to provide key school improvement services such as monitoring, challenging, supporting, and intervening in schools to ensure they meet statutory requirements and providing performance data to support school improvement by identifying underachieving pupils and prioritising areas for development. Successful local authorities have developed their education provision in various ways by strengthening and refocussing their school improvement service or creating school partnership services as autonomous organisations. The government itself has developed MATs to run schools that have no geographical boundary. In particular, LAs play a key role in promoting community cohesion and valuing diversity so that all pupils understand and appreciate others from different ethnic and linguistic backgrounds in the area they live in. Our recommendations for local authorities and MATs are:

1. LAs, MATs, and school improvement practitioners should attach great importance to the use of data and evidence from research on good practices to raise standards and close the school achievement gap.
2. Continue to gather and use data effectively to support school improvement, identifying underachieving groups early and targeting interventions accordingly.
3. Audit the workforce in the school and develop a workforce that reflects the local community.
4. Provide schools with programmes of centrally based training to share good practices for raising attainment and closing the achievement gap.
5. Value and celebrate cultural diversity.

Implications for diversifying the curriculum

We would argue that this book also raised

> many relevant questions and challenges for UK curriculum issues including What is British history being taught in schools? Many people involved in education now recognise 'the need for the decolonisation of the current Eurocentric curriculum, employing a more diverse workforce in schools, and making diversity and racial equality part of the curriculum.
> *(Demie 2021:2)*

Britain is a multi-ethnic and multicultural country, and there is, therefore, a need to develop and use an inclusive curriculum that recognises that students in schools come from a range of different backgrounds. This inclusive curriculum reflects and takes into account factors such as ethnicity, gender, language, socioeconomic status, and faith. Our research is about successful schools that have developed and used inclusive curriculum to meet the needs of Black and Minority Ethnic (BAME) students in their schools and provide good practices that schools can share to transform their curriculum and improve teaching and learning in primary and secondary schools. The recommendations based on this study and previous research are that:

- The government should ensure that every school develops a curriculum that reflects the rich local cultural diversity.
- The schools should develop an inclusive curriculum that engages ethnic minority students. The curriculum should reflect and value cultural diversity and have relevance to their lives.
- Students in the UK should be taught Black British History as part of the national curriculum with the whole range of Black and ethnic minority experiences that cover the lives of famous BAME people in Britain, the achievement of early civilisation such as Benin in West Africa, Cushitic and Merotic civilisation in North East Africa, the transatlantic slave trade and its abolition, and the history of the Windrush generation. In addition, students should be taught the pre-colonial Black presence in Britain, migration patterns, ethnic and cultural diversity in Britain, the positive contribution people of all ethnicities have made to Britain, and the role of the countries of the former British Empire in both world wars. In essence, the curriculum must be more relevant, decolonised, and inclusive to meet the challenge of today's multicultural Britain.

Implications for parental engagement and involvement.

Parental engagement in this book refers to teachers and schools involving parents in supporting their children's academic learning. The lesson learned from our study suggests parental engagement has a large and positive impact on children's learning. The EEF (2019) research also shows that the average impact of the effective parental engagement approaches is about an additional four months' progress over a year and a higher impact for pupils with low prior attainment. It is therefore a priority for schools to identify interventions that are effective in supporting parental engagement, including:

- School staff should receive parental engagement training in their initial teacher training or CPD.
- Schools should design and deliver effective approaches and programmes to support parental engagement which aim to develop parental skills such as literacy or IT skills; encourage parents to involve and support their children's reading, homework, and children's learning activities; and supportive programmes for families in crisis.

Implications for the research community

More 'what works research' is needed to inform policymakers' and educators' decisions about what constitutes effective approaches to addressing inequality and narrowing the achievement gap in schools (Demie, 2019c). Previous researchers who have analysed the study literature and focussed on the best evidence of 'what works' have generally backed this kind of research method (see Perry and Morris, 2023; EEF 2019; Demie 2019a, b; Sharples et al., 2011). Our review of the literature in this book also found several research studies into what works in driving school improvement and closing the achievement gap. A substantial body of evidence from the USA, England, and other English-speaking nations indicates that there is a performance gap in schools based on factors such as gender, socioeconomic level, ethnic background, and kind of school. There is limited research on strategies to decrease the achievement gap in schools, as well as at the national and international levels (Demie 2019a,b, 2023a, Hung et al. 2020, Rudasill et al. 2023, Gershenson et al. 2023). Broader insights into the learning possibilities available to school children would come from research on what works in transforming education and longitudinal studies conducted by schools, local authorities, MATS, and central government to close the performance gap. Additionally, we would support a more quantitative and qualitative approach to research at the national and international levels to improve the evidence supporting the most promising strategies for closing the attainment gap and to support and encourage educationalists and policymakers in their efforts to pursue greater academic success.

Our study did not consider schools' external factors beyond schools; instead, it concentrated on effective schools with a significant impact. There is little research that investigates what can be done to tackle factors that are beyond the school's control. Previous school effectiveness and improvement research suggests that around 80% of the variation in pupil academic achievement and progress in the school is attributable to factors such as wider family environment, social and economic factors, family background, and the neighbourhoods where pupils live (Clifton and Cook, 2012; Rasbash et al., 2010). Others also suggested that the problem beyond school gates is not much of school-making and is beyond the control of individual schools. We would argue schools cannot solve these factors by themselves (Ofsted 2014; ASCL 2014). There is, therefore, a need for further research beyond the school gate to study the extent to which factors such as social class, parental attitudes to authority, family relations, poverty, and economic circumstances affect Black and ethnic minority children's performance. The absence of such research evidence is responsible for pupil failure in schools and the community school serves. Addressing these factors that are beyond the school gate is a necessary condition for successful educational attainment.

There is also a necessity to research the schools as agencies that are failing to meet the demands made by Black and ethnic minority children. Our research in successful schools stressed the importance of examining the school's leadership, quality of teaching and learning, targeted interventions approach, tackling racism and teacher training, as well as providing more appropriate training for all teachers to make a difference. There is a need to investigate the effect of these factors, particularly on ineffective schools, or underachieving schools to address inequalities. Black and ethnic minority communities were emphatically against any research that blamed the Black and ethnic minority community for their children's difficulties in schools, which located causes of underachievement with the Black and ethnic minority community's family structures. The evidence of our research is successful schools suggest it was the education system which needed to ensure that it was achieving the type of education children needed. Hence, further research needs to investigate how to improve ineffective underachieving schools.

In the meanwhile, nevertheless, this book offers a regularly replicated model of research that shows indisputably what works in schools. It also tells a story of the search for lessons about how to improve schools.

References

ASCL. (2014) *Association of Schools and College Leaders written evidence to House of Commons Education Select Committee by, In Underachievement in Education by White Working Class Children*. House of Commons 142, The Stationery Office Limited, London, June 2014.

Baars, S., Bernardes, E., Elwick, A., Malortie, A., McAleavy, T., McInerney, L., Menzies, L. & Riggall, A. (2014) *Lessons from London Schools*. London: CfBT and Centre for London.

Cabral-Gouveia, C., Menezes, I. & Neves, T. (2023) Educational strategies to reduce the achievement gap: a systematic review. *Frontiers in Education* 8: 1155741. doi: 10.3389/feduc.2023.1155741 https://www.frontiersin.org/articles/10.3389/feduc.2023.1155741/full

Clifton, J. & Cook, W. (2012) *A Long Division: Closing the Attainment Gap in England's Secondary Schools*. London: Institute for Public Policy Research (IPPR).

Demie, F. (2019a) *Educational Inequality: Closing the gap*. London: UCL IOE Press, July.

Demie, F. (2019b) The experience of Black Caribbean pupils in school exclusion in England.

Demie, F. (2019c) *Tackling Educational Inequality*. British Educational Research Association (BERA) Blog. https://www.bera.ac.uk/blog/tackling-educational-inequality

Demie, F. (2021) *Transforming the Secondary Curriculum*. British Educational Research Association. https://www.bera.ac.uk/blog/transforming-the-secondary-curriculum

Demie, F. (2022a) *Understanding the Causes and Consequences of School Exclusions: Teachers, Parents and Schools' Perspectives*. London: Routledge.

Demie, F. (2022b) 'Tackling teachers' low expectations of Black Caribbean students in English schools. *Equity in Education and Society Journal* 1(1): 32–49. https://doi.org/10.1177/27526461211068511

Demie, F. (2023a) *Raising the Achievement of Black Caribbean pupils: Barriers and Good Practice in Schools.* London: Lambeth Research and Statistics Unit. https://www.lambeth.gov.uk/sites/default/files/2023-05/Raising_Achievement_of_Black_Caribbean_Pupils_-_Barriers_and_Good_Practice.pdf

Demie, F. (2023b) *Tackling Educational Inequality: Lessons from London Schools.* Equity in education & Society. https://doi.org/10.1177/27526461231161775

Demie, F. & Mclean, C. (2015) *Narrowing the Achievement Gap: Good Practice in Schools.* London: Lambeth Research and Statistics Unit.

Demie, F. & Mclean, C. (2017a) *Black Caribbean Underachievement in Schools in England.* Lambeth LA: Lambeth Research and Statistics Unit.

Demie, F. & Mclean, C. (2017b) *The Achievement of Black Caribbean Pupils: Good Practice.* London: Lambeth Research and Statistics Unit.

Dietrichson, J., Bøg, M., Filges, T. & Klint Jørgensen, A.M. (2017) Academic interventions for elementary and middle school students with low socioeconomic status: a systematic review and meta-analysis. *Review of Educational Research* 87: 243–282. doi: 10.3102/0034654316687036

Dirmeyer, H. (2021) *Black and White Student Achievement Gaps in Tennessee.* Electronic Theses and Dissertations. Paper 3862. https://dc.etsu.edu/etd/3862

Easterbrook, M.J. & Hadden, I.R. (2021) Tackling educational inequalities with social psychology: identities, contexts, and interventions. *Social Issues Policy Review* 15: 180–236. doi: 10.1111/sipr.12070

Edmonds, R. (1982) Programmes of school improvement: An overview. *Educational Leadership* 40 (3): 8–11.

EEF. (2019) *Teaching and Learning Tool Kit.* London: Education Endowment Foundation. https://educationendowmentfoundation.org.uk/evidencesummaries/teaching-learning-toolkit/

Gershenson, S., Lindsay, C., Papageorge, N.W., Campbell, R. & Rendon, J. (2023) *Spillover Effects of Black Teachers on White Teachers' Racial Competency: Mixed Methods Evidence from North.* https://papers.ssrn.com/sol3/papers.cfm?abstract_id=4631011

Hung, M., Smith, W.A., Voss, M.W., Franklin, J.D., Gu, Y. & Bounsanga, J. (2020) Exploring student achievement Gaps in School Districts Across the United States. *Education and Urban Society* 52(2): 175–193.

Hutchinson, J., Bonetti, S., Crenna-Jennings, W., & Akhal, A. (2019) *Education in England: Annual Report 2019.* Education Policy Institute. https://bit.ly/3ETGflu

Lindsay, C., Monarrez, T. & Luetmer, G. (2021) *The Effects of Teacher Diversity on Hispanic Student Achievement in Texas. Policy Brief.* Texas Education Research Center.

Mortimore, P. (1999) *The Road to Improvement: Reflections on School Effectiveness.* London: Taylor & Francis.

Mortimore, P. & Whitty, G. (1997) *Can School Improvement Overcome the Effects of Disadvantage?* London: Institute of Education, University of London.

Muijis, D., Harris, A., Chapman, C., Stoll, L. & Russ, J. (2004) Improving schools in socioeconomically disadvantage areas - a review of research evidence. *School Effectiveness and School Improvement* 15(2): 149–175.

OECD. (2020) *Education at a Glance 2021: OECD Indicators.* Paris: OECD. https://www.oecd-ilibrary.org/sites/db0e552c-en/index.html?itemId=/content/component/db0e552c-en

Ofsted. (2002) *Achievement of Black Caribbean Pupils: Good Practice in Secondary Schools*. London: Office for Standards in Education, HMI 448.

Ofsted. (2009a) *Twelve Outstanding Secondary Schools: Excelling Against the Odds*. London: Office for Standards in Education, HMI: 080240. https://dera.ioe.ac.uk/id/eprint/11232/2/Twelve.pdf

Ofsted. (2009b) *Twenty Outstanding Primary Schools: Excelling Against the Odds*. http://dera.ioe.ac.uk/11216/1/Twenty%20outstanding%20primary%20schools.pdf

Ofsted. (2014) *Written evidence to House of Commons Education Select Committee, In Education Committee (2014). Underachievement in Education by White Working Class Children*. London: House of Commons 142, The Stationery Office Limited.

Perry, T. & Morris, R. (2023) *A Critical Guide to Evidence-Informed Education*. Open University Press.

Rasbash, J., Leckie, G., Pillinger, R. & Jenkins, J. (2010) Children's educational progress: partitioning family, school and area effects. *Journal of the Royal Statistical Society* 173(3): 657–682.

Rudasill, K., McGinnis, C., Cheng, S., Cormier, D. & Koziol, N. (2023) White privilege and teacher perceptions of teacher-child relationship quality. *Journal of School Psychology* 98: 224–239.

Sharples, S., Slavin, R., Chambers, B., & Sharo, C. (2011) *Effective Classroom Strategies for Closing the Gap in Educational Achievement for Children and Young People Living in Poverty, Including White, Working Class Boys*. Technical Report. York: Institute of Education, University of York https://pure.york.ac.uk/portal/en/publications/effective-classroom-strategies-for-closing-the-gap-in-educational

Strand, S. (2012) The White British-Black Caribbean achievement gap: tests, tiers, and teacher expectations. *British Educational Research Journal* 38(1): 75–101.

Strand, S. (2014) School effects and ethnic, gender and socio-economic groups in educational achievement at age 11. *Oxford Review of Education* 40(2): 223–245.

Strand, S. (2015a) *English as An Additional Language and Educational Achievement in England: Analysis of National Pupil Database*. Department of Education, University of Oxford.

Strand, S. (2015b) *Ethnicity, Deprivation, and Educational Achievement at Age 16 in England: Trends Over Time*. University of Oxford.

INDEX

Pages in *italics* refer to figures and pages in **bold** refer to tables.

achievement gap 5, 23, 66, 79–80, 96, 122, 127, 148, 181, 196, 198–199, 202, 216, 220, 223, 233; *see also* closing the achievement gap; ethnic achievement gap; gender difference; socio-economic status difference
African American 24, 171, 174, 182, 184–189, 191, 194–197, 201–203, 221
Ahram R. 202
Anderson, L. W. 198, 202
Andrews, J. 26
Ansell, S. 181–182
Archer, L. 3, 5, 7
Armstrong, D. 172–173
Arnot, M. 31, 35
Asian America 181–182, 184, 187–188, 190–191, 194, 202–203
aspirations 26, 41, 44, 48–49, 56, 69, 89, 111, 129, 133, 136, 138, 156, 233–234
Assari S 182, 185–186
Assistant headteacher 115, 117
Association of Schools and College Leaders (ASCL) 233
Atherton, J. S. 73
attainment: KS2 26–32, **33–34**, 35–36, 66, 76, 85–86, **104**, 105–106, 114, 121–122; GCSE 4, 11–14, 25–32, **33–34**, 35–36, 43, 55, 66, 75–76, 93

Attainment: GCSE attainment gap 25–26, 32, 37, 90, 181–182, 233; *see also* the achievement gap
Australia 17, 31, 154, 171–174, 199–201, 222

Baars, S. 8, 10, 84, 90, 96–98, 227
Ball, S. 7
Banerjee, A. 189
Barber, M. 73, 80
barriers to learning 14, **33**, 40–42, 44–45, 47, 49–50, 52, 54, 57, 63, 78, 87, 112, 159–160, 215–216, 222; *see also* curriculum barriers; diversity; institutional racism; lack of funding; language barriers; low expectations; low literacy; low teacher expectations; poverty; school exclusion
Barton, A. C. 47, 186, 195
Berkowitz, R. 193, 195, 202
Biddle, B.J. 198
Black African 4–6, 9–10, 31–32, **33–34**, 35, 64, 92, 101–102, **104**, 120–121, 127, 135, 138, 153, 156, 160, 166, 201–202
Black Caribbean 4–12, 24–25, 29–32, **33–34**, 35, 44, 49, 52–54, 64, 67, 85, 93–94, **104**, 127, 139–140, 149–152, 156, 160–166, 174, 219

Blair, M. 8, 10, 66, 69, 217
Blake, J. 191
Blatchford, P. 198, 204
Blazar, D. 190
booster classes 48, 76, 79–80, 83–84, 86, 89–91, 94, 96, 113
Borg JR 195, 202
Borman, G. 195
Boyle, A. 10
Bradley, K. 182, 185
Brooms, D. 190
Brown, B. 10
Burgess, S. 10
Burris C. 197, 202

Cabral-Gouveia, C. 193, 202, 227
Callender, C. 148
Canada 17, 172–174, 201, 222
Card, D. 188, 202
Carter P 202
case study research 12, 219
Cassen, R. 23, 26, 32, 36, 149
Castro, A. 190
Catherine Snow, M. 190
cultural diversity 50–51, 64, 65, 72, 91, 142, 147–148, 161, 217, 228, 231–232
Chan, M. 190
Charles, C. 188
Choudry, S. 4
Clifton, J. 9, 149, 233
closing the achievement gap 9–15, 23, 63–64, 79–80, 96, 122, 127, 148, 181, 196–199, 202, 216, 220, 223, 231, 233; *see also* achievement gap
Clotfelter, C. T. 182, 189
Coard, B. 4
Codrington, J. 202
cognitive ability tests (CATs) 75
Coleman, J. S. 181, 197, 221
common factors in educational success 109, 167
Condron D. J. 202
Continuing professional development (CPD) 11, 88, 159, 199, 203, 215, 221, 228, 232
Cooc, N. 191
Cook, C. 4, 9, 149, 233
Cooper, C. E. 47, 186
Corallo, C. 193, 195–199, 202
Crain, R. 188
Crosnoe, R. 190
Crozier G. 4, 216

curriculum barriers 7, 14, 40–42, 50–51, 56, 149–150, 159, 216, 228

Daniels, K. 189
Darling-Hammond. L 27
data *see* use of data
Day, C. 66, 73, 135, 142–143, 228
DCSF 40, 216
Dee, T. 181, 189
Demie, F. 3–10, 13, 23–26, 30–32, **33–34**, 35, 37, 40–76, 83–85, 90–103, 109, 116, 127, 147–149, 157, 159–168, 174–175, 216–223, 227, 230–231, 233
deputy headteacher 139
Desforges, C. 143
DfE. 5–6, 10, 27, 29–32, **33–34**, 35–36, 40, 52, 55–56, 75, 90, 92, 96–97, 101–102, 105–106, 109, 147, 159, 163–166, 169, 174–175, 216, 233
Diamond J. B. 202
Dietrichson, J. 181–182, 193, 195, 227
Dirmeyer, H. 181–182, 185, 191, 221, 227
disadvantaged pupils 23, 25–26, 32, **33–34**, 35–37, 41, 43, 48, 56, 64–66, 80, 86–90, 94–97, 216, 219, 222, 228
diversity 5–15, 40, 42, 49–50, 56, 64, 65, 66–67, 72, 91, 101–103, 110–112, 140, 142, 146–149, 152, 160–161, 167–168, 174, 189–190, 192–193, 216–217, 219, 222–223, 228–232

EAL support 84–85, 87, 94, 105–106, 115–118, 218
Early Years Foundation Stage (EYFS) 130, 154
Easterbrook, M. J. 26, 185, 221, 227
Easton-Brooks, D. 189
Edmonds, R. 8, 63, 66, 219–220, 227
Education Committee 27
Education Endowment Foundation (EEF) 10, 15, 79, 83, 94–97, 166, 172, 227–233
education policy 3, 10–11, 13–14, 23, 29, 36–37, 163
educational inequality 8, 10–16, 23, 36, 50, 74, 84, 202, 215–217, 219–221, 227, 230
effective feedback 91–92
effective teaching and learning 10, 15, 66, 88, 111, 202, 219, 221

EHRC 40, 44–45, 52, 163, 176, 216
Ehrenberg, R. 189, 198
empirical evidence 10–11, 14, 36–37, 67, 103, 121, 164, 171, 219
English as an additional language (EAL) 12, 101; achievement 103, **104**; English proficiency assessment 105–106; strategies 109, 121; targeted support 115–116; teaching and learning 111–115
England 3–4, 14, 17, 25–32, **33–34**, 35–37, 49, 51, 74–75, 78, 90, 93–97, 101–103, 109, 122, 140, 147–149, 163–174, 181, 199, 201, 216, 218–222, 227, 229–230, 233
enrichment activities 49, 83–84, 89–90, 95, 156, 186
EPI 4–5, 9, 23–25, 37, 149, 163, 176
equal opportunities 6, 66, 72, 91, 167–175, 181–203, 215–223
equality 7, 17, 66, 110–111, 149, 160, 167, 174–175, 217, 219, 228–229, 231
ethnic achievement gap 28–29
Ethnic Minority Achievement Grant (EMAG) 93–94, 229
ethnic minority pupils 3, 7–8, 15, 26, 40–41, 50–51, 54–56, 64, 66, 84, 90, 93–94, 97, 127–129, 156, 159, 216, 229–230; *see also* African American; Asian America; Black African; Black Caribbean; Gypsy Roma; Māori and Pacifika; Mixed race; Native American; Turkish
ethos of a school 10, 71–72, 91, 132, 138–139, 152, 168–169, 172, 219, 229

Fan, X. 186
Finn J. D. 202
focus groups 11–12, 140, 143, 150, 158
Free school meals (FSM) 12, 25–26, 30, 33, 37, 48, 64, 66, 75, 79, 86, 90, 102, 165

Gaddis, S. M. 201
Galton, M. 198
General Certificate of Secondary Education (GCSE) *see* achievement gap
gender difference 31, 35
Gershenson, S. 8, 53, 181–182, 190, 192, 227, 233

Gillborn, D. 3–9, 30–32, 66, 127–128, 149, 216
González, T. 171, 173–174, 176
Gorard, S. 8–9, 23, 26–27, 31
Gottfried, M. 181–182, 188–189
Greaves, E. 4
Gregory, A. 170–176
Gypsy Roma 4, 24, 163–166, 174, 219, 222
Governors 10–11, 15, **65**, 65, 69, 74, 78, 140, 142, 146, 156, 158, 215, 217, 227, 229

Hanushek, Eric A. 197, 202
Harper S. R. 202
Harris, A. 66, 83–88, 147
Harris, A. & Chapman, C. 66
Harwell, B. 185–186
Hattie, J. 73, 198
Haycock, K. 195–197, 202
headteachers 43–45, 48–53, 67–77, 84–88, 110–111, 115, 117, 120, 130–143, 151–155, 158–159, 228–229
Hemphill, F. 187
Hill N. 47, 186
home languages 114–115, 133
homework 46, 73, 84, 134, 153–154, 186–187, 232
Hong Kong 171, 174
Hopkins, D. 8, 10, 63
Hornby, G. 47, 127
Hsin, A. 187
Hughes, D. 182, 192, 195
Hung. M. 27, 181–182, 185, 227, 233
Hutchings, M. 4, 90
Hutchinson, J. 9, 26–27, 37, 219, 227

IFS 5, 24–25
Igbal, K. 5
implications of research findings 227; for headteachers 229; for local authorities 230; multi-academy trusts 230; for parental engagement 232; for schools 227; for the central government 229–230; for the research community 232–234
inclusive curriculum 6, 10, 15, 66, 79, 109, 146, 148–150, 156–161, 167, 197, 217–218, 221–222, 232
Ingersoll, R. M. 189
institutional racism 14, 40, 53–54, 56, 163, 174, 188, 216
IPPR. 163–164, 176

Index **239**

Jencks, C. 187, 201
Jeynes W. H. 47, 127, 186

Kao, G. 24, 187, 201
Kaushal, N. 185–186
Kirby, S.N. 189
Kirkup, C. 74
Kober, Nancy 195, 197, 202
KS2 *see* attainment

lack of funding 42–44, 56, 216
Ladson-Billings, G. 27
Lambert, M. C. 47, 127, 186
language barriers 14, 45–46, 56, 121, 186, 188
Leach, A. 9, 147–159, 185–186
Leadership of schools: strong leadership 10, 66–67, 72, 78, 83, 97, 110–111, 167, 203, 219–220, 228; *see also* headteachers
Lee, J. 188
Leithwood, K. 70, 196
lessons to be learned from outstanding schools 222–223
Leung-Gagné, M. 191–192
Lindsay, C. A. 181–182, 191–192, 227
local authorities (LAs) 11, 16, 169, 171–172, 230–231
local communities, recruitment of school staff from 151, 158
London Challenge 94–95
Looney, J. 197
Losen D. 176, 202
low expectations 5, 14, 26, 40, 52, 54–56, 174, 188, 193
low literacy 40, 46, 48, 56, 216
low teacher expectations 7, 54, 202
Lucas, Samuel R. 189, 197

Macpherson W. 6–7, 40, 54, 147, 149, 159
Māori and Pacifika 200
Marks, H. 148
mastery learning 94, 96–98
Maylor, U. 4, 40, 53–54
McCluskey, G. 171, 173–174, 176
McDermott 47
McKenley, J. 10, 216
Mckown, C. 54–55, 182, 202
Meier, K.J. 189
meta-cognition & self-regulation 84, 88, 94, 98
Michael, E. 173

Miller, P. 10
Milliard, W. 4, 54
Minor, E 190–191
Minus-Vincent, D. 182
mixed race 4, 7–8, 12, 55, 64
Moncrieffe, M. L 147–149, 159
Mongon, D. 8, 26, 41, 56, 64, 84, 96–97, 218
Monk, T. 194, 197, 199
Moore, D. 166, 170, 174, 176, 199
Morris, R. 233
Morrison, N. 69–70
Mortimore, P. 6, 8–9, 27, 36, 63, 148–149, 198, 219, 230
Mueller, D. 195, 202
Muijis, Daniel 8, 63, 195, 220, 227
multi-academy trusts (MATs) 227, 230–227, 231
multicultural education 4, 6–7, 223, 230

NACEP 184–185, 202, 221
NAEP 85, 182–183, 186, 189, 201
National Pupil Database (NPD) 14, 23, 27–28, 30, 92
Native American 182, 185, 190–191
Navarro, M. S. 195, 202
Neuman, Susan B. 194
New Zealand 17, 172–173, 199–203, 215–222
Noguera P. A. 176, 186, 201–202

OECD 181–182, 200, 221, 227
Ofsted 4, 8–10, 12, 27, 36, 46, 56, 64, 66–80, 84, 91, 94, 96–97, 111, 127, 131, 133–134, 152, 154, 157, 176, 218–220, 227, 233
Ogbu, J. U. 185–186, 191
Olneck, N. 181
Orfield, G. 188, 202

Papageorge, N. 190–191
parental engagement 12, 14–16, 26, 40–42, 47, 56, 67, 79, 83, 94, 127, 131, 141, 143, 216–217, 232
Parsons, C. 165, 171–172, 174–175
pastoral care 83, 90, 94, 96, 170, 222
Peisner-Feinberg, H. 194
Perry, L. 185, 233
Peterson, K. 173, 199
Phillips, M. 182, 187, 201
PISA 200–201
phonics 89, 94, 97, 130, 140
Pollard, C. 182, 190

poverty 5, 9, 14, 26, 32, 36, 40, 42–45, 56, 64, 66, 78, 83, 89, 97, 103, 174, 186–187, 196, 199, 201, 203, 216, 221, 223, 228, 233
Power, S. and Taylor, C. 163, 227
Proctor, K. 48
Pupil premium funding (PPF) 26, 80, 88, 90, 95

qualitative study 11–12, 233
quantitative study 11, 233
Quinn, D. 190, 197

Race, R. 5–7, 40, 53–54, 56, 59
racism and racial discrimination 5, 7, 10, 14, 37, 40–42, 53–54, 56, 141, 147, 163, 174, 188, 192, 216, 220, 233–234; *see also* institutional racism
Raffaele Mendez LM 164, 173
raising achievement 63–66; quality of teaching 73–74; successful strategies 10, 64, 78, 196, 229; strong leadership 66–72; use of data 74–78; *see also* parental engagement; targeted interventions
Rampton, A. 3, 216–219, 37, 40, 56, 149
Rangel, M. 24, 190
Rasbash J. 9, 233
Reardon, S. F. 182
Redding, C. 190–191
research questions 16–17, 56, 83, 101, 146, 215
restorative approach 169, 170, 174
Reynolds, D. 8–9, 63, 147, 195–197, 202
Rhamie J 10
Richardson B 4
Robinson, V. 67
Rothstein, R. 188, 202
RSA 165, 170–171
Rubie-Davies 199–200
Rudasill, K. 181, 190, 233
Rudd, P. 75
Runnymede Trust 52
Rushing, W. 188
Rutkowski, D. 186
Rutter, M. 186

Sammons, P. 8–9, 63, 66, 73, 83–84, 97, 219
Sanders, W 197
Sandy J 186

SATs 51, 86, 182, 184–185, 202, 221
school ethos 72, 168–169, 172
school exclusions 12, 15–16, 40, 42, 50, 52, 56, 163–175; exclusion statistics 165–166; *see also* tackling exclusion: good practice
school leaders 10, 13–14, 43, 49, 66, 71, 79, 83, 87, 97, 147, 158–160
school leadership 12, 15, 53, 66, 68, 90, 114, 132, 196, 217
school performance 35, 71, 186
self-evaluation 12, **65**, 65, 70–71, 75
SENCO 13, 43
Sharples, S. 233
Sherman, L. 181, 188, 192, 194, 196
Shirrell, M. 221
Shortell, D. 188
Singham, M. 197
Skiba, R. J. 173
Small group additional support 88, 94, 203, 221
Smalley, S. Y. 199
Snipes, J. 197–199
Snyder, K. 96–98, 218
social class 27, 31, 35, 40–41, 47, 55–56, 216, 233
socio-economic status difference 32, 35; *see also* achievement gap
Song, S. 199–200
Special educational needs (SEN) 43, 76–77, 79, 85, 87, 95, 116, 118, 120–121, 163, 166, 175, 198
Stamou, E. 147, 162
Steele, C. 185
Stoll, L. 8, 63
Strand, S. 4, 9, 31, 52–54, 101–105, 149, 163, 216, 219–220
strongest teachers to teach English and maths 85, 88
Suárez-Orozco, C. 186–187
Success factors to drive improvement: Good practice 13, 15–16, 64, 78–79, 83, 109, 121–122, 127, 140, 174, 195, 216–217, 220
Swann, L. 3–8, 37, 40, 56, 149, 216

Tackling exclusion: good practice 167–174
Talbert-Johnson C. 185–186
targeted interventions 13, 64, *65*, **65**, 66, 78, 83–84, 90, 93, 96–97, 117, 199, 218, 223, 233; *see also* Booster classes; EAL support; effective

feedback; Enrichment activities; homework; London Challenge; mastery learning; meta-cognition & self-regulation; parental engagement; Phonics; Small group additional support; strongest teachers to teach English and maths
Taylor, B. 52, 163
teacher 42, 51, 77–78, 111, 136, 152, 154–155, 157
teaching staff 47, 49, 89, 168
Thompson, S. 24, 176, 194, 196–197, 199–200, 208
Thrupp, M. 8
Tikly, L. 91, 93–94, 216, 219
Timpson, E. 163, 174, 176
Tomlinson, S. 4–6
Turkish 12, **104**, 105, 200, 222

United Kingdom 5, 9–10, 23–27, 31, 36, 51–52, 84, 105, 120, 135, 142, 146, 149, 159–161, 166, 172, 221–232
United States of America: the achievement gap 181–192; assessment 198; inclusive curriculum 198; other countries achievement gap 199–201; quality teaching 196–197; school readiness gap 194; small class size 197; strategies to tackle inequality 193–194; the racial/ethnic achievement gap 181–195; target interventions approach 199
use of data 10, 15, 64–68, 71–79, 83–84, 95, 109–110, 122, 202, 217, 221–222, 228, 231

Valdebenito, S. 173–174
VanderHart, P. G. 188
Vanneman, A. 182
Villegas, A. M. 54–55, 189
Vincent, C. 182

West A. 185–186
what works 8–11, 14, 63, 96, 101, 109–110, 112, 166, 215, 217–218, 220, 223; lessons from England 218–220; lessons from USA 220–222; successful school experience 222–223
White British 9, 12, 24, 29–32, **33–34**, 35–37, 52, 54–55, 92–94, 102, **104**, 122, 166, 219, 229–230
White European 190
Williams, T. 9, 185–186, 220
Wood, C. 69–70
Wood, D. 91
Wright C. 163

Yarnell, L. M. 189

Zion S. D. 202